≈ A Sporting Century ≈

To the members of WAGBI and BASC, past, present and future.

A Sporting Century

Graham Downing

The History of the British Association for Shooting & Conservation

Quiller Press

First published in the UK in 2007
by Quiller Press, an imprint of Quiller Publishing Ltd

British Library Cataloguing-in-Publication Data
  A catalogue record for this book
  is available from the British Library

ISBN 978 1 84689 026 0

Printed in Malta by Gutenberg Press Ltd.

Quiller Press
An imprint of Quiller Publishing Ltd
Wykey House, Wykey, Shrewsbury, SY4 1JA
Tel: 01939 261616 Fax: 01939 261606
E-mail: info@quillerbooks.com
Website: www.countrybooksdirect.com

Contents

FOREWORD

HRH The Duke of Edinburgh KG KT

Writing a history of an organisation must always be quite a challenge. In this case, Graham Downing has made an excellent job of it, and I am sure that members, as well as other readers, will be impressed by the trouble he has taken to trace the origins and development of what has become the national authority for all the game shooting sports in Britain.

I am glad that the author has recognised the immense contribution made by Stanley Duncan to the formation of the Wildfowlers Association of Great Britain and Ireland a hundred years ago. I have happy memories of the 60th anniversary dinner held in his honour at the Guildhall in Kingston-upon-Hull in 1968. Wildfowling has always been a free-for-all sport for individuals, but Stanley Duncan realised that there was an urgent need to establish a basic code of practice and standards of behaviour for a rapidly expanding sport at a critical time for all wildlife in this country.

The Association was lucky to get the late John Anderton OBE, as its Secretary, and to guide it through its most formative years. 73 years after its founding, the Association, appreciating changing public attitudes, changed its name to the British Association for Shooting and Conservation. As this book makes abundantly clear, shooting and conservation have become hugely popular, and I have no doubt that this is largely due to the leadership given by the Association, and the many facilities that it provides for all those who appreciate the need to ensure that game shooting has to remain a sustainable sport.

Philip

'It would be a thousand pities if the wildfowler, with all his qualities of energy and perserverance, should fail to use them for the protection, purification and the perpetuation of his sport'

Stanley Duncan

Morning light on Welwick Strays, Humber estuary

INTRODUCTION

O ne hundred years ago, a young man strode along the tideline at Patrington Haven on the north shore of the Humber estuary, dreaming of how he might turn his vision of a new organisation for the defence and promotion of wildfowling into a reality. Little can he have imagined that his brainchild would grow from a small band of local enthusiasts into a fully fledged national organisation, or that it would survive – just – two world wars and go on to become the British Association for Shooting and Conservation, Britain's largest shooting association with 124,000 members and one hundred full-time staff.

This is the story of that association. It has been a long time in the telling, for amongst the day-to-day activities of a lobbying organisation such as BASC, recording the glories of the past quite rightly takes second place to tackling the problems of the present and future. Some thirty years ago a few WAGBI stalwarts, well aware that those who had fought the many battles which the association had faced in the 1950s were getting long in the tooth, made a start by amassing the personal reminiscences of some of the principal figures from the immediate postwar years. One of them, Les Brockbank, who joined WAGBI in 1930 and who was a former honorary treasurer of the association, advertised far and wide for the recollections of those who had been involved with the association at the time. The documents and tape recorded interviews he collected, still sorted and catalogued in their original brown envelopes, provide a unique and very personal insight, but although Brockbank worked hard at his research, he never committed the history of WAGBI to paper, and the nearest anyone got to doing so was when John Marchington wrote a chapter 'The birth and life of WAGBI' in his 1980 book *The History of Wildfowling*.

John Anderton, who ran the association for over thirty years and who was the architect of today's BASC, was adamant that what had been achieved in those early years should not be forgotten, although he himself never actually wrote anything for publication. His original intention was to launch a WAGBI history during the association's seventy-fifth anniversary celebrations in 1983. He even went so far as nominating a person to research and write it: 'It is my view that after we have appointed an information officer, he should regard the history as part of his brief. There can be no better way for him to learn exactly what the association has achieved than to study it closely since its inception.'

Perhaps, when Anderton wrote those words in 1976, he was having a particularly acute attack of clairvoyance, for BASC's first press officer did indeed go on to research and write the history, albeit thirty years later. When I joined the staff at Marford Mill in 1982, there were of course far more important things to do than wade through the old WAGBI minute books or surround myself with Stanley Duncan's glass photographic negatives, and I do not recall 'JA' ever mentioning to me that he wanted me to tackle the project. Even so, when I discovered that typewritten memo, I couldn't help feeling that in some mysterious way, I was fulfilling a predetermined destiny.

In doing so I have been granted access to all of BASC's remaining archives, some of which were snatched from the flames in 1981 when fire so nearly destroyed Marford Mill. Scuffed and grubby with age, those minute books still smell of smoke, and their yellowed pages are still wrinkled where they were soaked by the water from the firemen's hoses. It is sobering to dwell upon how close they came to destruction, taking with them those first-hand accounts of battles won and lost and of decisions made. Many of Stanley Duncan's original glass photographic plates still remain, as do the 'magic lantern' slides which he used when speaking to gatherings of wildfowlers, and it is a peculiar feeling to hold and handle those fragile pieces of glass with which he actually recorded his photographs a hundred years ago, their images of sportsmen in Norfolk jackets and high Edwardian collars frozen forever in time. The people they depict have long gone to their graves, but the negatives themselves are as crisp and sharp today as they were when they first emerged from Duncan's darkroom, and one can only wonder what he would have made of the technology by which they have been digitally scanned and reproduced on the printed page. Another invaluable source of material has been the 'Life and Times' of WAGBI, the scrap book of press cuttings, photographs, invitations and other personal memorabilia which John Anderton and his personal assistant Jean Morris kept religiously from 1957 to 1988. Particularly enjoyable were the volumes from the early 1980s through which marched so many familiar faces, most of which are now lined with age or fowling upon that great foreshore in the sky.

But whether from the record of times which I personally remember or from the minutes taken down by Stanley Duncan in the years before the Great War, one thing in particular struck me constantly during my research: despite the immense changes that have been wrought upon Britain's culture, society and countryside over the last hundred years, how much remains the same. Today's wildfowler may stomp the marsh in neoprene waders and wear camouflaged garb which would have startled Duncan and his colleagues, but the wigeon he pursues still haunt the same creeks and gutters and require the same skill and cunning to put them in the bag. A cock pheasant, hurtling across the bare twigs of some ancient oakwood against a grey January sky, is just as difficult to hit in 2008 as it was in 1908 and the thrill when one does so is just as keen. Thanks to the introduction of the syndicate shoot and the greater availability of wealth and free time amongst every section of society, many more people are able to shoot now than was the case when WAGBI first set out its stall, but the guns we use today are essentially little changed from what they were a century ago and much of the old sporting tradition remains.

So too do the issues which trouble us. Proposals to reduce the shooting seasons and restrict quarry species were matters over which WAGBI issued dire warnings in the 1920s and have been the stuff of debate at Council and committee meetings ever since. Night shooting and punt gunning have both been declared dead a thousand times over the decades, yet we still steal out after wildfowl beneath the full moon and those narrow grey boats still slip down into the tide on a still winter's morning. While their turn of phrase appears curious and quaint to modern eyes, many aspects of the old minute books and annual reports would be familiar to the BASC policymakers of today.

I am grateful to the many people, staff and volunteers, old and not so old, who have spent time talking to me about WAGBI and BASC. Their recollections have added colour to the narrative, fleshing out the bare bones of the written record. They are too many to list in full, but my particularly special thanks must go to Mary Anderton, Peter Turner, Richard Bream, Arthur Leek, Malcolm Lyell, Peter Keyser, Tony Laws, John Batley, Brian Hughes, David Gray, Ian Grindy, John Bishop and John Richards. Thanks also to Alan Credland for his research on the 'black hut', to Tony Jackson for Stanley Duncan's diaries, to David Frost for copies of Duncan's correspondence, to Keith Sykes for the recollections of Morecambe Bay wildfowlers, to David Upton for his help in gaining access to valuable information about Stanley Duncan and of course to those long-serving members of BASC's present staff who still remember the highs – and lows – of the 1970s and 80s as though it were yesterday, and in particular John Harradine, Colin Shedden and John Swift.

This is their story. It deserves to be told not merely because it is an interesting tale in itself, but because it may perhaps help those who carry BASCs torch in the future to inform their decisions with what has gone before. For I firmly believe that an organisation, like a person, is the product of its history. Its future is inevitably, if sometimes unknowingly, shaped by its past.

Graham Downing
Chediston 2007

Local wildfowlers at Patrington shot from hides or 'huts' built from the chalk boulders used by land reclamation engineers

Chapter 1
BEGINNINGS

When the sun rises on a winter's morning over the long, low shore of the Humber estuary, the light glinting off the wet foreshore mud to the wild shriek of the redshank and the curlew's haunting whistle, it is still possible to be transported back in time. Back to the days before drainage and land reclamation turned mud and salt marsh into arable fields, to a time when the grey gunning punts slipped quietly at dawn down Patrington west channel and shoulder gunners clad in oilskins and leather thigh boots sat out the morning flight in their hides or 'huts' thrown up from old baskets, driftwood and chalk boulders.

The year is 1908 and among those wildfowlers is a young man by the name of Stanley Duncan, a railway engineer by profession, a naturalist, photographer and writer by inclination. A man of boundless enthusiasm and huge passion for wildfowling, Duncan looked at the world around him and saw changes which worried and concerned him.

Britain at the turn of the twentieth century was indeed changing, and changing fast. It is tempting to think upon that time before the outbreak of the First World War as some sort of golden age, when the traditions of the countryside followed their ancient pattern year on year as they had done since time immemorial and the social fabric of Britain remained rooted in a deferential class system from which escape was well-nigh impossible. But in truth the Industrial Revolution had put paid to all that. Manufacturing industry, coal, steel and rail were bringing huge wealth to Britain, but they were also bringing filth and grime. Pollution was poisoning rivers and estuaries, new industrial development and the housing which went with it was gobbling up thousands of acres, many of them adjacent to tidal waters which once had provided habitats for wildfowl but which now formed the international highways for commercial shipping. Agriculture was in deep depression and land was changing hands. New money was staking its claim over old estates, and sometimes the new owners had ideas about traditional shooting rights which were very different to those of the farmers and landowners who had gone before.

Descending from a long line of wildfowlers, Duncan looked about him at the fast-changing landscape, revisited his old fowling grounds on the north east coast of England and found that they had altered beyond recognition. Where those changes had been brought about through natural causes or even for agricultural improvement, then he accepted them. What upset him, though, were the changes in attitude that were stealing, as Duncan saw it, the common heritage of the ordinary wildfowler by denying him access to marshes which he and his forebears had shot for generations. On one occasion Duncan visited a stretch of foreshore where three generations of his family had enjoyed wildfowling, and found himself warned off by someone who claimed the shooting rights as his own. Duncan refused to leave the shore, stood his ground and argued his case. Cards were exchanged and the other party departed in high dudgeon. Clearly the incident affected Duncan deeply, because he wrote about it afterwards in an article which was published in *Fry's Magazine*. It crystallised in his mind the need for wildfowlers to take a stand against the threats to their sport, to secure legal recognition for it, to weed out the undesirable

A young Stanley Duncan (left), his father Thomas Duncan and Thomas Waddington (right) after a morning's shooting around 1900

elements within it and to ensure that its participants conformed to a code of conduct which was both acceptable and enforceable.

'The sport needs no apology,' Duncan concluded. 'A search through ancient literature shows that, as far back as the life of the world is recorded, the pursuit of wildfowl is alluded to in some shape or form. Many pages might be written on the subject of its attractions, and very interesting they would prove. I will content myself by closing with the remark that it would be a thousand pities if the wildfowler, with all his qualities of energy and perseverance, should fail to use them for the protection, purification and the perpetuation of his sport.'

Thomas Elliot Wang Duncan, as he was christened, was born in 1878 at Heaton, Newcastle upon Tyne, the son of a railway engineer. He moved to North Yorkshire and married, but later settled in the thriving port of Hull where he came to work as an engineer with the London & North Eastern Railway. All Duncan's family were shooters. His father, Thomas, was a keen shot as were his uncles and his brother Norman, so guns, shooting and particularly wildfowling came naturally to the teenage Stanley. He had a lively and enquiring mind, was never afraid of voicing his opinion and at the early age of sixteen he started contributing to *Shooting Times* and to the other sporting magazines and periodicals of the time, slowly building up for himself an extensive network of friends and correspondents across the length and breadth of the British Isles. Nor was he afraid of meeting and talking to people across all classes of society, indeed, he was as much at home conversing with a humble wildfowler from Hull as he was when meeting and greeting the most eminent sporting gentlemen of the era. This ability was crucial when it came to drawing together the core of what was to become the embryonic wildfowlers' association, for its earliest members were not lowly longshoremen but tradesmen and local businessmen, timber merchants, trawler owners, undertakers, men of means and substance. Without the support of such as these it is unlikely that WAGBI would ever have taken wing.

Duncan was an avid shooter. His exploits are recorded in detail in the diaries which he kept throughout his shooting career, and there is no doubt that he was a marvellous shot who killed almost every time he pulled the trigger, though his secret was simple – he used a cylinder gun and rarely fired at anything beyond thirty yards. This of course meant that he had to be a master of fieldcraft, and his ability to call waders and wildfowl by whistling at them was legendary. He and his brother Norman both demonstrated on many occasions to rapt audiences the calling of curlew and wigeon and though the story may be apocryphal, it is said that once, when Duncan hailed a taxi in St James's Park, a pack of wigeon lifted from the park lake and circled over him. He shot regularly at Patrington Haven, some twenty-two miles east of Hull on the north shore of the lower Humber estuary, taking as his base the famous black hut where he stayed for two or three days at a time, often with fowling pals or his own sons. The season in those days started in late summer, so August weekends were spent at the hut shooting, fishing, busying with sketchbook and pencil or taking pictures with the cumbersome plate camera with which he became a

The Duncan family and friends in around 1894. Left to right *Thomas Duncan, Thomas Waddington, Stanley Duncan, Dr Compton, Norman Kingsley Duncan*

As a young man, Duncan shot anything which presented itself. Here he is with a bag of gulls

Duncan with the results of a morning flight

highly proficient photographer. In the winter Duncan would flight curlews from his favourite 'hut' built from chalk blocks on the tide's edge or launch his punt from Patrington Haven and ghost down the Haven channel out onto the grey, misty waters of the estuary. He had gained his initial punt gunning experience on the Tees, and punting was a sport which he found especially captivating. In later years Duncan spent a great deal of time building and designing gunning punts or working on the sleek grey ordnance with which they were armed.

Shooting wild birds in the period before the First World War was characterised by the phrase 'what's hit is history, what's missed is mystery' and Duncan was most definitely in the former camp. He shot anything which presented itself. His diary for 12 August 1911 opens with the note 'shot 1 barn owl, 3 waterhens, 2 curlews & 4 pigeons' the bag for the remainder of the two day visit included a gull, a grey plover, a knot, two immature shelducks, two greenshanks, a redshank and a kestrel. The season continued in a similar vein thereafter: herons, kingfishers, waders, gulls, wildfowl and

Many local wildfowlers used the black hut *as a base for their shooting expeditions*

Stanley Duncan was an accomplished wildfowl artist

waterbirds of all sorts fell to his gun on a weekly basis, though 1 September would see him walk the drains and marshes for the coveys of wild grey partridges which abounded in the East Yorkshire countryside, plus hares, rabbits and anything else which he could stow aboard his bicycle for the journey back to Hull.

Big bags were not in his nature, although he was not averse to enjoying a bonanza when conditions were right, once shooting one hundred and fifty curlews in two tides with his brother Norman. In his younger days, Duncan went pigeon shooting on his bicycle and could only carry one hundred cartridges at a time, but even so, his best bag was sixty-five pigeons which were carried home on his bike. Times improved and he got a car, enabling him to increase the number of cartridges which he carried with him. On one occasion he fired two hundred shots at birds coming into newly sown peas and bagged one hundred and forty-five. 'I enjoyed the sixty-five got on the bike better than the one hundred and forty-five,' he commented later.

A somewhat florid communicator in the written word, Duncan thought long and hard before he opened his mouth in public. But when he did so, his words were short and to the point. *Shooting Times* editor Tim Sedgwick once described a meeting

ABOVE:
Duncan believed in introducing his offspring to wildfowling at an early age. He is shown here shooting from a punt with one of his sons

LEFT:
Duncan modified his bicycle to enable him to carry his gun and one hundred cartridges

The Humber in Duncan's day was a popular location both for local and visiting punt gunners

Sir Ralph Payne-Gallwey, first president of WAGBI

which he had attended at which Duncan had been present. Discussion had raged over some point or other whilst all the time the old man had remained silent. Then, at an appropriate pause in the conversation there started a deep rumble from somewhere down in Duncan's stomach and out came the few choice words which cut straight to the point of the debate.

Duncan took the opportunity to meet and talk to any shooters of note who visited his part of the east coast and one of these was Sir Ralph Payne-Gallwey. One of the greatest of all the Edwardian gentleman wildfowlers, Payne-Gallwey, of Thirkleby Park, Yorkshire had devoted his life to shooting and most especially wildfowling. The third volume of his *Letters to Young Shooters* published in 1896, was – and in some respects still is – the text book on the subject. Payne-Gallwey was constantly investigating, experimenting and researching on matters such as ballistics, duck decoys and the design and construction of gunning punts, and travelled all over the British Isles in pursuit of wildfowl. Early in January 1904 he visited Patrington over a period of two weeks to shoot the area around Sunk Island, lodging at the Holderness Arms. He noticed that an old fisherman and fowler spent every winter all alone on board a smack moored in the very creek where, concidentally, Duncan launched his punts. 'I envy him,' observed Payne-Gallwey in his diary, adding that he at once engaged the old man to attend him when he was afloat. But the weather was not favourable and Payne-Gallwey must have spent hours kicking his heels by the tideline, no doubt talking with the local gunners one of whom was, of course, Stanley Duncan. The railway engineer shared with the baronet his dreams of founding an association for the protection of wildfowlers, to be told that such an organisation had indeed been formed, but that it had foundered through lack of support. However, Duncan was undaunted and pressed on with his vision. It must have been obvious to anyone intent upon forming a wildfowling association at the time that the support of such a formidable authority as Payne-Gallwey would be invaluable, and in due course Sir Ralph gave his personal blessing to Duncan's endeavours and consented to become the association's first president.

The exact date upon which WAGBI came into existence remains something of an enigma. Long established tradition holds that it was in the year of 1908, and this assertion has been celebrated on countless thousands of badges and car stickers, not to mention the fact that it was emblazoned on the association's letterhead for many years. Imagine WAGBI director John Anderton's embarrassment, therefore, when at the association's diamond jubilee celebrations at Hull in 1968, 'young'

Stanley Duncan confided to him that WAGBI had actually been founded by his father in 1907. The earlier date is alluded to in a brief reference in a typewritten article by Duncan senior, undated but probably written at some time in the 1950s. In it Duncan states: 'It was not until 1907, at a meeting in the Imperial Hotel, Hull, that the Wildfowlers' Association of Gt Britain and Ireland was formed, and Sir Ralph Payne-Galwey (sic) consented to become its first President.'

With the jubilee celebrations in full swing, Anderton kept the discrepancy quiet, and stuck to the 'official' line that the association's birth was in 1908 and not the previous year. He was probably right to do so, for Duncan's memory in his later years was failing and there exists no other independent corroboration of the comment made in that brief typewritten statement. We know that on 26 October 1907, Duncan sought the assistance of the Editor of *Shooting Times* with the words: 'Sir, I have been asked to suggest a Wildfowlers' Association, to which you, Mr Editor might give some assistance by permitting your paper to be the organ through which proposals might be considered and views obtained...' Those words do not suggest that the association was already in being, so if indeed it was formed in 1907, then the formation did not occur before the very end of that year. So far as the documentary evidence is concerned, the first entry in the minute book is a record of a committee meeting held on 4 March 1908. Furthermore, a minute dated 2 April 1908 reads: 'Mr Procter proposed that the year of membership should run from July 1st to June 30th in each year, so that present members' *second* year subscriptions will not become due until July 1st 1909...' It seems, concluded Anderton, that while a *decision* to form the association may indeed have been taken in 1907, there was no record of any meeting taking place earlier than the following March.

The fact remains that six persons were present at that first recorded committee meeting in March 1908 held at 44 De la Pole Avenue, Hull, all of them local men: Alec Holt, Percy G Timms, J W Barchard, Norman Duncan, William Lancaster and Stanley Duncan himself. Lancaster, a local undertaker, acted as treasurer and of course Duncan was secretary. In his minute book he recorded that the London, City & Midland Banking Co Ltd, Hull, would be the association's bankers, that the rules were approved by all present and that the Imperial Hotel, Hull, had been selected as the place to hold a general meeting. In the closing minute of that brief account, William Lancaster 'considered progress to date highly encouraging and favourable'. In response, Norman Duncan 'wished success to attend the efforts of the association'.

Minutes of the first recorded WAGBI committee meeting, held on 4 March 1908

Progress was rapid as the founders threw their energies behind the infant association, and another committee meeting was held on 18 March. Then, on 2 April a further committee meeting was combined with a general meeting, most probably the first full meeting of the association. While it was claimed in later years that this first meeting of WAGBI was held in the black hut, the tarred and weatherboarded structure beside the tidal channel at Patrington which formed the base camp for so many of Duncan's fowling expeditions, the gathering was in fact held in the rather grander, if somewhat less romantic, surroundings of the Imperial Hotel, Hull. The structure of the fledgling Wildfowlers' Association was already becoming established and at that general meeting simple administrative tasks were set in motion, such as the purchase of receipt books, the ordering of the first metal badges and the printing of membership cards and five thousand letterheads at a cost of £2 10s. Impressive stationery designed by C H Stafford of Nottingham was adopted to ensure a gravitas appropriate to a national organisation – WAGBI maintained the tradition of having a pictorial letterhead until after the Second World War. A network of regional contacts was also drawn together. While the original executive Committee members were from Hull, WAGBI's sights were set high from the

The Imperial Hotel, Hull, where the first general meeting of WAGBI took place on 2 April 1908. This photograph was taken in August 1966, two months before the hotel was demolished

outset, and honorary secretaries for Scotland and Ireland were immediately appointed, with five shillings being voted to W A Nicholson (Scotland) and Thomas B Gower (Ireland) to 'to defray or assist in expense of postage stamps'.

From its inception, WAGBI was recruiting from all over the British Isles. The bulk of the founding members were, not surprisingly, from Hull and its locality, but the membership records for 1908 show addresses in Surrey, Kent, Essex, Warwickshire, Lancashire, Sussex, Yorkshire, London, Norfolk, Bedfordshire, Shropshire, Cheshire, Devon, Worcestershire, Northumberland and several from Scotland and Ireland. That first year saw the recruitment of an impressive one hundred and forty members.

Relationships with other bodies were discussed and settled. Nicholas Everitt, WAGBI's first Hon Solicitor, was a Norfolk lawyer and author of the book on shooting law *Shots from a Lawyer's Gun* who also, incidentally, had the first motor car registration in Norwich. In July 1908 he suggested that WAGBI should affiliate to the Amalgamated Game Guild and Field Sports Association, but the committee cherished its independence and wrote to Everitt explaining that it did not, for the time being at least, 'see any means whereby a benefit would be derived or any compensation for its outlay by affiliation'. The invitation stood, however, and affiliation was eventually agreed, on the basis of a £5 subscription. This was later, in 1914, altered to 10% of turnover – WAGBI's income in that year being £46 5s.

From the outset it was clear that WAGBI was to be a politically active organisation which fought for the interests of wildfowlers. At the general meeting held on 12 November 1908 in the Imperial Hotel, indicated in the minute book as the 'First General Meeting' but more likely merely the first such meeting in the second subscription year, it was resolved to seek additional short-period game licences at a cost of 10s per week or 2/6d a day, an extension of the open season until 15 March and free rail travel for members' dogs accompanying their masters 'when bent on shooting'. A letter was sent by Duncan to the Railway Clearing House and two leading Railway Managers on this latter point. Naturally there was discussion about the very issue which had fired Duncan's enthusiasm in setting up the association in the first instance – access to the foreshore. There was concern over a court case which threatened to stop public rights over the foreshore, and it was agreed that sporting MPs should be written to on the subject 'with a view to increasing public interest on matters relative (to) foreshore & public rights'. Members were also exhorted to ascertain the attitude of their local county councils with regard to wildfowling, open seasons and the protection of birds, a particularly important matter at a time when local authorities had considerable powers to determine when certain species of wild birds could be shot. Finally, it was agreed that meetings should also be entertaining and instructive. A decision was made to obtain a lantern and slides with a view to an illustrated address being given at the next meeting. These 'magic lantern' talks became a feature of early WAGBI meetings.

And so WAGBI was launched onto an unsuspecting shooting world: a confident, energetic organisation with big ambitions and a spirited determination to get things done. Few if any in that meeting room at the Imperial Hotel could have guessed that their association would still be in business in a hundred years, let alone could they have dreamed of the size and breadth of what it would become.

The black hut

Beside the tidal channel leading from the Humber estuary towards the East Yorkshire village of Patrington Haven stood the black hut. A simple structure, time-worn and weatherbeaten from a century's exposure to the keen east wind, the black hut has assumed a mythical status in the iconography of WAGBI and BASC as the place where the idea of a wildfowlers' association was first conceived. Indeed, so many legends have been woven around Stanley Duncan's shooting hut that it can be hard to disentangle myth from reality.

In their introduction to *The New Wildfowler* in 1961, John Anderton and Col James Vallance, then honorary secretary and chairman respectively of WAGBI, related that 'our founder called an inaugural meeting which was held in Stanley Duncan's wildfowling hut, which stands to this day at Patrington Haven, not many miles from Hull'. Yet even this simple sentence is incorrect in two basic respects: neither was the inaugural general meeting of WAGBI held in the hut, nor did the hut even belong to Stanley Duncan.

To understand the background to the hut it is necessary to cast the mind back to the mid 1800s, when the marshes around Patrington were being drained for agriculture. Land reclamation in those days was a laborious process which involved huge gangs of navvies armed only with picks, shovels and wheelbarrows, but then as now, the engineer in charge would require some form of temporary site office. In 1850 a new bank was constructed to enclose a section of the Patrington marshes, the date being carved in the stone capping of a bridge over which today passes an unmetalled track leading to the river, and although there is no evidence to support the theory, it seems likely that the drainage gang erected a small weatherboarded hut to the south of the Haven channel to serve as a headquarters.

Drainage works were an evolving process and at some time in the late 1800s the Haven channel was reconfigured and a sluice, the 'New Clough', was built across it to mark the head of the tidal river. At that point, the old hut was most probably dismantled and moved to a new site on the bank of the channel beside the sluice, possibly to serve again as a site office. Those who knew it confirm that the hut's rough and ill-fitting planks bore holes and splits which indicated that it had indeed been taken to pieces and reassembled. So the black hut was not Stanley Duncan's – it was built and reassembled instead by the drainage commissioners.

That is not to say that it wasn't used extensively by the local fowlers. At one time it is said that a professional fowler lived there, and by the turn of the twentieth century Duncan and his friends used it on a regular basis. It was a long journey by train and bicycle from Hull to Patrington, and Duncan would regularly arrive for two or three days' fowling, sleeping overnight in the hut where no doubt he and his shooting friends filled the long evenings with yarns spun by the flickering light of a spirit lantern. Given the passion with which Duncan pieced together his plans for a new wildfowlers' association, it is inconceivable that his hopes and dreams were not shared with other like-minded souls on such occasions. To that extent, then, the black hut may indeed have been the spiritual home of WAGBI.

In due course the black hut was joined by two other similar structures, one of which certainly was built by Stanley Duncan. By 1908 the complex of huts beside the sluice had become the winter headquarters for several fowlers. Punts were moored in the narrow tidal channel or pulled up on the bank, though it was a long pull in a gunning punt from the sluice down to the shootable waters of the open river.

In later years, many other fowlers stayed in the black hut, using it as a base for their shooting as did Duncan

Wildfowlers outside the black hut after a successful morning flight c.1908

A party of wildfowlers outside the black hut with Jeffery Harrison, centre. By the late 1950s the hut had assumed considerable importance as WAGBI's purported birthplace and visiting shooters regularly had themselves photographed outside it

and his friends. Others visited out of curiosity and, as the legends surrounding the hut grew and developed, wildfowlers had their photographs taken beside it, much as any tourist might want a picture of himself in front of a famous or historic landmark.

So what became of the hut? It stood well above the high water mark of the biggest spring tides, and even the epic tidal surge of 1953 did not reach it. Indeed, the morning after that devastating event, local fowlers Alan Credland and John Ormerod cycled to Patrington Haven fearing that the hut might have been washed away. They found it safe and sound. In fact the hut survived until 1969 when, following an exceptionally wet nine months, the rivers board had to install two powerful pumps to lower the level of the floodwaters. Duncan's old punt shed was pulled down and it was thought unlikely that the black hut itself would withstand the constant vibration. However, it survived this ordeal, only to succumb after the dismantling of the pumping equipment in September. *Shooting Times* reported the following month that the hut had been washed away by a big spring tide on 28 September which flooded the whole area. However, given the high ground on which it was standing, it would seem more likely that some anonymous digger driver simply bulldozed it into an ignominious death as he cleared the site after the removal of the pumping gear.

This massive canvas by Julian Novorol depicts a wigeon's eye view of the famous 'black hut' as it may have appeared in Stanley Duncan's day. The painting hangs in the Duke of Westminster lecture hall at Marford Mill

Today the place is marked by a permanent memorial, recognising the part which the hut undoubtedly played in the history of BASC and of wildfowling as a whole. But just to add to the confusion of the unwary, the memorial stone, surrounded by a low iron railing, stands on the south bank of the Haven channel, not the north bank where the hut was when Duncan knew it. This fact is made clear in a small plan which is inset into the top of the memorial, showing the location of the three huts which comprised the 'black hut complex' – together with that of the sluice, which itself was removed and of which no trace now remains. Perhaps the most atmospheric reconstruction is captured in Julian Novorol's magnificent painting *Wigeon over the Black Hut* which hangs at BASC headquarters, and thanks to Julian's detailed research we can catch a glimpse of what Duncan's fowling quarters must have looked like.

The shoreline of the Humber continues to change, as it has done so many times down the ages. Today, the old sea walls are being partially dismantled, and under a 'managed retreat' scheme the tide now flows once more across newly established saltings and foreshore beside the Haven channel. Perhaps the ghosts of those nineteenth century engineers who built the black hut look down in horror at the reversion of drained farmland to salt marsh, but if they do, then Duncan's ghost must surely gaze approvingly at the restoration of habitat where curlew and redshank call once more and wigeon pitch into the flooding creeks at evening flight.

Chapter 2
EXTENDED DIRECTIONS

Securing foreshore shooting was an important theme throughout the early years. Rights over mudflats and tidal waters at Bosham, the Blackwater in Essex and at Wells in Norfolk were all under threat. 'Wildfowling on estuaries will be doomed if things are allowed to go on as they now are,' complained Duncan. But WAGBI did not simply wring its hands in despair, it reasoned that if its own members were seen to be responsible people who kept to the rules, then deals might perhaps be struck in their favour. In his capacity as secretary, Duncan therefore wrote to the Lord of the Manor at Bosham asking that local members be allowed to enjoy the privileges of wildfowling as they had done in the past, on the understanding that the fowlers would assist in the suppression of poaching. The same approach was proposed at Wells, where it was suggested to the landowner, The Earl of Leicester, that the 'fact of a person being a member might be a sufficient guarantee of his sincerity as a sportsman and thus aid him to obtain the necessary permission to shoot over the marshes in question'. The suggestion bore fruit. In December 1911 Lord Leicester agreed to permit members of the Wildfowlers' Association to shoot wildfowl freely over the salt marshes at Wells. That same year foreshore rights were under discussion at Lough Swilly in Co. Donegal and in Lancashire, where an approach was made by WAGBI to the Hesketh estate. In September 1913 the secretary was asked to investigate and obtain legal advice and opinion over foreshore rights at Blakeney Point in Norfolk. Evidently this dispute was concluded successfully, for a vote of thanks was given to the National Trust and the local members.

Shooting seasons were also up for debate, and the early minutes reveal much wrangling and disagreement over what was appropriate. While shooting seasons for game birds had long been fixed by the 1831 Game Act in England & Wales and the Game (Scotland) Act 1772 north of the Scottish border, those for wildfowl were regulated by county councils. In January 1910, Holland (Lincolnshire) CC proposed extending its wildfowling season and not surprisingly the Wildfowlers' Association wrote in support. Likewise Yorkshire's East Riding CC was asked to get its open season extended from 12 August to 15 March. In the event the dates were amended, and an open season of 1 August to 1 March was carried by two votes.

But this was all piecemeal stuff. What WAGBI wanted was uniformity across the country, so that wildfowlers knew where they stood no matter which part of Britain they might happen to be shooting in. Eventually, after long debate, the committee proposed a close season from 31 March to 31 July for curlew, godwit, whimbrel, green, golden and grey plover, redshank, knot, snipe, woodcock, teal, wigeon, mallard, shoveler, pochard, pintail and greylag. Clearly there was much argument on this list right up to the final decision, for brent, barnacle, pink-footed and white-fronted geese were all deleted from the hand-written minute. 'This resolution', wrote Duncan in 1911, 'is the unanimous decision of the Committee (after three years research and careful consideration) as the most preferable in pure fairness to bird protection to all sections of gunning sportsmen (the wildfowling community) and also that the period mentioned being contended as quite adequate for all necessary and generally beneficial protection for these birds.' Again, the degree of argument and dissent is indicated by the heavy crossings out and amendment of the handwritten record, but the fowlers had at last agreed upon a universal close season for shore-birds and wildfowl throughout the British Isles. How were they now to implement it? A minute from 1912 gives us a clue, where the committee cites as admirable a Wild Bird Order framed by Suffolk CC and recommends it to other counties. In due course, WAGBI set about approaching councils and encouraging them to adopt its preferred open and close seasons.

Making recommendations to county councils was all very well, but the committee fully realised the powerlessness of a small group of wildfowlers sitting around a table in Hull and acknowledged 'how little the association is yet known'. They needed more members and more support, and this in turn required more publicity. From the outset Arthur Bonsall, editor of *Shooting Times*, had given his support to WAGBI. Indeed, in the Christmas 1908 issue the magazine carried a supportive article about the newly formed association, funds being subsequently voted by the committee to purchase one hundred copies of the 'Shooter' so that the good news could be spread far and wide to current and prospective new members. Three years later, advertisements were taken in *The Field* and, at a cost of £5, in Stanley Duncan and Guy Thorne's new book *The Complete Wildfowler, Ashore and Afloat*.

This advertisement set out WAGBI's stall for all to see. It included a complete list of officers, starting with the association's illustrious president, Sir Ralph Payne-Gallwey, and its list of vice presidents which included gentleman gunner of the Essex Blackwater, Count de la Chapelle, Arthur Bonsall and Guy Thorne. By now there was not only an executive committee of seventeen, but also a corresponding committee comprising wildfowlers from around the principal fowling areas of Great Britain and Ireland. The stated aims of the association were to uphold the legal rights of wildfowlers, to foster courtesy and etiquette in the sport, to amass information about different wildfowling quarters, to acquire fowling grounds where possible, to create a spirit of sportsmanlike respect and suppress jealous shooting, to encourage an interest in wildfowl ornithology, to record its proceedings and to publish them amongst its members.

The copywriter – almost certainly Duncan himself – confidently proclaimed: 'The association has now reached a stage of success that demands the attention of all directly or indirectly interested in its objects. Those who participate in the joys of wildfowling should help forward its good work in extended directions.' WAGBI was up and running, and in business.

Meetings in the early days were serious matters – there were, after all, no fewer than three undertakers on the executive committee. Charles Proctor, a contracting plumber who specialised in leaded church windows would take the chair, and with his waxed moustache and easy, yet authoritative manner, would take complete control of the assembled members. Those who attended were all knowledgeable wildfowlers, and the discussion continued earnestly into the evening until it was time to finish with a lantern slide lecture in which Proctor, a wonderful storyteller, would speak over slides of wildfowl, birds of prey and vermin trapping. Occasionally, Sidney H Smith, a regular visitor to Sudan, would bring a touch of the exotic, with slides of African wildlife, while of course Stanley Duncan's own slides of wildfowling, punt gunning and shotgun ballistics were a regular staple. His son, 'young' Stanley, made the 3¼ inch square slides from his father's glass negative plates, occasionally embellishing the tedious pictures of shotgun patterns with extra dots of Indian ink if the shot holes looked a bit sparse. Evidently the audience seemed not to worry and concentrated intently upon what the speaker had to say, the only laughs occurring when the projectionist burnt his fingers on the arc lamp or inserted his slides upside down.

To add gravitas to the association, Duncan adopted for WAGBI the Latin motto *'non sibi cunctis'*, translated loosely as 'not for himself, for others also', the words being borrowed from Old Kingston High School in Hull, the school which Duncan's sons Horace, Cyril and 'young' Stanley attended. The motto was used with aplomb for many years on letterheads, annual reports and official documents, though some ribald comment was occasioned when in the golden jubilee annual report in 1958 the motto was printed without the second 'c'.

As well as dealing with the legal issues such as shooting seasons and access to foreshore, the association started to take an interest in services to its members, and one of these was the provision of guides to travelling wildfowlers planning to shoot in unfamiliar parts of the country. There were at the time a substantial number of 'professional' wildfowlers. These tended to be longshoremen in the small towns or fishing villages around the coast, who tended their nets, crab pots or mussel beds in the summer, but who in winter turned to the shoulder gun or, very often, the gunning punt to eke out a precarious living by shooting ducks and geese for the market. An alternative source of income to the professional longshore gunner was the money which he might receive from visiting gentleman fowlers who wished to be taken out shooting by a person with an intimate knowledge of local geography, tidal patterns and wildfowl movements. WAGBI was particularly interested in supporting the professional wildfowler, and one of its earliest objectives was the compiling of a register of such professionals 'who are prepared to assist and be hired by amateur members who require a few days shooting in their district'.

One of WAGBI's original objectives was to support the professional wildfowlers, many of whom were engaged by visiting gentlemen gunners as local guides. Here a visiting sportsman shoots seabirds off Flamborough Head with two local longshoreman wildfowlers in the early 1900s

Likewise, the association also invited hotel proprietors and those having apartments in wildfowling districts to forward their names and addresses so that these might be placed on a wildfowlers' register which would in turn be accessible to the membership at large. Those seeking the services of professional guides or information about local accommodation were asked to write directly to the honorary general secretary.

The idea of a wildfowlers' register was a good one, but if indeed it took off then it can only have had a short life, as references to it within the proceedings of the association are very limited. It seems, though, that WAGBI dabbled in a range of areas which were peripheral to the central objects of the association. Another of these was the recommending of particular types

Many professional wildfowlers used single-handed gunning punts

of gun, ammunition or equipment. In February 1914 certificates of merit were awarded by the Committee to Messrs Burberry Ltd for the excellence of their waterproof garments, while in May of the same year, WAGBI debated the relative merits of leather as against rubber for the manufacture of thigh waders. It concluded that leather was superior by a margin of twenty-eight points to sixteen. There was also a lively debate on the question of what is the perfect wildfowling gun. Duncan's own views on this must have been well known, for in *The Complete Wildfowler* he wrote: 'I have a double 10 bore built for me by Mr Greener which is an absolutely perfect weapon. Its range is enormous; its hitting power is very great, and as a duck gun for fast flighting work incomparable. It comes to the shoulder – weight 9½ lbs. – with the greatest ease, and I can shoot redshank and snipe with it with comfort…'. Clearly he argued his case with his usual energy, for the outcome of the debate by a decision of six votes to three, with two abstentions, was 'that a 9lbs 10 bore to take 3 inch perfect cases was the handiest and most generally useful (shoulder) weapon for dealing with ducks and geese.'

By the time that the first frosts had arrived and the wigeon were crowding the estuaries on that fateful autumn of 1914, it must have been clear to all that debates about rubber waders and wildfowling guns were about to be overshadowed by a different and much uglier form of shooting that was taking place in the trenches of northern France. The Committee met on 15 January 1915, and the seventh Annual General Meeting of the association was held two weeks later. There was no meeting the following year, and at the 1917 AGM it was decided that the financial audit be suspended 'until more favourable times,' that no further meetings be held during the war and that the affairs of the association be left to the able management of the Secretary. Duncan's copy of the agenda for that meeting still exists, annotated by his own hand. With it is a circular letter to members which reads:

'It is with regret we have to record a sad decrease in our members due to the War. In consequence the Association is suffering lamentably in its resources by the fact that much in the way of "assistance" & "investigation" is at present drawing hard upon time & effort. We have strived to continue the good work of our Society by securing concessions where regulations have been imposed, and aiding returned Warriors in quest of wildfowling. Unless, however, adequare (*sic*) support is forthcoming we shall not be able to carry on much longer. We sincerely trust you will give us your kind attention and early support that when happier times arrive we shall be able to progress again with vigour.'

WAGBI, like countless similar bodies, had been overtaken by the national emergency. It was foundering and could so easily have stopped functioning altogether but for the secretary's own personal determination. He clearly regarded wildfowling as an activity which supported the war effort and his diary notes with strong approval that the Board of Agriculture and Fisheries, through the efforts of the association, extended the 1917 season until the end of March and the period within which wildfowl could be sold until the 15 April. He himself celebrated the event by going afloat in his punt on the evening of 31 March and shooting a single mallard drake with his punt gun. Indeed, Duncan continued wildfowling throughout the war and his shooting diaries record the Zeppelin raids over Hull on the nights of 6 March and 5 April 1916. 'Saw Zeps on both occasions "Fearful Machines". Height probably 3 miles. Saw bombs drop. All the people terrified. Damage considerable.'

After the war ended in 1918, the association remained at a low ebb for several years, although the committee remained in being and Duncan himself continued to dispense advice. Members

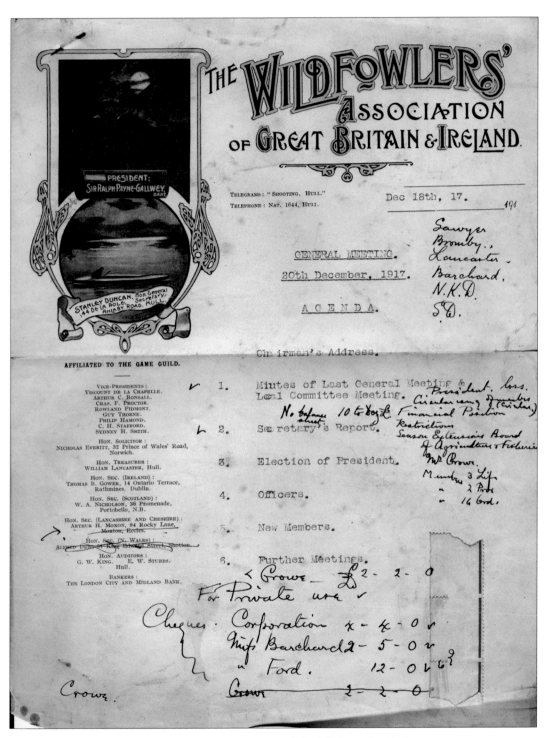

Duncan's own annotated copy of the AGM agenda, 1917

were anxious about the plight of the professional wildfowlers and warmly welcomed in 1919 the generous offer by Dr Charles Heath which resulted in the creation of a fund, the interest from which was used to benefit the professional fowlers. In the following year, with civil war in Ireland, a motion was passed expressing sympathy in the 'present lamentable sporting and other conditions' with the Irish membership, though by 1921 it was already being proposed that the network of corresponding committee members in Ireland should be revived once again.

Another sign of the times was the fact that in 1925 one of the original campaigning objectives of WAGBI, the gaining of concessionary rail travel for shooters, was placed on the back burner, since 'most shooters now travel by road in Motor Cars'. The campaign for cheap rail tickets for fowlers was finally dropped altogether three years later. Even so, the then president, Dr Charles Heath, travelled by train. On one occasion he arrived in Hull for a winter meeting, and 'young' Stanley drove his father to meet him from the station in a four-seater open-topped tourer with a hood and side curtains. Trains were not heated in those days and Heath emerged from the station in a deerstalker, travelling coat and cape with a rug over his arm. Upon being greeted he took one look at the car and another at the young driver, then turned to Duncan and said 'Stanley, get me a cab.'

The prospect of bird protection legislation was very much a concern during the inter-war years. Duncan was particularly incensed when

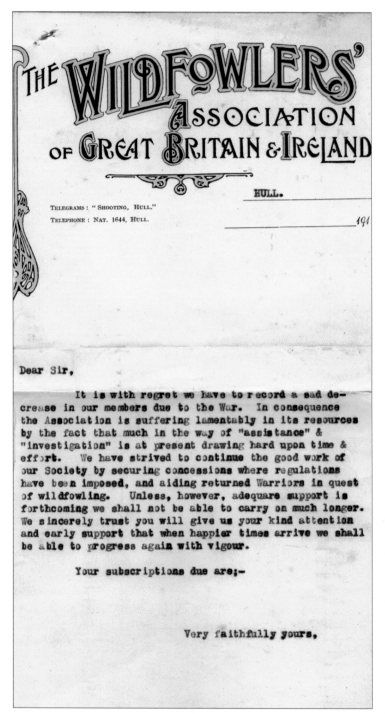

A circular letter to members from 1917 warning of the difficulties faced by WAGBI as a result of the war

Duncan poses for the camera with his guns and decoys after a goose shooting expedition near Hull

decisions were made without adequate – or indeed without any – input from the wildfowlers who were most directly affected by them. In October 1921 he wrote to County Hall, Beverley, about protection of the lapwing in the East Riding: 'The lapwing is the mainstay of the rough shooter's general and wildfowler's winter sport...Now with the green plover banned the estuary shooter is with good reason, very deeply aggrieved and finds his humble sport denied him, not because of the weakness of his cause but because he has overlooked the necessity of representation, where it appears to be very much needed...We pray you to reconsider your decision to prohibit the shooting of the non-local lapwings which come to the East Riding in winter.'

When a new Wild Birds Protection Bill was published, the wildfowlers' association immediately resolved to oppose strenuously any measures likely to become law, including a ban on wildfowling from mechanically propelled craft, 'unnecessary protection' and the 'curtailment of shooting in any form'. The prospect of new legislation must have had a galvanising effect upon Duncan and his supporters, for in July 1925 WAGBI held its first extraordinary general meeting at the Charing Cross Hotel in London. Dr Charles Heath, who had become president upon the death of Sir Ralph Payne-Gallwey, was in the chair and it was agreed that a London branch and a parliamentary committee should be formed immediately.

WAGBI deplored what it saw as the meddlesome and unnecessarily mischievous provisions of the proposed legislation, and in December a deputation consisting of Dr Heath, Messrs S Duncan, E Valpy, C Proctor and Count de la Chapelle met Lord Gray, chairman of the Wild Birds Advisory Committee to ensure that the views of wildfowlers were expressed with due vigour. The campaign over the Wild Birds Protection Bill was regarded as a creditable effort, but it was clearly not felt that there was any great need to continue with parliamentary activity in the long term and shortly afterwards the London branch became defunct. However, this brief involvement in high politics was a foretaste of what was to come in later years.

Unlike game birds, wildfowl migrate across national boundaries, and wildfowlers quickly realised the need to become involved with the developing international conservation movement if they were to ensure that the needs of wildfowl populations were properly considered throughout the length of their entire flyways and that some of the unique traditions of British wildfowling were not to be lost. Flyway conservation became established in the United States during the 1930s when the loss of huge areas of wetland during the 'dust bowl' led to the formation of

Ducks Unlimited. In Britain it was as early as 1928 that a proposal was made to set up some form of co-operation with representatives of wildfowling in other European countries. Two years later, international co-operation was again up for discussion at the general meeting, but the resources of WAGBI at the time were very limited, and it was decided that the best way of exchanging notes with foreign sporting societies was through the medium of the British Field Sports Society. In 1935 Stanley Duncan was appointed to the committee of the BFSS. International co-operation may not have moved forward very much, but at least communication between Britain's sporting organisations was underway.

Even before the First World War Duncan had started to trade from his home in guns and ammunition, selling the odd shotgun or box of cartridges to one or other of his shooting chums. The gun dealing continued and increased in volume, and eventually Duncan set up a gun shop in Hull. He was still working for the railway at the time, and Stanley put his son Cyril into the shop, the business being set up in the name of C V Duncan & Co although it was soon known simply as 'Duncans'. It became a meeting place for shooters of all sorts, a clubhouse where fowlers and game shooters could drop by for a chat and pick up the latest gossip. Because of this, Duncan got to know everything that was going on in the shooting world. He would be the first to hear when the newly arrived teal or wigeon were spotted on the river, how many hares the local keepers shot on their end of season hare shoots, what guns were being sold and who was buying them: he became a veritable mine of local sporting knowledge. But he was not loose or injudicious with his tongue, indeed he was very correct in his manner, turning up in the shop in later years in his trademark three piece suit and bowler hat. On one occasion the young Arthur Leek, later to become founder of the Hull and East Riding Wildfowlers' Association, was casually chatting to 'young' Stanley, who manned the shop with his brother, when the 'old man' entered. Arthur was told in a few well chosen words that the finely polished counter was not for sitting on, and the crestfallen Leek departed with his tail between his legs.

The association did not meet frequently during the 1930s. Dr Heath died in 1935 leaving the association several hundred pounds known as the Richards Memorial Fund in memory of his late friend Dr Richards, of Darlington, and Captain Brook of Annan accepted the presidency. Stanley Duncan continued with the business of advising members on a myriad matters relating to shooting, while his son Cyril assisted with the administration, typing up technical articles and letters for his father, keeping the

Duncan's gun shop in Hull was a meeting place for local shooters. Here the celebrated wildfowling guide Kenzie Thorpe talks to Cyril Duncan

books straight and chasing the subscriptions of late payers with a polite letter. Duncan also paid visits to local wildfowling clubs, speaking at general meetings and perhaps illustrating his talk with lantern slides. Such an evening is mentioned in the earliest records of the Lancaster, Morecambe & District Wildfowlers' Club, as the Morecambe Bay WA was then known. Its 1932 hotpot supper was attended by Duncan and his magic lantern, helping to further cement the warm relationship which had existed between WAGBI and the club since its formation ten years before. Duncan put in several appearances at such events during the 1930s and in 1939 invited the club to nominate three members to sit on the WAGBI general committee. He was very supportive of initiatives by local wildfowlers, especially initiatives which sought to defend fowlers' rights against unnecessarily restrictive close seasons and shooting dates, which were still in the hands of county councils. Records from the period are very sparse, however correspondence does exist between Duncan and Eric Phillips of Pagham Harbour regarding proposals by West Sussex County Council to alter the local shooting dates. Duncan advised the wildfowlers there to hold a meeting and form a local branch of the association – in other words an affiliated wildfowling club – in order that effective protest could be mounted against the county council. In due course he wrote in support to the Home Office advising that they should adopt the close season date of 20 February on tidal waters as proposed in the Wild Duck and Goose Act 1939.

For the second time in a generation, international events cast their shadow over national life, and with the clouds of war gathering, simple pleasures of the coast and countryside such as wildfowling now seemed but trifling matters when weighed against Britain's fight for survival. Fowlers and field sportsmen played their part in the struggle of course, their skills in fieldcraft and marksmanship being turned to deadly effect, but how many of them, straining their eyes into the grey dawn from some lonely observation post, from the spray-lashed deck or from an aircraft's cockpit, must have yearned for the sound of wild geese or the whistle of wigeon over the moonlit saltings and pledged that, if they returned home when it was all over, they would ensure that shooting sports were there for their children to enjoy into the future.

Others were planning the exact opposite. The birth of the organised anti-field sports movement between the wars had drawn into its arms those who hoped for the overthrow of everything connected with privilege and tradition. In the Labour movement it found a natural ally; one which saw in the foxhunting British Establishment of the 1930s the antithesis of its own bitter struggle against the rise of fascism. When the ideological war of words turned to a war of bombs and bullets, first in Spain and later throughout most of the rest of the world, the Britain it was fighting for was a brave new world of egalitarianism, one in which scarlet coats, pheasant coverts and grouse moors had no place. Even with the tanks still rolling through Europe, the seeds of a campaign which would lead to the Hunting Act 2004 were being scattered on fertile soil and were taking root.

Though it was yet six months before Labour's 1945 landslide election victory would bring Clement Attlee into office, Duncan's circular letter to members in January of that year was stangely prescient: 'At the present moment, when so many of our active members are away on service the affairs of the above (association) are consequently apt to drift into abeyance and become almost adamant (*sic*).

'There is grave evidence and belief that Societies in this country, with immense funds, opposed to Sports Afield are very energetic and efforts are being made through legislation, to bring about the total prohibition of Hunting, Shooting and Fishing, while opportunities prevail. The Wildfowlers' Association and Shooters' Union is very desirous that its prestige and high standard of efficiency be maintained and in consequence anxious that Sportsmen generally support the cause. Membership subscriptions and donations will be welcomed.'

Whether the appeal for funds had any effect is not known, for the association, which had not met since before the war, did not assemble again until May 1946 at the Imperial Hotel, Hull. Accounts were approved and basic business was transacted, but WAGBI was a threadbare organisation and a little over a year later, at the age of sixty-nine, Stanley Duncan gave notice of his resignation after forty years of service. It must have been a shattering moment for him, for WAGBI had been a major part of his life. Charles Proctor chaired the meeting at which the matter was discussed, and it was agreed that a committee should be appointed in order to find a suitable successor.

In truth, there was not much of an association for any new secretary to take charge of. A mere three hundred members, a couple of handwritten minute books, the Richards Memorial Fund and Colonel Hawker's famous double punt gun must have seemed little to show for so many years of hard effort, and there was a strongly held view amongst some of the committee that WAGBI should give up the struggle altogether and throw in its lot with the British Field Sports Society, which was by now facing a furious fight at Westminster to save foxhunting. Independence or amalgamation, which was it to be? The debate was hotly contested, and it was finally agreed that the matter should be put to a ballot of all the membership. An extraordinary general meeting was called at the Imperial Hotel on 12 February 1949 to hear the result.

Of the three hundred and six ballot papers sent out, one hundred and sixty-four were returned in favour of the Wildfowlers' Association retaining its own identity, twenty-nine favoured amalgamation with the BFSS and seven were returned void. The die was cast and Berger Andersen, who had conducted the poll, was appointed secretary *pro tem* while a new constitution and set of rules was drafted. A temporary executive committee of twelve was formed, and Stanley Duncan was invited to become delegate to the BFSS for the coming year.

At a meeting at the Grosvenor Hotel, Manchester on 17 September 1949, the new rules were adopted and new personnel stepped onto the scene: Major James Vallance, J W (Judge) Johnson and Clarence A Devall, who was elected as the association's secretary. It was a meeting barely less auspicious than the one which had been held in Hull more than forty years earlier, because it signalled the determination of a new group of individuals to pick up the ailing WAGBI by the scruff of its neck and set it moving once more in the right direction. Of particular significance in the new rule book was the rule which determined that affiliated clubs might send representatives to the new executive committee on the basis of one for every one hundred and fifty of their own members, for this signalled the beginning of a bond which was to exist between the national association and its affiliated clubs, a bond which would lend untold strength and support to both parties in the coming years. Representatives of the Morecambe, Frodsham and Southport clubs were present at the meeting.

Equally important was the inclusion of conservation objects within the constitution of the association. Duncan had himself been a formidable practical naturalist and was a fellow of the Zoological Society, but now for the first time, WAGBI determined that it was its duty to 'Encourage and organise the rearing and ringing of wildfowl and co-operate in the study of migration and other relevant scientific investigation'.

The new organisation may have arisen, phoenix-like, from the ashes of the old, but there were still shades of the old WAGBI present, and during an adjournment a new punt gun breech block for converting muzzle loaders was inspected, while Norman Duncan entertained members with a demonstration of wader and wildfowl calls.

There was one further closure. Inevitably the debate and ballot over amalgamation with the BFSS had caused friction and upset. Once the dust had settled, the society's secretary,

The Wildfowlers' Association
Of Great Britain & Ireland

CONSTITUTION AND OBJECTS OF THE ASSOCIATION.

THE Wildfowlers' Association of Great Britain and Ireland consists of a body interested in the sport of wildfowling, having a president, vice-presidents, executive committee members, ordinary members, life members, lady members, trade members and professional members—*i.e.,* professional wildfowlers.

The aims of the Association are to uphold the rights of its members as wildfowlers, to foster a mutual understanding amongst shooters with regard to certain acts of courtesy or etiquette of sport; to amass and disseminate information of general value, relating to various and different wildfowling quarters, to help wildfowlers in every possible way; to create a spirit of sportsmanlike respect; to suppress jealous shooting; to assist in the study of wildfowl ornithology; to encourage and organise the rearing and ringing of wildfowl, and co-operate in the study of migration and other relevant scientific investigations; to record and periodically publish all proceedings.

The objects of the Association are to uphold and protect the sport of wildfowling. A beneficial regulation of the close and open seasons for wildfowl is advocated in such a way that a better state of protection may be obtained.

The Association requests the attention of all directly or indirectly interested in its objects. Those who participate in the joys of wildfowling are desired, as members, to help forward its good work in extended directions.

The Shooting Times and British Sportsman is the official organ of the Association.

The rules adopted by WAGBI on its re-formation in 1949

JW Fitzwilliam, addressed WAGBI members in order to clarify misunderstanding and to smooth troubled waters. He said that he personally would rather see all specialist associations as independent bodies. The address was much appreciated.

The Hawker punt gun

The mighty Colonel Peter Hawker, soldier, sportsman and diarist, was nothing short of a fanatic when it came to developing new equipment and techniques for wildfowling, and his celebrated double punt gun is BASC's oldest and proudest possession. When Hawker's contemporaries armed themselves with ever larger punt guns, he pondered how he too could cram massive firepower into a punt gun which combined modest recoil with a service weight that would be sufficiently light to enable his punt to carry it in the shallowest of waters. Eventually he hatched the idea of building a double gun which was capable of discharging a pound of shot from each barrel or, if required, a murderous two pounds to a double discharge.

Detail of the right (flint) lock. The momentary delay in ignition between this and the left (percussion) lock was calculated to minimise recoil and maximise killing power

The Hawker gun has remained one of WAGBI and BASC's proudest possessions for more than seventy years. This view shows the revolutionary spring-dampened loop breeching beneath the massive damascus barrels

Gunner's view of the Hawker gun

In Hawker's *Instructions to Young Sportsmen* he described 'a pair of barrels put together so as to fire two circles, each one partly eclipsed with the other: the one ignited by percussion, and the other by flint, by which means the trifling difference of the two separate modes of ignition makes such an immense difference in the recoil'. The combination of flint and percussion ignition also ensured that 'at the moment when one part of the birds are being killed by the detonater (*sic*), the others are just conveniently opening their wings for the flint barrel', thus ensuring a doubly effective execution.

Hawker tells us that during its construction the double gun, built in 1824, went through several hands, including those of 'best' gunmakers Durs Egg and Joseph Manton; Fullerd, who made the barrels, and Westley Richards, who manufactured the revolutionary loop breeching upon which the gun is mounted. Hawker was careful, however to ensure that he was credited with the conception and on the top rib he is described as 'Inventor and Director'. Although it was later claimed that the gun cost £250, Hawker actually paid £210 for it, after a bitter dispute with Egg. The deal box and cleaning rod for which Egg wanted to charge an additional £4 11s Hawker received free of charge after a meeting attended by Hawker's solicitor and Manton, in which both parties agreed to decide the matter on the toss of a coin. Hawker believed that Egg was able to cheat by tossing 'tails' so allowed him to toss, called 'tails' and won. After an initial trial in October 1825 on the park lake at Alresford House, in which Hawker loosed off at a huge company of starlings, killing an estimated 500 of them, he used the gun with great success against more conventional quarry at Keyhaven, his fowling ground on the south coast, for twenty-five seasons.

The Hawker gun at the Birmingham Proof House, photographed for Colin Willcock's The Gun-Punt Adventure *1958*

Although manufacture was entrusted to some of the best gunmakers of the day, Hawker ensured that his contribution as inventor and director was recorded

In 1889 the gun was purchased for £12 by the equally devoted punt gunner Sir Ralph Payne-Gallwey Bt, and it is pictured with him in a painting completed in 1914 by Anthony de Bree of the gunroom at Thirkleby Park, Sir Ralph's home near Thirsk, N Yorkshire. It also almost certainly features in the magnificent painting of 1892, also by de Bree, of punt gunning at Lindisfarne which hangs at Marford Mill. In 1919 Sir Ralph died, leaving much wildfowling equipment to disperse, and his widow sold the Hawker punt gun to Stanley Duncan who in turn sold it to Dr Charles J Heath, successor to Sir Ralph as president of WAGBI. When Dr Heath died in 1935 he left the association the Hawker gun.

A brass plate affixed to the gun provides a brief, if slightly inaccurate, outline of its history

One of the most celebrated Edwardian gentleman wildfowlers, Sir Ralph Payne-Gallwey consented to become WAGBI's first president. This painting of him with his double punt after a shot at brent geese at Lindisfarne was painted in 1892 by Anthony de Bree and hangs in the library at Marford Mill

As WAGBI had no permanent home, the gun for some years endured a peripatetic existence and on occasions it was almost sold to raise funds. It was moved in 1946 from Lancaster to the York Philosophical Society's museum in York, and thence, three years later, to the Wildfowl Research Institute in Tring. However, the executive committee was anxious that it should be seen by the shooting public and in 1951 they decided to loan it for display at suitable gunshops. Blands valued it at £300 in 1952 and put it on display at their premises in the Strand before carrying out repairs to the gun. It travelled the following year to an exhibition arranged by the Dee Wildfowlers and in 1956 it went on semi-permanent display at the Birmingham Proof House.

In due course, WAGBI acquired its own headquarters at Marford Mill, Rossett, and the gun took pride of place in the entrance lobby before eventually being moved to the newly opened Duke of Westminster lecture hall, where it currently resides.

Many gunmakers and engineers have since manufactured double-barrelled punt guns, but the Hawker gun still holds a unique place in wildfowling history. Its barrels measure 8 ft 3½ in in length and the muzzle diameter is 1½ ins. The gun's overall weight is 193 lb.

Chapter 3
THE WILDFOWLERS' CHARTER

ritain's postwar Labour Government lost no time in setting about its task of rearranging the country's political geography. Health and housing were uppermost on its agenda, but the countryside was not far behind. Agriculture was reorganised and revitalised after the superhuman efforts it had made to feed the nation in wartime, while the National Parks and Access to the Countryside Act 1949 fulfilled the dream of those who saw the prospect of countryside recreation as just reward to the British people for the six years of suffering which they had endured in wartime. However, the Act, described by Town and Country Planning Minister Lewis Silkin as 'the most exciting Act of the post-war Parliament', was concerned with much more than countryside access.

The Huxley Committee, set up to investigate the nature conservation needs of England and Wales, had reported in 1947 and had recommended the creation of a string of new nature reserves plus an official advisory body to oversee them and to advise generally on conservation policy. It also proposed the creation of Sites of Special Scientific Interest in which protection would be provided to plants, wildlife and other natural features outside the designated reserves. In due course the Nature Conservancy was established, and it was to be the 1949 Act which gave the infant organisation its teeth. This restructuring of conservation policy would ultimately have huge influence on shooting, particularly wildfowling.

A full Government review of wild bird conservation was to follow shortly. Thus far bird protection had been dealt with in something of a piecemeal fashion, and it was recognised by all, wildfowlers included, that a new Act was required. What cannot have been appreciated at the time by WAGBI's new executive and officers, however, was the sheer immensity of the lobbying effort which a full-scale battle over a new bird protection Bill would involve and the strain it would place on resources, for although the Wildfowlers' Association had undergone a revival, it was still very much a part-time, amateur outfit. The accounts for 1950 show that its income for the previous year, at just £68 15s 2d, was little more than half the expenditure of £123 10s 11s, of which nearly £64 comprised postage. The total assets were only £864 1s 7d, of which £546 was tied up in the Richards Memorial Fund. There was £185 cash in the bank and the Hawker punt gun, valued at £100. Something had to be done to increase subscription income and put the association on a sound financial footing.

Huge efforts were made by the secretary, Clarry Devall, and the treasurer, G M Bowden, to reorganise and regroup. A new membership register was prepared, together with an index card system. Accounting procedures were revised and stationery, rule books and membership cards were printed. Stanley Duncan was no longer involved in the day-to-day running of the association, but even after his retirement as secretary he still remained as WAGBI's representative on the vitally important Home Office Wild Birds Advisory Committee and the International Wildfowl Inquiry Committee, and as the association's delegate to the BFSS. Duncan was also nominally on the executive committee, and it must have been hard for him to see the reins slip from his

Members of the WAGBI executive committee were guests of Morecambe Bay Wildfowlers for morning flight on the day of the association's AGM at the Ship Hotel, Overton, in 1950. Back row (left to right) E L Parish (WAGBI), Ted Berwick (MBWA), Mr Dixon (MBWA) G M Bowden (WAGBI treasurer). Front row (left to right) Geoff Mitchell (MBWA) C Devall (WAGBI secretary), Mr Shepherd (WAGBI), E Houghton (MBWA), Col J Vallance (WAGBI chairman). Morning flight was entirely blank: the wigeon was found dead on the tideline.

hands into those of the new guard. He was offered a vice presidency, which he refused, and an appeal was launched for a presentation fund.

Morecambe Bay Wildfowlers hosted the general meeting in November 1950. Prior to the meeting, which was held at the Ship Hotel at Overton, morning flight was arranged by a contingent of local fowlers, armed with 8 bores, for their honoured guests from the WAGBI executive, who were more lightly kitted out with 10 bores and a magnum 12. It was reported afterwards in the *Shooting Times* that the geese came and went, four gunshots high, and the only bird to be bagged was a wigeon that had been found dead on the tideline. Even so, two Morcambe members were elected to the WAGBI committee. Frodsham wildfowlers played host the following year, for the wildfowling clubs were by now taking a much more active part in the life of the association and WAGBI's leaders, conscious of the political battles which lay only just around the corner, realised that the vigorous involvement of ordinary fowlers who represented the grass roots of shooting had a very significant part to play in strengthening the sport's bargaining power. Not only that, but it also meant a large number of new potential members.

The call went out for the creation of new clubs. Pagham Wildfowlers were formed in response to a proposal to protect the whole of Pagham Harbour as a nature reserve, and very soon there was a string of new affiliations. In January 1952 the Home Counties, Westmorland and Strangford Lough clubs applied, then later that year the Fenland, Little Oakley, Wells & District, South Durham & N Yorkshire, South Cumberland, South Lincolnshire, North Lincolnshire, Essex and Dee clubs affiliated and the following year more clubs joined: Teeside Gun and Wildfowlers' Club, Blakeney & District, Dorset, Hull & District, Blackpool & Fylde, Holbeach & District, while proposals were made to get a Scottish group going. It was also suggested for the first time that members of affiliated clubs should be admitted as full members of WAGBI at a reduced subscription rate, thus making membership of the national body far more attractive to local fowlers. Although this proposal was eventually withdrawn and referred to the executive committee, the efforts at boosting membership bore fruit and by December 1952 a 340% increase in numbers was reported.

Even Stanley Duncan, an old man by that time, was still actively giving his support to the creation of new wildfowling clubs. When Arthur Leek, the young fellow who had so foolishly parked his bottom on the counter in Duncan's gunshop, came in one day to bemoan the troubles which were afflicting the local fowlers, the old man overheard him from the back of the shop, came to the counter and said: 'Arthur, you ought to get a club going.' Leek had a notice posted in the shop announcing the proposal to form a wildfowling club in Hull and within a couple of weeks it was full of signatures from prospective members. Flushed with enthusiasm, Leek called a meeting and the Hull & East Riding Wildfowlers' Association was formed, with L Trevor Field, a clay shooting competitor at

Stanley Duncan, Trevor Field and Captain Bysom decoying geese at Eastoft, beside the Humber

the 1936 Olympics and an old fowling companion of Stanley Duncan, accepting the post of president.

Naturally the clubs wanted their own local issues and disputes to be addressed, and Colonel Vallance, now honorary solicitor, turned his attention to local rights of way, sea wall disputes and complaints about out of season shooting. James Vallance's role as both chairman and legal adviser was a very significant one. A Nottinghamshire man, he had trained as a solicitor and became senior partner in a Manchester firm, but had a wide range of other business interests and a huge breadth of commercial experience. Serving in Anti-Aircraft Command during the war, he was promoted to Lieutenant Colonel and went on to command the Robin Hoods until 1955, when he was appointed OBE. Vallance shot his first goose at Wells, Norfolk, at the age of ten and became a keen wildfowler, pigeon shooter and game shot for the rest of his life, often shooting with a matched trio of 20 bore guns. He was a member of the Bols Woodcock Club, having shot his left-and-right, but he was averse to shooting hares.

Wildfowlers too were becoming involved in a growing debate about the ethical basis of their pastime, and in particular the commercialisation of wildfowling. Support for the professional fowler had long been at the heart of WAGBI, but the old-time professional was fast disappearing and feelings were running high about the disposal of wild ducks and geese into the marketplace as a mere commodity. Members were horrified at the 'terrible toll' of 300,000 ducks per annum being taken by the Dutch decoy ponds and alarmed that in Lincolnshire, young fowlers were 'clamouring for stuffed decoys' to enable them to make big bags of geese for sale. It was a difficult problem for wildfowlers to wrestle with; after all, food rationing was still part of everyday life in Britain, while in continental Europe the terrible privations of the late 1940s were still raw in the memory. The sale of ducks and geese yielded a valuable source of fresh meat and it represented an important income to local shooters in districts such as the Fens. The majority of members, however, saw wildfowling primarily as a sport, not a profession and slowly the view of the association came round to support for a ban on the sale and importation of dead wild geese.

Whether he was 'leaned on' to resign is not clear from the surviving records, but in April 1950 Devall informed the Home Office that, owing to ill health, Stanley Duncan would not be attending the next meeting of the Wild Birds Committee and that he had consented to attendance at that meeting by another person. The nominated successor was James W 'Judge' Johnson. Nicknamed because of his wise counsel, Johnson had first become a member of WAGBI in 1935 and he was among the small group of enthusiasts who revived the association in 1949. A Cleethorpes man and a long-standing member of the North Lincolnshire WA, he worked in the electricity supply industry, and his utter devotion to WAGBI can be measured by the fact that in 1952 he turned down promotion and the offer of a substantial salary increase as it would have meant his having to cease any active work on behalf of wildfowling. Johnson was appointed to the Wild Birds Advisory Committee on 2 April 1951, and attended his first meeting a month later. He was horrified at what he heard.

It was clear that the committee had gone a long way towards setting out the basis for a new Protection of Birds Act to replace the existing legislation, which dated from 1880 and which had subsequently been modified by several successive measures into an ungainly and almost incomprehensible hotch potch. Close seasons, Sunday shooting, sale of wild birds, duck decoys, semi-automatic shotguns and punt gunning were all under scrutiny, and it was painfully evident that WAGBI's man on the committee, Stanley Duncan, had been less than vigilant in dealing with the gathering threats or at the very least had failed adequately to alert others to them. So far as the Wild Birds Advisory Committee was concerned, such matters had been discussed and dealt with to the satisfaction of WAGBI's then representative, Duncan; they were not interested in reopening the debate. But Johnson was not prepared to take 'no' for an answer and wrote to the chairman, Lord Ilchester, setting out the point of view of the new WAGBI hierarchy on these matters and he went on to argue his corner at the committee's next meeting. Johnson's terrier-like worrying of the committee effectively forced it to reconsider and established a series of hugely important principles: a universal February foreshore season, acceptance of Sunday wildfowling and semi-automatic shotguns and a restriction on the muzzle diameter of punt guns to 1¾ inches rather than an outright ban on punt gunning.

Johnson reported back to the WAGBI executive and at a meeting in London it planned a full scale fight against the growing threat. He appealed for wildfowlers to become aware of the current position 'namely the activity of protectionists and anti-blood sport societies'. He did, however, make a clear distinction between the two groups, and recognised that while the anti-hunters were philosophically opposed to all killing for sport, the bird protection lobby wanted to pursue a progressive path and was not intrinsically opposed to all shooting. The only satisfactory answer in the face of the threat, he said, was unity among fowlers. He said that the anticipated

Stanley Duncan (left) receives a presentation from Dr Vincent Walsh, chairman of Hull and East Riding Wildfowlers, in 1953

new Bill would touch upon Sunday shooting, species protection and police powers of search. Attempts were still being made to prohibit punt guns, restrict semi-automatic and pump action shotguns to two shots only, and to protect the brent and barnacle goose. New shooting seasons were proposed, which would extend from 1 September to 31 January, with an extension for wild ducks and geese over tidal waters to 20 February.

Evidently WAGBI's views had been taken very seriously by the Wild Birds Committee, indeed Lord Ilchester had written in response to one lobbyist who was attempting to obtain total protection for wild geese above the high water mark: 'I am afraid that what you say is not likely to be acceptable to the committee because it would practically mean that all goose shooting would be at an end, and that would not at all suit the Wildfowlers' Association, which is a very strong one.' Johnson's tough and uncompromising attitude had saved the day.

WAGBI delegates met the new Committee of Inquiry which was set up by the Government. One of their principal concerns was over a wholesale plan to designate wildfowl sanctuaries where shooting would be prohibited. However, WAGBI recognised the need for local reserve areas, and suggested that some clubs might like to set aside their own local sanctuaries in order that their value might be assessed. They raised the matter of punt gunning, and were relieved to hear that the committee was no longer opposed in principle to the sport, and that it had accepted instead the concept of restriction upon the size of guns which could not be fired from the shoulder.

During the succeeding months the temperature steadily increased. The association's AGM was held in 1953 at Caxton Hall, Westminster, and Johnson gave a full report on WAGBI's most recent meeting with the Committee of Inquiry, noting that 'several individuals who do not see eye to eye with the sportsman were left with plenty to ponder over. At the same time, I do emphasise that, if shooters wish to preserve their privileges, these people will have to be closely watched.'

Particularly worrying was the proposal to protect the brent goose. In June 1953 the committee suggested that the brent should be protected for ten years. This was described by Johnson as 'farcical'. Even so, it was supported by the Nature Conservancy – as was the total abolition of February wildfowling. The WAGBI executive met in January 1954 at the Great Northern Hotel, Peterborough, and the seriousness with which the threat to shooting was taken may be judged by the fact that no fewer than sixty-one executive and club representatives attended the meeting.

A key matter for discussion was the February foreshore season, but deep concern was also expressed about the one-sided nature of the press reporting of the bird protection issue so a fighting fund was set up and a public relations campaign initiated which would include the writing of letters to local newspapers and the BBC, plus the publication of an insert in the *Shooting Times*. It was vital that the shooting public was made fully aware of the danger posed by the Bill, and the *Shooting Times*, as ever, rallied to the fowlers' support.

WAGBI focussed its attentions for the time being on the need to remove the wildfowl sanctuary clause from the Bill and to reverse the proposed bans on the shooting of brent and barnacle geese and the use of pump action and semi-automatic shotguns. A few weeks later, however, a bombshell was dropped upon its plans in the shape of new and potentially devastating allegations made by Peter Scott, director of the Wildfowl Trust. Scott had been an ardent wildfowler and punt gunner before the war, but had become increasingly ambivalent towards shooting and was now campaigning openly to restrict it. He and his former punting partner Christopher Dalgety claimed publicly that punt gunners had shot two tons of brent geese over a period of just six weeks. Intense investigation had not substantiated the allegation and neither Scott nor Dalgety were prepared to divulge their sources. The Wildfowl Trust had hitherto been seen as an ally in the cause of wildfowl conservation but Scott's claims changed the position overnight. One young member of the WAGBI executive committee, John Ruxton, now posed succinctly the question which wildfowlers were asking: 'Can we trust the Trust?' WAGBI was adamant that Scott's claims were entirely without foundation, but the damage had been done and the allegations were being freely quoted and no doubt embellished. Brent geese were all but lost and to make matters worse, it was now being proposed that the curlew – described by WAGBI as the 'poor man's grouse' – should be added to the protected list.

Edward Parish was chairman of the executive committee. An active wildfowler, he shot on the Suffolk coast in the company of local professional fowler Fred Upson and on one occasion collected eel grass from the Deben estuary in an effort to restock the dwindling eel grass beds in Pagham Harbour. Parish shouldered much of the burden as two Bills made their way through Parliament. He spent endless hours travelling back and forth to Westminster and lobbying MPs, he wrote hundreds of letters and spent days in the House of Commons. Dr Geoffrey W Storey, the secretary at the time, said of him on his retirement in 1958 that he had placed his family and business second to the interests of the wildfowler and done more for the sport than any man living: 'Never in the association's history have its members owed so much to the activities of one man as they have to the retiring chairman. Were it not for his knowledge, wisdom and boundless enthusiasm the situation today would be inconceivably worse than when the Protection of Birds Act filled us with misgivings.'

Eddie Parish and his colleagues fought like tigers. The most famous victory which they secured concerned February foreshore shooting which was first taken away and then snatched back after relentless lobbying in the House of Commons in which the wildfowling clubs weighed-in with their own strong and determined effort. It was recognised by all sides of the House that wildfowling was the sport of the working man, and eventually MPs lent it their support. There were long discussions over unnecessarily restrictive proposals for bird sanctuaries, and while these were not ditched altogether, they were considerably reined back. In Parliament a pitched battle was fought over the quarry list. The curlew was first protected but was won back at the eleventh hour, though the brent and barnacle goose and some waders went onto the protected list, leaving many wildfowlers disgruntled, dissatisfied or plain furious with the outcome. The bird protection lobby, however, had expected to achieve much more from the Bill and was

When Stanley Duncan died in 1954, he was buried in an unmarked grave in Anlaby cemetery. It was nearly fifty years before the wildfowling community rediscovered the grave of WAGBI's founder and raised a subscription to erect a headstone. The memorial was dedicated on 19 October 2003

equally disappointed. Amongst some of them the Wild Birds Protection Act 1954 became known as the 'Wildfowlers' Charter'.

On 1 December the new law came into force and it was time for both sides to take stock after a bruising battle. The annual general meeting in December 1954 was hosted at the New Manchester Hotel, Hull, by the Hull & East Riding Wildfowlers' Association, and Trevor Field, president of the HERWA and a longstanding wildfowling colleague of Stanley Duncan, welcomed WAGBI back to its birthplace. Before the business of the meeting could commence, however, there was a sad duty to perform. Stanley Duncan had died on 30 August of that year, and the association honoured the memory of its founder by standing in silence. Speaking in tribute to his friend, Field commented that Duncan would rank second only to Colonel Hawker in the annals of wildfowling.

With a new bird protection Act in place, the Wild Birds Inquiry Committee had been wound up, and a WAGBI representative was once more appointed to a re-vamped Wild Birds Advisory Committee set up by the Home Office. Meanwhile the Nature Conservancy was flexing its muscles by attempting to regulate shooting over key reserve areas at Bridgwater Bay, Southport and the Humber. It was recognised that wildfowling clubs would have to keep their ears closely to the ground in order to ensure that their interests were not brushed aside in the rush to set up reserves, and a particular concern was expressed over those parts of the coast where there was not an existing club network to provide local intelligence. In such districts it was agreed that wildfowling interests would in future be monitored by the nearest club.

As for the executive committee, the sheer workload which it had been forced to carry over the course of the previous months and the prospect of more legislation to come in the future had made it think hard about the ability of voluntary part-timers to cope with the day-to-day business of the association. Clearly there was now a need for a paid full- or part-time officer to cope with the increasing scale of activities, and it was agreed that the executive should be empowered to pay such honoraria as were necessary.

More immediately there was a severely strained relationship with the Wildfowl Trust which had to be resolved. The obvious man for the job was Dr Jeffery Harrison, a Kentish GP who was both a keen wildfowler and at the same time an eminent ornithologist, being a vice president of the British Ornithologists' Union. Jeff Harrison's breadth of interest and the respect in which he was held both by shooters and conservationists would hopefully enable communications with the Trust to be restored. A meeting was agreed. It would be chaired by Harrison with the object of clarifying outstanding difficulties and establishing future co-operation in the common objective of wildfowl conservation. For its own part, WAGBI was keen to set up a range of shared scientific studies of wildfowl and other activities of mutual benefit with the Trust, and to establish a permanent means of maintaining future liaison. The meeting took place in September 1955 and was attended by members of both the Wildfowl Trust's council and WAGBI's executive committee. There was a good deal of straight talking as the still-smouldering coals of the 1954

Both WAGBI and the Wildfowl Trust worked hard to heal the rift which occurred during negotiations over the Protection of Birds Act. Peter Scott (centre) was guest speaker at a Hull & East Riding Wildfowlers open meeting and film show in 1954. On the left is Dr V Walsh, club chairman and right is L Trevor Field, club president

Members of the Hull & East Riding Wildfowlers releasing mallard on the Humber. In the mid 1950s wildfowling clubs enthusiastically took up WAGBI's call to rear and release ducks and geese as a practical contribution to conservation

Act were raked over once again. Why had the Trust upset the compromise when WAGBI had conceded August shooting in order to maintain the February foreshore season? Why had the Trust forced a ban on the shooting of all brent geese when WAGBI would have accepted the compromise position of a prohibition on shooting of the rarer light-bellied population provided the dark-bellied brent goose remained on the quarry list? And what about those spurious punting records? Peter Scott apologised on the latter count, but commented that the Trust had chosen the safer course by supporting protection. In cases of doubt, he warned, it would always do so.

There was still a good deal of wariness shown by both parties and a suspicion by some on the WAGBI side that the Trust was being secretly funded by the Government. However, there was also plenty of common ground over matters such as research, wildfowl counts and ring returns, and at least the hatchets were buried. Harrison summarised: 'I think the feeling is that we have entered quite a new era in our relationships and a great deal of good will come out of it for both sides. As wildfowlers we are also naturalists and we are closely related.'

Wildfowlers were indeed naturalists. It had been one of the founding principles of the Wildfowlers' Association that those who pursued ducks and geese should have concern both for them and the wild places which they inhabited, and there were many who wanted to do more to ensure the well-being of their quarry. In the mid 1950s it was envisaged that the simplest and most efficient way of increasing numbers of wildfowl would be to set up a rearing and releasing programme, and such a scheme was the subject of a long discussion in 1955. Jeff Harrison was solidly behind the idea. He saw duck rearing as an activity which the wildfowling clubs could take to their hearts, one which would increase local duck populations, stimulate interest in conservation among wildfowlers and at the same time demonstrate publicly the shooter's commitment to conservation. At the 1955 annual general meeting, hosted by the Fenland WA, Harrison held aloft a duck nesting basket and appealed to wildfowlers to rear mallard, commenting that 'there is no other equally positive way of getting more ducks in the air'. The Fenland club had already initiated its own rearing scheme and was able to report with pride that it had produced over one hundred birds. 'If only a few pairs survive it will have been worthwhile and who knows, it may eventually become nearly as big as Ducks Unlimited,' said club secretary Ray Butt. By the following year, over one thousand duck leg rings had been sent out to clubs and Harrison was investigating the introduction of Canada geese to new parts of the country.

WAGBI's brand of conservation was not just about producing more ducks and geese to shoot at, albeit that was an objective which every wildfowler could understand. It was also driven by genuine altruism, based on a desire to understand more about wildfowl species and the habitats upon which they depended. Alongside the rearing and releasing programmes, there was also a scheme, run jointly with the Wildfowl Trust, to sample the gut contents of wildfowl in order that more could be learned about the plants and invertebrates which ducks fed on. Wildfowlers were asked to provide the samples of viscera from the birds which they shot, while the Wildfowl Trust

Members of the Hull & East Riding Wildfowlers releasing mallard and Canada geese on Hornsey Mere. Wildfowlers were instrumental in establishing breeding colonies of Canada and greylag geese across Britain

was to undertake the analysis. By 1957 Harrison was able to report that his own club, the Kent WA, had forwarded three hundred and fifty-seven samples to the Trust's laboratories whilst the Home Counties had forwarded eight, Blakeney thirty-one and S Cumberland six. A league table was fast developing.

First fruits of the rearing and ringing scheme were also starting to be seen in the form of ring recoveries. With one thousand five hundred mallard now carrying WAGBI rings, seventy recoveries had been reported, though 80% of these were from within a few miles of the coast.

Conscious of the need to work alongside the bird conservation bodies rather than against them, as had been the case during the passage of the 1954 Act, the executive committee decided that it would also be prudent to set up a meeting with the RSPB. Clearly they wanted to avoid any prospect of a public bust-up, such as had occurred with the Wildfowl Trust, so feelers were put out and a round table discussion was held between, for WAGBI, Edward Parish, Brigadier Geoffrey Holmes and The Hon Aylmer Tryon and, for the RSPB, Lord Hurcomb, Geoffrey Dent and Philip Brown. There were several useful points of agreement, such as the need to ensure that protected birds were not shot, the discouragement of excessively long-range shooting and the provision of sanctuaries. The meeting was seen as both useful and constructive, and a channel of communication was set up between the two organisations.

Conservation issues were aired in the association's first magazine, *The Wildfowler* a publication which was started by the Dee WA but which was swiftly adopted by WAGBI and of which one thousand copies were printed in 1957 at a cost of £200. Side by side in the first issue, which sold for 2s 6d, were features on wildfowl hybridisation, eel grass and wader plumage, as well as anecdotal articles about sport on the coast, home loading, fishing in the west of Ireland and shooting in occupied Germany. In his introduction the editor, Peter Smith, highlighted the changes which had taken place in wildfowling following a postwar growth in the number of those taking up the sport and the ready accessibility of shooting areas resulting from the availability of motorised transport. The problems which beset the sport had, he said, been addressed through the energy of local wildfowling clubs which now not only provided their members with the opportunity to go wildfowling, but with pigeon shooting, clay shooting, film shows, lectures, and the tuition of young shooters 'so that they have become focal points for shooting men in the neighbourhood'.

Wildfowling clubs had indeed found their feet, and more were being formed every year, steadily spreading the network of club activity around the coasts. One of their principal goals, especially in the light of the increasing pressure on shooting opportunity, was to secure sporting rights. WAGBI thus saw it as a priority to give guidance on how best to approach the Crown Commissioners, who controlled much of the foreshore, and a detailed paper was prepared on how to obtain shooting rights within an estuary by contacting river boards, landowners and local councils. The advice it proffered to clubs was sound: 'No matter how forbidding or important is the personage involved, have a go – he can only say no. Never write when you can phone. Never phone when a personal visit is possible.'

Where wildfowling clubs did not already exist, WAGBI was urging the formation of new ones. Where they did, the clubs themselves were starting to group together and form local joint councils, in order that matters of common interest in a particular locality or district might be aired and shared. The Cheshire Joint Council of Wildfowling Clubs, comprising the Dee, Frodsham, N Cheshire, the Northern Roughshooters and Warrington clubs, was among the first of these. By the beginning of 1957 no fewer than sixty-one clubs were affiliated, causing the chairman to comment that 'the association, which had started fifty years ago as an association of individual wildfowlers had become a federation of wildfowling associations'.

WAGBI officers photographed at the association's AGM and annual dinner, 1957. Standing left to right Dr G W Storey, vice president; Col J Vallance, honorary solicitor; W L I Brockbank, honorary treasurer; P Smith, chairman publications committee; J Moffatt, vice president. Seated left to right Brig G D Holmes, vice president; J Hirst, past honorary secretary; Lord Gifford, vice president; E L Parish, chairman; N M ('Tim') Sedgwick, vice president and editor of Shooting Times

And not only were wildfowlers joining the association. WAGBI itself was changing, and for the first time there were long debates about whether or not rough shooters should be brought into what had always been a wildfowlers' organisation. To a large extent the discussion was a pointless one, because the rough shooters were already voting with their feet and joining what they recognised as a body with values which they respected, an organisation with a track record of fighting on behalf of the sporting shooter. Membership was multiplying by the month, overloading the voluntary staff and making it impossible for the executive committee to deal with the everyday business of the association. Sub-committees were formed to handle such matters as finance, legal matters, publications, duck rearing and relations with the Wildfowl Trust, but what was needed above all was an energetic part-time secretary. In March 1957 such a man was appointed. His name was John Anderton.

It has been said, and with some justification, that WAGBI/ BASC was the creation of two men. If Stanley Duncan was the powerhouse behind the founding of the association, the person with the foresight to see that wildfowling needed to organise if it was to survive, then John Anderton was the man who picked up the struggling WAGBI in the late 1950s, re-energised it and gave it the new sense of direction and purpose which set it on course to become the major representative body for shooting that it is today.

Born in Southport, Lancashire on 8 August 1923, Anderton was educated at Worksop College, Nottinghamshire and joined the Royal Navy in November 1941 as an ordinary seaman. His service career was impressive. He rose from the lower deck on warships with the Russian and Atlantic convoys and was commissioned in 1943, going on to command small ships in combined operations in the Mediterranean and during the Normandy landings, then continuing his war in the Far East. After the cessation of hostilities, he joined the Royal Naval Volunteer Reserve, in which he reached the rank of Lieutenant Commander. In 1946 he entered the family textile business in Manchester and hated every minute of it so, under some pressure from his father-in-law, he joined in 1952 his wife's family property business based in Liverpool. The string of companies for which he was responsible was profitable enough and provided the Andertons with a good standard of living but John, eventually becoming frustrated at the conservative policies and the rigid control exercised by his father-in-law, needed to turn his energies to something else. A voluntary appointment as honorary secretary of WAGBI appealed to him and he initially ran the association's business out of his own office in Liverpool, devoting an hour or so a day to WAGBI activities.

A complex character, Anderton worked incredibly hard and played hard too. He sailed yachts and dinghies, he became a passionately keen gardener who, with his third wife Mary, produced three exquisite gardens, and he devoted much time to running the Cwm shoot in North Wales of which he was the tenant. He was an exceptional man manager, who always knew how to get the best out of somebody, and although he could be a hard taskmaster, he had an innately generous spirit.

Anderton's great gift, however, was the fact that he could get on with people from every background and station in life. With his piercing blue eyes and a handshake which made grown men wince, he was as comfortable conversing with a peer or the chairman of a multinational company as he was talking with a plasterer or a postman, and moreover

John Anderton in 1983. Stanley Duncan may be hailed as WAGBI's founder, but it was Anderton whose vision turned it from a relatively small organisation for wildfowlers into Britain's largest shooting association

he had the powers of persuasion that enabled him to sell his vision to the belted earl and the bricklayer alike. And what he sold was an organisation that defended wildfowl and their habitats just as much as it defended wildfowlers. At a time when WAGBI was regarded with great suspicion by the emerging conservation bodies, Anderton engaged with their leaders and convinced them that shooting was good for conservation.

THE WAGBIRD.

Due to great efforts at conservation this species is on the increase.

CALL: Quack-quack, Bang-bang.

Frequently migrates all over the country from its nesting site in Liverpool.

Feet webbed for paddling in troubled waters →

John Anderton, as caricatured by Christopher Curtis

Indeed, one of his greatest contributions to the cause of shooting was to tear down the barriers which existed between the shooters and the conservationists and, with the committed support of a small group of colleagues, to create a new level of understanding with the conservation movement. Philip Brown, at one time secretary of the RSPB, recalled later: 'John and I were soon on the same wavelength. If the broad lines of WAGBI and the RSPB might be different, they certainly ran parallel to one another.' The level of understanding which existed may be illustrated by the occasion when the wildlife film-maker and sporting writer Colin Willock, a mutual friend, arranged for Anderton and Brown to be interviewed together by Anglia Television. Anderton turned up for the interview wearing an RSPB tie and, without any prior connivance, Brown arrived with a WAGBI one.

Chapter 4
THE PURIFICATION OF THE SPORT

New legislation had ensured a uniform approach to wildfowling seasons and the quarry list across the country, but local authorities still had the power to determine whether or not wildfowl could be shot on Sundays. In some counties, including those parts of Wales with a strict chapel tradition, Sunday shooting was frowned upon. However, working men who could only go about their recreation at the weekend, and who often worked on a Saturday, placed great value upon the opportunity to go shooting on their day off.

One of John Anderton's first skirmishes occurred when Flintshire County Council in North Wales proposed a ban on Sunday shooting. WAGBI was determined to take a firm stand and the Dee Wildfowlers' Association, whose fowling grounds straddled the borders of Cheshire and Flintshire, successfully applied to the Home Secretary for a public inquiry to contest the proposal. The Inquiry was held at Mold on 4 July 1957. The wildfowlers mounted a formidable team, including their own honorary solicitor, J Lumley Williams and a barrister, R M Bingham, together with fifteen witnesses and a solid phalanx of forty supporters from the Dee club, many of whom had given up a day's pay to attend. Flintshire County Council relied upon the services of its own solicitor, who called no witnesses and had not a single supporter in the chamber. He rested his case upon Sabbatarianism, wildfowl protection and uniformity of law within Wales, but his arguments were systematically demolished by the wildfowlers, who called representatives of the Nature Conservancy, the Wildfowl Trust and the Cambrian Ornithological Society to the witness box to confirm that there was no conservation reason for imposing a ban. John Anderton himself gave evidence, arguing that Sunday observance was a matter for each individual and that intolerance as to how a man should spend the sabbath was no Christian virtue. Seven weeks after the close of the inquiry, the Home Secretary decided the matter in the fowlers' favour.

Another highlight of 1957 was WAGBI's first public exhibition. The association had received an invitation from the *Daily Express* to take a trade stand free of charge at the Boat Show at Olympia. Judging that many wildfowlers were also boat owners who used small craft in pursuance of their sport, the committee decided to accept the offer. What they had not fully allowed for, unfortunately, were the costs of building the exhibition stand and manning it for the duration of the Boat Show itself, both of which were considerable. While much interest was expressed in wildfowling by the no doubt curious boat owning public, the show was not an unqualified success. As a first toe in the waters of show attendance, however, it was certainly a learning experience.

And what was to happen to the exhibition stand after the show? There was nowhere to store it and by the time a few months had elapsed it was becoming something of an embarrassment. 'Burn it' was one suggestion. 'Throw it in the river' was another. But the stand was not destroyed, which was just as well, for shortly afterwards WAGBI received an invitation to participate in a new shooting and fishing event at Stetchworth, near Newmarket, which called itself the Game Fair. The exhibition stand was thus transferred into the keeping of Ray Butt of the Fenland WA, in whose care it remained for most of the following twelve months.

Jeffery Harrison and John Anderton at the CLA Game Fair, Longleat, in 1962

The concept of the Game Fair had originally been that of Nigel Gray of the Game Research Association, which was in due course to join the Eley Game Advisory Service to become the Game Conservancy. Gray eventually approached the Country Landowners Association with the idea and, following the promise of a £500 guarantee from Essex landowner Sir John Ruggles-Brise, they agreed to sponsor it. Central to the success of the event would be the support of the London gun trade, so a meeting was convened at the RNVR Club to which key personalities in the trade were invited. Opinions were mixed. Boss said that the last time they had exhibited at a fair – the 1899 Paris Trade Fair – they had not sold a gun, so company policy was opposed to such events. In the end, however, sufficient representation from the trade was promised.

Three thousand visitors were expected at that first Game Fair on 25 and 26 July 1958 but eight thousand five hundred turned up, and its future was assured. The event was an outstanding success for WAGBI. Many hundreds of visitors saw the association's stand, seventy-one new members were enrolled – small beer by today's standards but a huge number in the late 1950s – and twenty-three ducks were 'adopted' in a duck adoption money-raiser which was run from the stand.

'Placing WAGBI before the public was without a doubt a sound decision and it is only to be hoped that the Game Fair becomes an annual event and that we appear on all future occasions,' wrote John Anderton after the event. These were prophetic words on both counts, for this novel show, which brought country sports together for their own summer festival for the first time, went on of course to become the huge international event it is today. Moreover, WAGBI was in at its birth and the association has been a central exhibitor at every Game Fair since, the annual pilgrimage to some great country estate becoming one of the immovable bodies in the firmament around which it and the other country sports organisations move in their annual cycle. And as for the exhibition stand, it got the reprieve it needed and went on to feature in the even bigger and better WAGBI enclosure at the CLA Game Fair at Hackwood House the following year.

The year of 1958 was significant for another reason. Given that the association, as received wisdom had it, was founded in 1908, this was WAGBI's golden jubilee year, and the executive committee was determined to ensure that the occasion was celebrated in style. As with every major anniversary, it was a time to reflect upon the history which had made WAGBI the substantial and respected organisation it had become, whilst laying the foundations for further growth and development or, as John Anderton phrased it, 'hats off to the past, coats off to the future'.

From the beginning of the year, wildfowling clubs had been encouraged to garner whatever publicity for wildfowling they could in their local newspapers, with guidelines being offered as to how they might go about attracting the attention of journalists to the sport. 'The young and the old' was suggested as a theme, with clubs being invited to identify both their oldest member, who could remember the sport as it had been in years gone by, and the youngest, who would hopefully carry fowling's traditions forwards into the future.

The first major celebration, however, was the golden jubilee annual general meeting and dinner, hosted by the Kent WA and held at the Coniston Hotel, Sittingbourne on 10 May. The meeting itself was an opportunity to report on the burgeoning growth of WAGBI and its activities, the successful first year of a permit scheme at the Caerlaverock reserve on the Solway, the proposal to make a film, jointly with the RSPB, on wildfowling and the formation of eight new clubs. The evening finished with a gala dinner attended by the association's president, the Earl of Mansfield and captured by cartoonist Fred May who produced a page of caricatures under the heading 'Wildfowlers' Identification' for *Shooting Times*. The magazine itself commented that the 'stubborn and well-founded success of the Wildfowlers' Association serves as a timely reminder and outstanding example that any sport can only survive if its supporters are prepared to unite in concerted and unselfish effort to protect it.

'Everyone who shoots or takes any interest in wildfowl, inland or on the coast, should be grateful for the existence of such a capable and active association, and show his appreciation by supporting it to the hilt.'

Shooting Times stored up its principal tribute, however, until the eve of the new wildfowling season, for on 29 August it published a special WAGBI golden jubilee issue, complete with the Wildfowlers' Association badge framed in gold on the front cover. It was an opportunity for founder member The Rev E A H Strong to recall the formation of WAGBI and for John Anderton and Leslie Brockbank to answer at length the question 'Where do we go from here?' Congratulations showered from the letters pages like confetti: Lords Mansfield, Leicester, Gifford and Hurcomb, the latter chairman of the RSPB, all heaped praise upon the association as did Peter Scott, director of the Wildfowl Trust; Brigadier Pepys, secretary of the British Field Sports Society; and Max Nicholson, director of the Nature Conservancy. Nicholson pointed out that the jubilee was one to be celebrated by conservationists as well as wildfowlers: 'But for the vigorous and courageous and statesmanlike leadership of WAGBI a futile and chronic guerrilla warfare between naturalists and wildfowlers would be almost unavoidable. Everyone would suffer through it, most of all the wildfowl themselves. Instead of this, we find growing mutual

After WAGBI's golden jubilee dinner in 1958, Shooting Times *published a cartoon by Fred May with caricatures of the officers and prominent guests who attended*

understanding and readiness for fair and commonsense practical arrangements for the improvement of wildfowl stocks and for the benefit of all interested in their welfare.'

The golden jubilee issue was a mark of the close relationship which existed between WAGBI and *Shooting Times*, the association's 'official organ'. This bond had existed from the time that Arthur Bonsall, editor back in 1908, had pledged his support for the formation of a wildfowlers' association to Stanley Duncan. However, under the editorship of Noel M 'Tim' Sedgwick, or 'Tower-Bird' as he styled himself in print, the support of *Shooting Times* became stronger than ever. Tim had farmed, worked as a part-time gamekeeper and as a rabbit catcher before taking the reins at *Shooting Times* in 1932. He was a born countryman and a great writer, having had his first article published in *Shooting Times* at the age of seventeen and being the author of several books. Though he could appear to be a tough and controversial character, Sedgwick had a heart of gold and was always ready to help anyone, especially a young shooter in search of advice or assistance. He was devoted to wildfowling, shooting regularly at Chichester Harbour with his shooting partner Matt Normington and in 1956 he was instrumental in setting up the Chichester Harbour Wildfowlers.

Writing to Sig Bjornsen, whom he brought in as club secretary, Sedgwick explained: 'Matt and I are in with all the boys down there, and a tough lot they are, but very keen. I think we can get about thirty local guns as members, and I want to get one hundred or many more members from different parts of the county, even from London. This I can do without much trouble.'

He was a joker, too. On one occasion Sedgwick had just tucked himself down under the sea wall at a convenient bend when a young lady birdwatcher strode up to remonstrate with him for shooting ducks. She stood firm on the flood bank twenty yards away waving her arms about, thereby making the ducks change their course. Sedgwick thought for a moment, stooped behind the reeds, found a large round stone and put his face mask and hat over it before bolting off about one hundred yards. Incredibly, the birdwatcher was taken in by the ruse and continued to wave bits of her clothing, thereby succeeding in diverting the ducks over the relocated Sedgwick, who shot two of them. When he offered one to the lady at the end of the flight, she curtly declined. He was also a hot shot with a catapult, which he used to shoot pigeons in the London parks. He carried a catapult in his pocket, even in the *Shooting Times* office or at his favourite watering hole, the Old Cheshire Cheese. It was there on one occasion that he settled a challenge to his accuracy by knocking the bowler hat off the head of an eminent barrister standing five yards away. The incident cost him several whiskies and a new bowler.

Shooting Times gave a particularly valuable form of support to WAGBI by carrying a membership application form in its golden jubilee issue, a novel method of promotion in those days. By 6 September it had yielded one hundred and thirty-six new members, and the following month there were supportive articles in *The Times* and *The Field*. It had been a good year for the association.

By the following spring, however, at least one of its policies was coming home to roost. Or to be more precise, the progeny of one of its policies were finding a good too many roosting places for the liking of some conservationists. Canada geese had been one of the principal species involved in WAGBI's wildfowl rearing and releasing programme, and local fowling clubs around the country had by 1959 done a very good job at translocating the birds and setting up new breeding colonies. There were by now a few murmurs of concern from the farming community at the damage these big, brash geese were causing, and the Nature Conservancy, itself worried about the spread of a particularly vigorous non-native species, asked for a clarification of WAGBI's policy. They received a very direct reply: 'It is our intention to continue both to rear and distribute Canada geese in Britain since this is a practical part of conservation and it affords

Rounding up Canada geese for breeding and relocation in 1964. WAGBI robustly defended its policy of introducing Canadas to new breeding habitats, though in the end the association decided that it would be better to focus its efforts on the native greylag

much pleasure to the populace to see geese on the wing and on public park lakes – particularly in those areas where the public never had the opportunity of seeing wild geese prior to our efforts.' WAGBI was sticking to its guns, for the time being at least. There was, however, some reflection upon the rapidly burgeoning Canada goose population, and increasingly the goose rearing programme focussed its attention to the less controversial greylag.

One of the greatest champions of goose rearing was John Ruxton, a blunt no-nonsense Cumbrian with a first class intellect. Of humble origins, Ruxton had served in the Far East during the war, ending up as a sergeant. He was a totally dedicated wildfowler who, although his old job in an engineering business in Kendal had been kept open for him on his return from the services, preferred to spend his 'demob winter' in a punt on the Solway. He returned from Scotland, set up his own business and proceeded to do very well. Ruxton had taken over a wildfowl collection in Kendal, and as secretary of the WAGBI Goose Conservation sub-committee he travelled far and wide through England and as far north as Sutherland catching up flightless goslings or wingtipped adult birds and bringing them back to the Lakes for breeding. Greylags were released in Norfolk, Lincolnshire and Cambridgeshire, but about fifty birds a year were released onto a reserve which had been established by the South Cumberland Wildfowlers at Hawes and within three years a thriving population of greylags had built up in the south Lakes. This was only one of several regional colonies established at the time with the express intention of reintroducing the wild greylag as an English breeding species, and many of the feral greylag populations which are to be found around Britain today owe their origins to enthusiasts like John Ruxton.

The end of the 1950s saw no let up in the formation of new wildfowling clubs. Four new clubs were formed in the spring of 1959 and another six were in the process of formation. Often, the creation of a club came in response to concerns by farmers and landowners over poaching and irresponsible shooting by outsiders who had little understanding of local traditions and even less respect for them. A good example of this was on the Blackwater estuary in Essex which was 'discovered' by unsavoury characters from east London and heavily poached, to the dismay of both the farmers whose land bounded the estuary, and the local fowlers from Maldon and the surrounding villages. It was decided that the best way of controlling the shooting on the river was by forming a wildfowling club for the locals who, with the consent of the farmers, would be able to continue shooting over their traditional marshes. Thus the Blackwater Wildfowlers came into being in 1960.

But irresponsible shooting was not merely an Essex phenomenon, nor even was it one which only affected coastal marshes close to the larger cities. Reports were increasingly coming in from all over the country of poaching, out-of-season shooting, killing of protected species, shooting at excessive range and sheer bloody-mindedness on the marsh. The phenomenon was put down to a number of factors, probably the most significant of which was the sharply increasing standard of living and disposable income of the broad mass of the British public. With postwar privation now becoming a distant memory, greater car ownership, increased spare time and more disposable income gave people the opportunity to try their hand at new leisure activities such as shooting. Wildfowling was particularly cheap and accessible. Following the introduction of myxomatosis in 1954 and the subsequent crash in the rabbit population it was one of the few forms of shooting that was readily available to the less well-off, and moreover it was being actively promoted and romanticised by writers such as James Wentworth Day, Denys Watkins-Pitchford ('BB') and Alan Savory. Not surprisingly, enthusiastic novices wanted to have a go at it, often without the faintest idea of how to go about doing so.

John Ruxton in 1964. Ruxton was twice chairman of WAGBI/BASC and devoted much of his knowledge, expertise and energy to the association

And so the reports started rolling in to the WAGBI office: fowlers shooting in statutory sanctuaries, visiting gunners swarming the access points at morning flight time on the Wash, outrageously long-range shooting on the Solway, the use of .22 and even .303 rifles at flocks of wild geese in Scotland, excessive bags of geese in Lincolnshire. And it was not only the 'cowboys' who were causing problems. Some of those who should have known better were also playing fast and loose with the rules. Indeed, some farmers were still openly shooting mallard over their laid wheat or stubble fields in late summer, despite the fact that the close season had been extended to 31 August since 1954. Anderton realised that if wildfowling was to be defended, then it had to be defensible, and if bad behaviour was bringing the sport into disrepute, then it had to stop. 'The anti-shooting fraternity is not our greatest enemy, but the man who through his own stupidity, ignorance or selfishness behaves against all the rules written or unwritten, and who by doing so manufactures the ammunition for the antis to fire,' he wrote, sentiments which were to be repeated on many subsequent occasions. Alongside the political defence of the quarry list and the conservation of wildfowl, WAGBI clearly had another important task: that which Stanley Duncan had described so many years before as the 'purification' of wildfowling. This became an increasingly significant part of the association's activities.

Initially, WAGBI arranged for the printing of notices bearing details of the legal shooting seasons, and these notices were distributed both to wildfowling clubs and more especially to police stations in coastal areas. Thus fowlers were at least made aware of the correct shooting seasons whilst at the same time county constabularies were encouraged to enforce the law. Disciplinary measures were available to deal with malefactors, and the minute books started to record instances of members who had broken the law being brought before the committee to explain themselves, such as the member caught poaching in the Humber wildfowl refuge, illegally using a mechanically propelled boat in pursuit of wildfowl. Initially relying for his intelligence upon sometimes not altogether impartial reports received from local wildfowling clubs, Anderton decided eventually to subscribe to a press cuttings agency which would send him reports of court proceedings and prosecutions relating to poaching, firearms offences and the illegal shooting of wild birds. A 'black list' was duly established of those convicted of such offences and membership was denied to those who had broken the law. Those who, in the opinion of the executive committee, were found to have brought the sport into disrepute, were expelled from membership and their names and addresses were published in *Shooting Times*.

Together with the stick came the carrot, for there was clearly a duty to educate newcomers in the ways of wildfowling, or as Anderton put it, 'the laws and the lores' of the sport. Tim Sedgwick's article on 'Elementary Marshcraft' in the 18 November 1960 issue of *Shooting Times*, was the forerunner of many similar pieces, providing warning and encouragement in equal measure and showing the reader how, by improving his fowling skills, he could enjoy more successful sport. As well as magazine articles, a text book was needed, and

Leslie Brockbank, former WAGBI honorary treasurer, photographed in 1959. Brockbank was later asked by John Anderton to research WAGBI's history and went on to record interviews with some of the association's leading figures from the 1950s

with Duncan and Thorne's classic *The Complete Wildfowler* now well out of print, discussions were held with the publishers, Herbert Jenkins, about the possibility of revising and reprinting the book. After some consideration, however, it was decided that this would be unwise as the book was so out of date. Instead, a new all-embracing book on wildfowling, to be published by WAGBI, was planned under the direction of a steering committee chaired by Sedgwick. This was eventually to see light of day as *The New Wildfowler*.

Chapter 5
FOWLING BY AGREEMENT

By 1960 WAGBI had one hundred affiliated clubs and as the first shots were fired at the start of the new wildfowling season on 1 September it had that year already enrolled one thousand new members. The organisation was growing fast, but the cracks were starting to show. WAGBI had always been staffed and run by amateurs, and whilst the secretary, chairman and the various senior committee members were by and large thoroughly competent in what they did, they were in the end merely a small group of enthusiasts who gave their time voluntarily, paying their own expenses and often arranging meetings around the opportunity of a day's shooting here or a morning flight there. John Anderton's influence had been huge, and with his powerful personality he had succeeded in focussing the leadership of the association, but the day-to-day administration of a rapidly growing body was becoming too much for one man working in an honorary capacity and it was recognised that very soon a paid official might have to be appointed. The reverse side of the same coin was that a full-time staff required more suitable office accommodation.

For four-and-a-half years WABGI had – sometimes uneasily – shared Anderton's office at Castle Street, Liverpool, but it was becoming increasingly clear that this was no longer an acceptable arrangement. When Anderton's secretary, Mrs Blowfield, died at the early age of thirty-eight, a typist, Miss Reid, was engaged to work exclusively on WAGBI business, and in December 1961 she was joined by WAGBI's first full-time assistant secretary, thirty-five year old Captain Mark Legg a former career soldier who had won the DFC whilst flying Austers in Malaya in 1956. Legg was appointed from a short list of four at a salary of £800. Meanwhile Anderton had found suitable offices just three hundred yards away from what were then his current premises. A 450 sq ft main office, a typist's room and entrance lobby were available at 1 to 3 Harrington Street, Liverpool, for just £120 per annum, plus rates of £198. Electrical work, joinery and decorating would be required, but after considering – and quickly rejecting – the suggestion that WAGBI might move to London, the chairman, Colonel Vallance, signed the lease and WAGBI moved into its new accommodation in early October. Anderton commented that any member wishing to visit would be made most welcome, except on Saturdays during the shooting season.

Two further administrative developments agreed at this time were to have far-reaching consequences on the growth of the association. The honorary solicitor, John Gow, had spent time in deep discussion with insurance brokers Bluett Smith over the possibility of their arranging a policy which would provide insurance cover for WAGBI members. He eventually hammered out a deal which would offer up to £50,000 cover for any one accident at a cost of 1/– per member. WAGBI was thus the first field sports organisation to proceed down the path of offering insurance to its membership and in the years to come the attraction of guaranteed public liability insurance within the membership package was to have a very significant effect upon recruitment.

The second development was the suggestion that affiliated clubs which operated a rule requiring all their members to be full members of WAGBI could be exempted from paying any affiliation fee other than a nominal charge of, say, one guinea. After Anderton had refined and revised the concept, the 'full membership' rule was to become a hugely important factor in membership growth, indeed it was seen by some as a turning point for WAGBI. Anderton set about visiting club functions in order to broadcast the association's message and at an annual dinner of the Leicestershire Wildfowlers he managed to persuade the club to adopt the rule. With its large membership of inland duck and goose shooters, this instantly brought a large number of members on board who were not concerned purely with shooting on the coast.

Indeed, WAGBI was becoming more than just an association of wildfowlers. Rough shooters and pigeon shooters were joining and even game shooters were expressing interest in becoming members. At the 1961 annual general meeting, Colonel Vallance told members that 'a rather remarkable thing happened this morning when I came in here with the secretary. A little boy of about sixteen in a white apron who was cleaning up the table came over to me and said "excuse me Sir, but does your organisation have anything to do with ordinary game shooting as well? I am very interested in game shooting and hope to have a gun of my own some day."'

Anderton was well aware of the need to broaden WAGBI's remit, and at a special meeting of the executive committee which was attended by representatives of twenty-seven affiliated clubs and three joint councils, he spoke passionately about the need to create an organisation with an interest which spread its mantle further than the narrow confines of coastal duck and goose shooting. 'Are we to turn people away because they shoot game, pigeons or vermin?' he asked. 'Many new affiliated clubs now don't have "wildfowl" in their title. Frodsham, one of the first clubs to affiliate, have a very good partridge shoot. Are they to be pushed to one side because their interests are split?'

He was strongly supported by Tim Sedgwick who pointed out that wildfowling would find it impossible to stand alone in the face of a major attack on shooting, and that all branches of the sport should be under the WAGBI roof. Club contributions to the debate were broadly supportive, one spokesman from Huddersfield pointing out that his club was midway between two coasts: 'There is nobody who calls himself a wildfowler who never shoots game,' he argued.

A note of caution, however, was expressed by Dr Geoffrey Storey, a WAGBI vice president and a former committee member of Morecambe Bay Wildfowlers, who commented that while he was not against progress, he wanted to see efforts directed to wildfowling and wildfowling matters and that he was concerned at the prospect of WAGBI being 'hoodwinked' by other forms of shooting: 'Experts on roe deer, partridges, pheasants and vermin mean the break-up of WAGBI as we understand it,' he warned.

The meeting concluded with an agreement that WAGBI would adopt a middle course, catering first and foremost for the wildfowler, but meanwhile extending its interests in other forms of shooting. It may have been the end of that particular discussion, but it was only the start of the debate, one which was destined to be argued out over the next twenty years and beyond, leading to successive changing nuances in the association's name and ultimately to the adoption of the present title in 1981. Indeed, some would say that the debate about the place of wildfowling within BASC still continues to this day.

Just before Christmas 1962 the weather changed for the worse when a belt of rain over northern Scotland turned to snow as it moved south. By Boxing Day the snow clouds were stationary over southern England and the following day the snow lay a foot deep. As the wind picked up, the snow drifted, bringing the country to a standstill. In many places the snow stayed until early

During the hard winter of 1962–63 wildfowlers distributed tons of food for wildfowl.
Here, members of Preston and District WA, led by their chairman and WAGBI executive
committee member Ted Conroy (in deerstalker) offload bags of grain

March, for that memorable winter turned out to be the coldest since 1740. Estuaries in southern England were blocked with pack ice and in the arctic conditions, foreshores froze and those wild-fowl which had not moved on to warmer climes struggled to find any available source of food. Responding to a joint appeal for voluntary restraint issued by WAGBI and the Wildfowl Trust on 8 January, the wildfowling clubs responded magnificently, several of them breaking ice and put-ting down supplementary feed for birds. John Ruxton travelled the Midlands collecting tail corn from seventeen farms to relieve starving ducks and geese. Around the worst affected parts of Britain wildfowling clubs took WAGBI's advice and ceased shooting when it became clear that the birds were in poor condition while others in areas where the conditions were less extreme contin-ued to monitor closely the condition of wildfowl. Even so, there were reports of irresponsible shooting and even 'wanton slaughter' during the prolonged hard weather, and within a few weeks, the bird protection lobby was arguing for changes to the 1954 Protection of Birds Act to allow temporary bans on shooting during hard weather. WAGBI was not in favour of a change in the law, and cited the way in which clubs had voluntarily laid aside their guns, though it acknowledged that Britain was out of step with other countries in Europe which already had legislation in place. Shooting, it argued, was well able to police itself. It did, however, support a proposal by Lord Mansfield to introduce a Bill in the House of Lords prohibiting the sale of dead wild geese.

The Earl of Mansfield, WAGBI's president, appeared to those who didn't know him to be a crusty old aristocrat, but beneath the dour exterior he was full of wisdom and knew his way about the corridors of power at Westminster. He was a seasoned operator, a moderating influence with-out being a restraining one, and John Anderton came to rely upon his wise counsel implicitly. Undoubtedly Mansfield's reserved political approach saved WAGBI from the gaffes it would otherwise have committed, for where the firebrands might have gone in with all guns blazing, Mansfield would, with a few carefully chosen words, moderate their approach and so achieve the desired result.

There was widespread concern at the excessive bags of migratory geese that were being taken, most notably in the east of Scotland, and while WAGBI wanted to do something to curb the annual massacre, it was anxious to do so in a way which would steer well clear of any ban on shooting. An obvious course of action was a prohibition on the sale of dead wild geese which would prevent the miscreants from disposing profitably of their large bags. This in turn would, it was hoped, moderate their behaviour. Unfortunately Lord Mansfield's Bill ran out of time during the Parliamentary session of 1962-3, but the sentiments which it encapsulated were to be resurrected in future legislation.

With their duck rearing programmes having released close on forty thousand mallard, with two thousand five hundred acres of local reserves having been established by wildfowling clubs, with the greylag goose re-established as a wild breeding species, with a bird ringing programme and wildfowl viscera and food plant research underway, Britain's wildfowlers had earned national respect for their conservation efforts. Jeffery Harrison and others, however, were well aware that migratory wildfowl could only be managed through international agreement and co-operation. Equally, they appreciated that international regulation could have unforeseen impacts upon traditional wildfowling practices here in Britain. In short, WAGBI realised that it had to participate in the politics of wildfowl conservation at an international level, and it was on the lookout for any opportunity there might be to play a role on the European stage.

Fleeting contacts with the French and Danish hunters' associations had not produced any lasting results, so when St Andrews was chosen as the venue for the First European Meeting on Wildfowl Conservation, WAGBI seized the moment to go international. Delegates from seventeen countries and several international conservation bodies were present for the three-day conference, which owed its origin to the enthusiasm of Max Nicholson, director general of the Nature Conservancy. WAGBI was the only shooting association present at the meeting, and at one point during the second day there was some tough talking to be done in defence of punt gunning, a branch of wildfowling which had in theory been banned under the Paris Convention and one which was particularly vulnerable. Geoffrey Storey, one of the WAGBI team and a former punt gunner on the Kent and Lune estuaries, spoke out in support of the sport, and he was joined by Peter Scott, who listened for half an hour to a sustained attack on punting before replying: 'There are only two people in this room who know anything about punt gunning and I am one of them.' He proceeded with a valuable defence of punt gunning which helped save the day. WAGBI later hosted a cocktail party at the conference for one hundred distinguished guests, and made a number of valuable friends and contacts. More importantly, the association had dipped its toe for the first time into international waters.

Peter Turner, a young Birmingham solicitor, had been a member of WAGBI from an early age. Turner had shot regularly in Wales and had joined the Red Wharf Bay Wildfowlers. Two weeks after he qualified, he had attended a WAGBI meeting in Birmingham at which he had signed-in as a member of the Red Wharf Bay club. The fact was remarked upon since never before had that club been represented in the attendance register. At the bar after the meeting, Turner got into conversation with John Anderton and made him the offer of any legal assistance which WAGBI might require in the future. Within a few months, John Gow decided to stand down as honorary solicitor, and the thirty-year-old Turner found himself invited to take over as the association's legal adviser. Meanwhile Colonel Vallance, who had given so much to the association over many years, retired as chairman, giving way to Captain Dan Hunt.

Conservation was a central plank in WAGBI's activities but its successes had been achieved

The decoyman's cottage at Boarstall decoy, which was leased by WAGBI and became a conservation centre

at second hand. The association could only rear and ring ducks and geese or create wildfowl reserves through the efforts of hundreds of volunteer members of its affiliated clubs. For some time it had been felt that more was needed and that WAGBI required its own field centre at which practical and scientific work could be undertaken, a place which members, and indeed the general public, could visit in order to see all that was best in wildfowl conservation.

It was with great excitement, therefore, that the WAGBI officers plus two members of the Aylesbury & District Gun Club made a first visit to Boarstall decoy, between Bicester and Thame in Buckinghamshire. Fully described in Sir Ralph Payne-Gallwey's *The Book of Duck Decoys*, the two hundred-year-old decoy itself was set in sixteen acres of woodland. It had three pipes which in former times had been used to catch thousands of wildfowl for the market, a three acre lake and a three bedroom decoyman's cottage. The whole property had been offered to WAGBI on a twenty-one year repairing lease at £100 per annum. Even better, Squadron Leader Sam McCoy, a former secretary of both RAF Patrington Wildfowlers and the Humber Area Joint Council, had offered to act as unpaid decoyman and warden in return for rent-free accommodation in the cottage until his retirement from the RAF in 1966.

A deal like this was impossible to refuse, and in March 1964 WAGBI signed the lease on Boarstall decoy. It was recognised that the setting up of the new field station, with possibly a breeding centre for ducks and geese, was not going to be created overnight, and as the operation to clear the site swung into action during the course of the summer, it became evident that the job was a very substantial one indeed. About 90% of the wire and the supports for the pipes were rotten and the pipes themselves were strewn with fallen branches and trees which would need removing. Volunteers were called for, and a swarm of local supporters from the Aylesbury Gun Club turned up to help, plus members of the Berkshire, Buckinghamshire and Oxfordshire Naturalists' Trust. Together, the working parties gradually removed the debris that had resulted from decades of neglect and made safe the dam which controlled the water levels.

One of the pipes at Boarstall decoy after restoration by local WAGBI members

Their Royal Highnesses Prince Charles and Princess Anne were visitors to the WAGBI stand at the 1965 CLA Game Fair at Shotover. Photographed with them were Nicholas Soames, Lord Mansfield, Dan Hunt and Lawrence Thompson

It was decided, if possible, to renovate at least one pipe and rebuild the screening fences which surrounded it in order that the decoy might be operated once more. However, work had also to be carried out on the cottage if it was to become habitable, and under the direction of Peter Turner and fellow management committee member David Lishman, this latter task was completed the following summer, when Lord Mansfield called in at the site during his visit to the 1965 Game Fair at Shotover Park near Oxford. Later that year, however, Squadron Leader McCoy found that he would be unable to take up the warden's post as intended and instead Jim Worgan, a former engineer on a cable-laying ship and a member of the

Royal Naval Bird Watching Society, was appointed. He moved into the cottage at Boarstall in December. Jim was soon to take on another job, that of driving WAGBI's new exhibition caravan around the county shows and of course the Game Fair.

There were staffing changes at headquarters too. John Anderton had since his appointment tried to combine WAGBI duties with his other business interests, but the continued growth of the association was now making this a sheer impossibility. In 1963 his father-in-law had died and he had been voted onto the boards of the property companies which he managed, but the failure of his marriage brought him to a crossroads in his

WAGBI president Lord Mansfield, John Anderton and WAGBI chairman Dan Hunt at the association's 1964 AGM

career. Anderton was faced with a difficult decision: was his future to lie in the property business, with all it offered by way of financial rewards and comfortable lifestyle, or should he tie his star to the shooting organisation which he had pulled up by its bootstraps and which was now poised to move on to greater things? He chose WAGBI, resigned his company directorships and in May 1964 took an honorarium of £1,000 per annum as full-time national secretary. The following year his role was re-styled and he became the association's first director.

By now, Anderton had three female administrative staff working under him, however, the assistant director's job had not worked out as well as had been hoped for. Mark Legg had quickly departed, to be replaced by Lieutenant Commander Gerald Culme-Seymour, whose WAGBI career was equally short-lived. A measure of stability was not to be achieved until December 1965 when Barry Bailey was appointed assistant director. Bailey, who had spent five years as honorary secretary of the Frodsham Wildfowlers and who was a former member of the Executive Committee, was a natural choice. A keen and knowledgeable shot, he was also a local man, farming five hundred acres at Frodsham, Cheshire. The following year, WAGBI's first full-time treasurer was appointed in the shape of Michael Capper. Gradually the headquarters team was growing, but the number of people who actually drove the association and the representation of shooting was still tiny. Anderton once commented that they could fit into one large family saloon, adding: 'I hope they are not all in it when it goes over the cliff edge – as well it might!'

Barry Bailey was appointed WAGBI assistant director in 1965

Access to the foreshore was of fundamental importance to wildfowlers. In the opening years of the twentieth century the muds and marshes which were washed by the tide were widely regarded as a 'no man's land' where the opportunity to shoot at ducks, geese, waders and indeed gulls and other seabirds was free to all. However, even in Stanley Duncan's day this was changing and landowners were starting to question the rights of fowlers to shoot over local saltings. By the 1960s the process had gathered speed and slowly it dawned upon the wildfowling fraternity that unless they had sporting rights over the marshes which they and their forefathers had traditionally shot, then their days were numbered.

One option was to purchase the marsh outright, and while this was out of the question in the case of most wildfowling clubs, a few pioneers saw land purchase as the way ahead. In 1963 members of the South Essex Wildfowlers were offered Bridgemarsh Island, in the River Crouch, at an asking price of £1,800. Two club members, John Fuller and David Gray, promptly got into a

The WAGBI caravan, photographed at the 1965 Bath and West show

car and drove to the WAGBI AGM where they put their case to the meeting and boldly asked for a loan to enable a group of South Essex members to buy the island. The two were asked to wait outside while the matter was discussed, but they did not have to wait long for an answer to their request: the loan of £600 was agreed, and Bridgemarsh Island was secured for wildfowling.

Most other fowlers had to rely on the opportunity to shoot over public foreshore, much of it owned by the Crown. Their shooting was thrown into turmoil by a new move to criminalise armed trespass which emerged as a result of a Private Member's Bill introduced into the House of Commons by B Goodman Irvine MP. The Government sympathised with his Bill, and proposed its own legislation which, not surprisingly, had wide support from the farming and countryside lobby. Wildfowlers, however, were not impressed, for the new law made it an offence to be in a public place with a loaded shotgun, and the Crown foreshore was nothing if not public.

John Anderton and Peter Turner sought their way out of what appeared to be an impossible conundrum by approaching the Crown Estate Commissioners with a view to obtaining an agreement which would create a licence allowing all WAGBI members to shoot on Crown foreshore where the sporting rights were not leased to another party. At first the Commissioners wanted nothing to do with the idea, but Anderton's powers of persuasion and all his political skills were concentrated upon the matter in question and further patient negotiation resulted in an historic agreement with the Crown Estate whereby WAGBI members would be permitted to be on Crown foreshore with a gun.

It was not long before the Crown Foreshore Agreement was put to the test in the courts. A case was brought against a member fowling on Crown foreshore in Wales by a policeman who was ill-disposed towards shooting. It was argued by the prosecution that irrespective of any agreement that might exist between WAGBI and the Crown which entitled the fowler to carry a gun on the foreshore, he still had no right

Peter Turner, WAGBI's honorary legal adviser, and John Anderton, seen here outside the Palace of Westminster with Jeffery Harrison, successfully cracked the deadlock which existed with the Crown Estate after the criminalisation of armed trespass by brokering the Crown foreshore agreement which allowed WAGBI members to retain access to their traditional fowling grounds

to shoot there. However, the judge took the contrary view, commenting that he couldn't envisage why anybody would want to take a gun on the foreshore unless he had the intention of shooting with it.

This judgment proved to have far reaching consequences, for it demonstrated that in order to take advantage of the Crown Foreshore Agreement, a wildfowler had to be a member of WAGBI – which in itself was a highly significant incentive to join the association. But the judgment actually meant more than that, for it enabled a wildfowling club which traditionally occupied unleased Crown foreshore to prosecute for armed trespass any non-member caught shooting there. That in turn gave sharp new teeth to WAGBI's disciplinary procedures, for if a fowler behaved badly and found himself excluded from membership, he could now lose the right to shoot over the foreshore.

Irish Tom

Many large punt guns have been built, but there are few as huge as the remarkable 'Irish Tom'. A massive piece of wildfowling ordnance weighing 300 lb and measuring 14 ft 1¾ in from stock to muzzle, the gun was originally made as a muzzle loader and was bought in the 1930s by Stanley Duncan from a professional wildfowler in Ireland. WW Greener subsequently converted the gun to breech loading under Duncan's supervision and Duncan first used the gun in 1936, continuing to do so until the war.

Punt guns outside Duncan's gun shop. At the top is the Hawker double gun and bottom is Irish Tom

James Robertson Justice, the much-loved character actor and star of such classic films as *Scott of the Antarctic*, *Whisky Galore*, *The Guns of Navarone* and *Chitty Chitty Bang Bang* was a friend of Peter Scott, with whom he went on to found the Wildfowl Trust, and like Scott he was also a keen punt gunner. Justice had been in touch with Duncan about the gun and eventually an agreement was made between the two of them that he would buy it by instalments. These payments were not always very promptly made, but in due course Irish Tom became his. Justice punted on the Wash, where the gun was used by HRH The Duke of Edinburgh on at least one outing, and where it survived many escapades, including an occasion in which Justice's punt capsized, depositing the gun on the bottom of the Welland. Fortunately it was recovered the following day at low water.

One indignity from which Irish Tom did not escape, however, was the removal of the end portion of its massive barrel. Justice used to travel to the Wash towing his punt behind his yellow Rolls Royce and because the gun's barrel was so long, it used to make contact with the boot of the car whenever the trailer was manoeuvred around a corner. Being fed up with this, Justice took it to a local blacksmith at Sutton Bridge who performed surgery with a hacksaw. In due course the gun ended up on the Dornoch Firth where the Justices had a home.

For many years Irish Tom could not be traced and was feared lost, but in 1981 Major John Rippingall discovered the gun in a boatyard in Inverness. Justice had died in 1975, but with the approval of his widow the gun was moved to Essex where it was restored by Rippingall and the noted punt gun engineer Allan Owens. Together they replaced the missing portion of the barrel, built a new stock, action, breech plug and cartridge case, and the restored gun was delivered to BASC headquarters on 27 April 1983.

The stock and action of Irish Tom were reconstructed by Major John Rippingall and Allan Owens

Irish Tom

Irish Tom salutes the crowd at the Holkham Country Fair in 1984

Irish Tom is proved to fire a phenomenal 50 ounces of shot and 10 ounces of coarse grain black powder, but with a bore diameter of $2\frac{1}{32}$ in at the muzzle and $2\frac{1}{16}$ in at the breech, it exceeds the maximum size permitted for use against wildfowl by modern legislation. It has, however, been fired in recent years, perhaps most notably by Squadron Leader Mike Townsend from his big double punt on the lake at Holkham, Norfolk – with a blank charge only – during a display of punt gunning at the Holkham Country Fair. The gun presently hangs in the Duke of Westminster lecture hall at BASC headquarters beneath Julian Novorol's painting *Wigeon over the Black Hut*.

Chapter 6
UNDER FIRE

*T*owards the end of 1966 rumours started circulating in shooting circles that the Government had it in mind to introduce new controls on firearms. For decades WAGBI had focussed its attention on maintaining the wildfowler's rights in the face of legislation designed to protect wild birds and the habitats in which they lived, but now a new front was to open up in the fight to defend shooting. Modern firearms legislation dated initially from 1920 when a Government with one eye over its shoulder at the turmoil in Ireland and the other fearful of communist revolution in mainland Britain, introduced controls on pistols and rifles. A further Act in 1936 extended the legislation and prohibited private possession of fully automatic weapons – the things most people refer to as machine guns. However, shotguns were not regarded as a major threat to security or public safety and they remained still largely uncontrolled in the early 1960s. All that was required in order to purchase one was a gun licence which could be obtained at a cost of ten shillings from the local post office.

As in other more recent instances, the spark which lit the fuse leading to a change in the law was a tragic multiple killing – the murder of three policemen in South Wales with a pistol. The Home Secretary, Roy Jenkins MP, was out of the country at the time, and when he returned, a journalist pushed a microphone under his nose and asked what he was going to do about the outrage. He replied that the Government would be placing stringent controls on firearms. There was no parliamentary time for an early Firearms Bill, but a Criminal Justice Bill was available so the Home Office adopted this as a vehicle for change and tagged onto it a licensing system for shotguns which would, as was already the case with firearms, be administered by the police.

A letter was quickly despatched by John Anderton to the Home Secretary requesting a meeting, and John Farr MP, one of shooting's principal supporters in the House of Commons and a WAGBI vice president, drew a small team together, consisting of the Conservative Norman Wylie MP, the Liberal Alasdair McKenzie MP and Ben Ford MP of the Labour Party. Significantly, from the outset, WAGBI's lobbying effort was to be cross-party.

Shotguns were being targeted by the Home Office principally because of a perceived increase in the use of the sawn-off shotgun by criminals, and it was proposed that they should be included within the general provisions of firearms licensing. The Government was determined to press ahead, but the consequences for ordinary sporting shooters of certification for shotguns on the same basis as rifles would have been horrendous, so at a discussion within its policy-making body, which had recently been transformed from the old and rather cumbersome Executive Committee into a more streamlined management committee, WAGBI decided upon the safeguards which it would require in order to make the Bill acceptable. Conditions on certificates restricting the place and time of use for shotguns were 'not to be tolerated and we must ensure that no such conditions can be imposed'. It was also agreed that there should be a uniform set of principles governing the obtaining of a certificate and that reasons for refusal of a certificate should be given, along with the right of appeal.

HRH The Duke of Edinburgh talks to Jim Worgan, decoyman at WAGBI's Boarstall decoy, at the association's exhibition at the Council for Nature's wildlife exhibition in 1966

Peter Turner focussed his attention on the Bill and realised quickly that the resources of all the sporting organisations would have to be brought together if there was to be any chance of amending what was a thoroughly bad piece of legislation. Lines of communication were therefore established with the British Field Sports Society, Clay Pigeon Shooting Association, Gun Trade Association, Gamekeepers' Association and others, leading to the formation in April 1967 of the Long Room Committee. Named after Purdey's famous Long Room in which the group met, the Committee was the fore-runner of today's British Shooting Sports Council. It mounted a stiff opposition to the Bill and chipped away at the licensing provisions proposed by the Government to ensure that the new shotgun regulations were less onerous than those for rifles and pistols. However, it was quite evident that the Home Secretary was not prepared to give way on the core of his proposals, and in 1967 the new law came into force. It was goodbye to the ten bob gun licence and hello to the shotgun certificate.

It had been a steep learning curve for WAGBI, and there can be little doubt that both it and the other shooting organisations had been ill-prepared and under-rehearsed. Policy on firearms matters had not even been considered in any detail prior to the introduction of the Bill, and the machinery with which to mount any credible opposition was clearly inadequate. WAGBI at least addressed this latter point through the setting up of a small permanent parliamentary group under the chairmanship of John Farr MP. Crucially, it also established a new and unified approach to firearms matters with the other shooting associations. Very soon it started receiving reports of uneven – and unfair – administration of the new law by different police forces around the country.

A further crucial piece of legislation came up for discussion in 1967. Bird protection law had now had a dozen years to bed-in and the Government had decided that in certain aspects it was found to be wanting. Wildfowlers had no argument with one of the main changes introduced under the Protection of Birds Act 1967, a ban on the sale of dead wild geese, for this had initially been the proposal of WAGBI's president, Lord Mansfield. The ban now became law, despite the opposition of some Scottish MPs who had been lobbied hard by farmers who were anxious to ensure that they could continue to hammer at the geese which they accused of raiding their crops. A second measure was brought in largely as a result of the experience of the severe winter of 1962-3, for although WAGBI had argued for self-regulation by wildfowlers during periods of exceptionally cold weather and had thrashed out a formula for it with the Nature Conservancy, the Government decided that voluntary action by fowling clubs was not enough, and introduced powers for the Secretary of State to ban wildfowling during periods of hard weather.

Sir Tufton Beamish MP, a shooting man, had undertaken responsibility for steering the Protection of Birds Bill through the House of Commons and it was felt, with some confidence, that the legislation was in safe hands. As it entered its committee stage, however, Nicholas Ridley MP tabled a surprise amendment to prohibit the use of guns larger than 4 bore. Suddenly punt gunning found itself holed below the waterline and sinking fast. Ridley's verbal assault on punt gunning was sugar-coated. He said that he did not regard it as cruel or unkind, and he conceded that the number of active punt gunners in Britain was very small indeed. However, he contended that there were still active commercial punt gunners who killed large numbers of ducks for profit and that excessive bags were sometimes made – in one case three hundred and sixty wigeon killed with one shot. The figure was entirely without foundation, but as usual it had the desired political impact.

Stanley Duncan Jr meets HRH The Duke of Edinburgh at the WAGBI diamond jubilee dinner, Hull Guildhall 9 July 1968

THE WILDFOWLERS'
ASSOCIATION

of

Great Britain and Ireland

(founded 1908)

ANNUAL DINNER

QUEEN'S HOTEL
CHELTENHAM
GLOUCESTERSHIRE

Saturday, 4th June, 1966

Host Organisation :
GLOUCESTERSHIRE WILDFOWLERS' ASSOCIATION

In the 1950s and 1960s WAGBI annual meetings, and the celebratory dinners which accompanied them, were hosted by affiliated clubs around the country

Within hours of the maroon rocket being fired over Westminster, Anderton was busy marshalling every possible source of support and rehearsing the arguments which had been used to defend punting at the international conference in St Andrews. Great play was made of the fact that Ridley's amendment had come out of the blue, without any prior discussion with WAGBI or even with the Nature Conservancy's Wildfowl Conservation Committee. Anderton had consulted expert punt gunners within the WAGBI membership and, armed with the information he had gleaned, he briefed MPs on the standing committee which was examining the Bill. John Farr, Sir Tufton Beamish and Marcus Kimball all spoke up for the sport and in the face of such opposition Ridley backed down and withdrew his amendment. Disaster had been averted, but another political lesson had been learned. Anderton quickly dispatched an appeal to all punt gunners to provide him with basic information on their equipment and activities in order that he could be better armed were the attack to be repeated. His fast footwork was hugely appreciated by the punt gunning fraternity, and in due course Ted Conroy, an enthusiastic Lancashire punt gunner with great commonsense who had assisted closely with the campaign, arranged for a painting to be presented to him. The gift was subscribed to by practically every active punt gunner from across the country. *Shooting Times* called the affair a triumph for WAGBI, but Conroy was probably closer to the mark when he placed the praise and appreciation on Anderton's shoulders alone. Anderton was to achieve many victories in his defence of shooting over the coming years, but the punt gunning fraternity was a highly influential force within WAGBI and never forgot what he had done for them. Some would argue that it was the successful defence of punt gunning in 1967 which cemented his reputation.

There had been little opportunity for Anderton to prepare for WAGBI's golden jubilee in 1958, just a few months after he took office as honorary secretary. Ten years on, he was absolutely determined to make the diamond jubilee a year to remember, and early in 1967 the management committee was told in confidence that HRH The Duke of Edinburgh had consented to become the association's first royal patron during its sixtieth year. Moreover, there was every prospect that Prince Philip would be prepared to attend a major event held to celebrate the occasion. Arrangements were put in hand as soon as the royal diary was sketched out, with Anderton visiting Buckingham Palace to discuss arrangements for a dinner to coincide with the 1968 annual general meeting. It had been decided that the event would be held in Hull, WAGBI's birthplace, on 9 July, and the celebrations took place at the town's Guildhall that evening following an AGM held at the Royal Station Hotel. Naturally all the WAGBI hierarchy attended, but pride of place was given to the host club, the Hull and East Riding Wildfowlers Association, its members and in particular its chairman, Trevor Field, who had been introduced to wildfowling by none less than Duncan himself. When Prince Philip arrived he was of course immediately surrounded by the top brass, but it was noticed by those who were there on the evening that he turned not to the dignitaries but to the local fowlers for conversation. Addressing one lowly HERWA member he asked which part of the river the fowler shot.

When you join WAGBI....

You are supporting the only organisation working solely on behalf of wild-fowlers and rough shooters and against those who would ban shooting

WAGBI needs the help of every shooting man

Join today and safeguard your sport and the conservation of your quarry

Cheque, cash, or P.O. to the Treasurer, WAGBI, Grosvenor House, Watergate St. Chester

This membership recruitment advertisement in a 1969 issue of Shooting Times *stresses WAGBI's wildfowling roots. But by the late 1960s its membership was rapidly diversifying*

The WAGBI exhibit at the annual CLA Game Fair, such as this one at Bowood in 1967, quickly became a fixture in the association's calendar and the single most important venue for membership recruitment

In 1968, John Anderton was invited to an international wildfowl conservation meeting in Leningrad. With the cold war becoming frostier, Anderton, a former naval officer, sought guidance from the Foreign Office as to whether or not he should attend. He was advised against travelling to the Soviet Union and declined the invitation

'Just to the west of Hull, Sir' was the answer. 'Oh, would that be Faxfleet?' enquired Prince Philip. The fowler beamed. Yes indeed it was, and a lively conversation ensued.

The printed menu card for the evening contained a number of photographs, one of Duncan's black hut, described – romantically but not entirely accurately – as the place where WAGBI had been founded, plus others of the impressive offices at Grosvenor House, Chester, to which the association had moved in February, the decoy cottage at Boarstall and hand-reared greylag geese in Lancashire. The implication was clear: WAGBI had risen from humble beginnings to a position of some greatness. When he rose for his after dinner speech, Prince Philip looked at the assembled gathering – the politicians, the local dignitaries, the illustrious guests, the great and the good from the shooting and conservation worlds alike, together with the ranks of ordinary members from Hull and elsewhere, and commented:

'Stanley Duncan certainly started something sixty years ago.'

He went on to speak about wildfowling, the international environmental issues with which he was so familiar and the inter-relationships between man and wild animals, pointing out that while man the hunter had had little adverse impact on his quarry over millions of years, man the businessman and scientist was succeeding in driving whole populations of wild animals towards extinction inside a couple of generations. 'I think Stanley Duncan would have been extremely impressed by the sense of responsibility, by the code of behaviour and by the attitude towards all forms of wildlife which the association is successfully encouraging among its members. There is no better discipline than self-discipline, there is no greater freedom than self-control. The association is the means chosen by sensible wildfowlers and rough shooters to exercise self-discipline and self-control for the benefit of all, and every wildfowler and rough shooter should be demanding to join.'

In September 1968 WAGBI held its first National Forum meeting at the Queen Hotel, Chester. Reformulation of its governing structure had meant that club representatives were no longer entitled to attend meetings of the policy-making management committee in the way that they had been able to attend the old executive committee meetings, and it was felt that there needed to be some form of gathering, outside the annual general meeting, at which clubs from across the country could share their views with the senior management. Forty-five members turned up at Chester, including delegates from eighteen affiliated clubs and three joint councils. The meeting opened with a film recording of The Duke of Edinburgh's speech at the diamond jubilee dinner in Hull, after which Peter Turner was able to answer questions on the new shot-gun legislation.

The meeting was a great success, but it highlighted once again the changing nature of WAGBI's membership, which year by year contained a reducing proportion of coastal wild-fowlers and an increasing proportion of rough shooters, pigeon shooters, inland duck shooters and even game shooters. Yet again it prompted the management committee into lengthy discussion over a possible change of name. There was strong opposition to the prospect of losing the famous WAGBI acronym and all that it implied, but did the present title convey the full breadth of the association's activities? Would game shooters join if the title was changed? Nobody knew the answer to these questions although Anderton was determined to press the discussion forward as far as he could, and it was agreed that WAGBI was recognised and accepted despite its name if not because of it. Parking the discussion once more on the side burner, the committee decided that even if WAGBI was to remain a wildfowling organisation in name, then at least it would have to turn its attention towards improving the services it offered to the burgeoning rough shooting membership within its ranks.

Woodpigeon control was the issue of the moment. Anyone walking in the English country-side in the early months of 1969 could have been forgiven for wondering what sort of deadly plague was affecting the nation's pigeon population. Stupefied and disorientated pigeons were to

Would you care to see a pluck-off Ma'am? HM The Queen is definitely amused as the feathers fly in the WAGBI Woodpigeon Plucking Championships at the CLA Game Fair, Stratfield Saye, 1974

Plucking spectacular! Competitors pluck against the clock for Her Majesty

be found feebly flapping about the woods and fields. Indeed, in some areas the landscape was littered with dead and dying birds – pigeons and pheasants alike. The idea of catching woodpigeons by the use of stupefying narcotic baits had first been mooted in the 1940s, and by the late 1960s researchers from the Ministry of Agriculture had evolved a method of using tic beans coated in alpha-chloralose. Treated bait was spread on a crop when it was at its most susceptible to woodpigeon attack, whereupon the local pigeon population would, in theory, descend upon the field in their droves, eat the beans and keel over. They could then be picked up by hand and dispatched. During seventy trials between 1964 and 1967 a total of 5,167 pigeons had been caught – together with one hundred and fifteen pheasants, one hundred partridges and sixty-two protected birds of various species, many of which had died. However, the collateral damage was considered acceptable by the Ministry scientists, who decided to press ahead with full-scale trials in Bedfordshire. They recruited twenty-seven farmers to participate.

With 1,393 Bedfordshire woodpigeons reported dead, the National Farmers Union hailed the trials as a success, though the Ministry expressed its satisfaction rather more mildly, noting merely that the control method 'was practical and reasonably economical in relation to labour'. WAGBI was not so sure. In fact it was downright alarmed at the prospect of widespread use of narcotics against woodpigeons. Chairman of the WAGBI Woodpigeon sub-committee was David Lishman of the Midlands Woodpigeon Club, who had been closely following the Ministry's research. Lishman immediately put the published report before his committee, which was by no means satisfied that the Government had got its sums right. In fact, on examining the economics of the exercise it was established that the cost of the narcotic bait and the labour involved made the price for killing each bird about 3s 2d. If the cost of Ministry direction and supervision were added into the equation, the price soared to 14s 9d. Furthermore, the WAGBI committee highlighted the worrying fact that only two of the farmers who went ahead with the trials strictly followed the instructions given for the use of the bait.

The implications for pigeon shooting over decoys if the widespread use of narcotics went ahead were obvious, and WAGBI decided that as well as questioning the cost of doping, it must also put more resources into woodpigeon shooting. Already it had fourteen affiliated specialist pigeon shooting clubs, while a further fifty fowling clubs also offered pigeon shooting to their members, so the membership interest in pigeon shooting even at current levels was considerable. Lishman reasoned that if the Government was prepared to put money into costly control by narcotic bait, it was worth seeing if it would consider providing financial support for pigeon shooting either as well or – preferably – instead. WAGBI thus convened a meeting with the Ministry of Agriculture, the NFU and the rabbit clearance societies with the aim of setting up and promoting a nationwide chain of shooting clubs offering pigeon control services to the farming community. However, while the Ministry was prepared to consider shooting, it had already invested too much technical and research capital in the narcotics experiment to throw in the towel on tic beans and alpha-chloralose, so it pushed on with its experiments. By 1970 it had conducted two hundred and eighty-six operations and collected three thousand two hundred birds. The Midlands Woodpigeon Club fought back with a comparative trial in which shooting and doping would compete side by side. This, so far as WAGBI was concerned, proved a huge success, the shooters bagging 1,500 birds over decoys and the boffins collecting none.

Lishman proposed a campaign to form more woodpigeon clubs, similar to the campaign which had been waged on the marsh and foreshore twenty years earlier and which had created the string of wildfowling clubs that had become WAGBI's backbone. He suggested a national roost shoot with entry fees, prizes and publicity and an All-Britain Pigeon Plucking Championship to be held at the Game Fair. This was eventually, and far more grandly, styled the 'WAGBI World Pigeon Plucking Championship' and it was run by the enthusiastic Martin Thompson and his brother. Together they devised a full-blown competition in which

The woodpigeon and rabbit control service offered relief for farmers and shooting opportunity for WAGBI members

Denis Graham-Hogg outside WAGBI's offices in Chester

ABOVE:
*Denis Graham-Hogg and John Richards in
1973. Graham-Hogg was to co-ordinate
WAGBI's National Woodpigeon Control
Service*

RIGHT:
*John Richards, Roy Jordan and David
Lishman were central to the success which the
WAGBI Safari became*

pigeon shooters vied against each other to shave fractions of a second off the record plucking time. Pigeon plucking at the Game Fair reached its zenith in 1974 at Stratfield Saye when HM The Queen toured the WAGBI stand during her visit to the Fair. Keen to demonstrate before royalty the speed at which WAGBI's finest could make the feathers fly, and in a comment which must have had the royal flunkeys aghast with consternation, it is recorded that the chief plucker approached his sovereign with the immortal words 'Ma'am, would you care to see a pluck-off?' History does not relate the response he received, but it was the difficulty of storing large quantities of pigeons in the sweltering heat of the Game Fair rather than a spell in the Tower which finally put paid to the World Pigeon Plucking Championships.

Pigeons were flavour of the month. In 1972 Lishman recommended in a paper to the management committee a formalised structure for a National Woodpigeon Control Service to be administered by headquarters and run by designated clubs which would offer a call-out service to farmers who required pigeon control. Participating clubs would guarantee a pigeon shooter on the ground within twenty-four hours and their members in turn would benefit from lots of extra shooting opportunity. Within a few months fifty-five clubs had applied to be included and a further twenty-eight had expressed interest. It seemed that demand for pigeon shooting was growing by the week, and it was established that WAGBI pigeon shooting clubs now shot over 1,046 farms and estates and in 1971 had killed 162,378 woodpigeons with a sales value of £13,000. Even to narcotics enthusiasts at the Ministry of Agriculture it must have been clear that shooting, not doped tic beans, was the way forward for pigeon control, but while government officials fought shy of committing money to the project, the Shooting Sports Trust weighed in with financial support, promising £2,000 to employ a part-time officer to promote and run the scheme and to liaise with the Ministry of Agriculture and the pigeon clubs. Concern was expressed by some members of the WAGBI management that the association might be over-stretching itself. Worried by the prospect of bad publicity were the clubs to be seen shooting pigeons for commercial gain, they counselled caution, but by now Anderton had got

HE'S GOING — ARE YOU?

THE SECOND

WAGBI SAFARI

CLAY SHOOTING & GUNDOG TESTS

Packington,

near

Coventry,

Sept. 9, 10 AM — 6 PM

OPEN 30 SPORTING SHOOT
(1st prize £20)
PLUS POOL AND PRACTICE

OPEN SOLO AND TEAM
(3 guns plus 2 dogs and handlers)
SHOOTING AND RETRIEVING TESTS
(Wedgwood Trophy for top WAGBI club team)

" WAGBI-QUALIFIED RETRIEVER " TEST

TOTAL PRIZE MONEY OVER £75

Crude but effective. An advertisement for the second Safari in 1973

John Anderton oversees announcements at the 1973 WAGBI Safari. The Safari was a new form of competitive event for the shooting man and his dog

the bit between his teeth and pointed out that if WAGBI failed to promote a pigeon shooting service to farmers, then others would almost certainly do so. On the strength of the SST funding he agreed to appoint a part-timer and in September 1972 Ernest Taylor, a sixty-four-year-old former officer with the Royal Canadian Mounted Police and chairman of the Three Counties Woodpigeon Club, was given the job. Unfortunately Taylor resigned within four months due to poor health and the following March Denis Graham-Hogg took the part-time post of Woodpigeon Shooting field secretary. Graham-Hogg was a former RAF pilot who had been a POW during the war and who had subsequently worked overseas for Shell before retiring. He was experienced in international conservation, having been a trustee of the Serengeti National Parks for four years, and he was a rough shooter and pigeon shooter. Within a short while he was promoting the National Woodpigeon Control Service in *Farmers Weekly* and meeting

The Safari had wide appeal. WAGBI members on the Safari catapult range in 1974

Ministry of Agriculture officials who agreed to publicise the service to all their regional and divisional offices.

Of even greater significance for the future development of the association were two other staff appointments. After a long period of wooing and courting by John Anderton, the Sports Council, which had resources available to direct towards development and training in sport shooting, agreed early in 1972 to provide £2,200 per annum in grant aid towards the funding of an assistant development officer who would help ease the rapidly increasing workload of Barry Bailey. At the same time Jeffery Harrison had been agitating for some time to raise WAGBI's conservation game. Boarstall had not been living up to expectations. It was costing around £3,000 a year to run and in 1972 its gross takings from visitor entrance fees was £612, only a few pounds up from its miserable out-turn of £495 the previous year and still nowhere near any prospect of break-even. Conservation within WAGBI needed a shot in the arm, argued Harrison and he put

forward the recommendation that a conservation officer with a degree in zoology should be appointed to the headquarters staff.

The candidates who were to fill both the development and conservation posts were interviewed, both joined the staff within weeks of each other and very soon Anderton reported that a 'blast of fresh air' was being felt throughout the entire WAGBI establishment. The two new staff members were John Swift and John Richards. Swift, an Oxford zoology graduate with a research interest in the

A young John Swift teaches duck ringing at a conservation course at Deal, Kent in 1975

common snipe and wildlife expedition experience in the European Arctic and Africa, got straight down to business at Harrison's fast-developing reserve at former gravel workings near Sevenoaks in Kent. His first work there was that of analysing invertebrate food in snipe pools blasted out by explosives and then laced with cow dung. Richards had trained at the Royal Agricultural College, Cirencester, and spent three years in Tanzania before studying at Bangor University with a view to returning to East Africa. Instead, however, his interest in wildfowling, which started on the south coast at Pagham and continued in North Wales during his university days, led him to

By 1975 WAGBI was still – in name at least – an association for wildfowlers. But it was recruiting from the ranks of rough shooters, game shooters and gamekeepers alike

WAGBI. Shortly after his arrival he was handed an altogether different project, another scheme from the fertile brain of David Lishman, developed with assistance from resident gundog expert Roy Jordan, Lord Aylesford and the Dorset Wildfowlers: the WAGBI Safari.

Billed as a new type of competitive event for the shooting man, the Safari was intended to test the prowess of both the individual shooter and his dog under conditions which would simulate as closely as possible those in the shooting field. It was to include an individual twenty-five bird sporting clay shoot, an individual dog and gun competition, plus team clay shooting and gundog events. A 'wildfowler' dog and gun competition would include two water retrieves. The WAGBI caravan and the entire HQ staff would be in attendance on the day and there would be full publicity. Packington Park, near Meriden in Warwickshire, the home of Lord Guernsey, was to be the venue for the first Safari. It was held on 17 September 1972 and was a stunning success. Never had so many members gathered in one place under the WAGBI flag and the event was immediately earmarked for an annual fixture, albeit with less clay shooting and more gundog handling. Furthermore, Packington itself proved to be such a perfect site that it was seriously proposed as a long-term location for WAGBI headquarters.

Development of the staff and the association was entirely dependent upon one thing alone: membership recruitment, a subject to which John Anderton's mind turned endlessly. In January 1972 he had presented a paper to the management committee which put the membership at 21,346. It was an impressive total for an organisation which had barely been able to stand on its own two feet eight years previously, but Anderton was not remotely satisfied. Annual recruitment was buoyant, but the turnover of members was also high, with the result that WAGBI had to run quite fast in order to stand still. 'We should be recruiting five hundred new members at the Game

Fair,' complained Anderton. 'What puts them off? The answer is plain and always has been – our title. Our title puts off the very great majority, but title change or no, anyone picking up our annual report can see at a glance that our main energies and cashflow are concerned with wildfowling. Therefore until we develop in the field of game birds, we cannot really expect a change of heart amongst shooters.'

In fact the title had changed at the 1970 annual general meeting at which John Ruxton had taken over as chairman, and although the change had not exactly been a startling one, it set the association on a track which was to have major significance inside a decade. At the meeting, and with the support of a large majority, the subtitle 'Representing Wildfowlers and Roughshooters' had been deleted and the phrase 'For Shooting and Conservation' had been inserted in its stead. The phrase neatly encapsulated what WAGBI was all about. Now, two years later, Anderton was looking further ahead and agitating once again for a full-blown name change. Purist wildfowling clubs might disaffiliate if the 'Wildfowling' title were dropped, he conceded, but the gun clubs, woodpigeon clubs and game shooting clubs would be in favour. 'The all-important consideration should be "what is best for the sport?" not "what is best for WAGBI?"' he insisted.

'In the 1950s WAGBI came out of the "troubles" well because it was seen to care for the sporting interests of the 'have nots' with mud on their boots. Things have changed since then. The slices of the economic cake are much more generous for a broader range of the people. Fish and chip shops now sell chicken and scampi, and the purist wildfowler of yesteryear shoots game birds as well as wildfowl and woodpigeons.'

Anderton was alert to the wider political ramifications of a name change, for this was something which would clearly affect the structure – or 'hotchpotch' as management committee member John Marchington put it – of other shooting organisations. Was there room for a merger between WAGBI, the Gamekeepers' Association and the Game Conservancy? What about a ballot of members on a name change? Perhaps it should be called the 'British Shooting Association', or even 'BSA (Incorporating WAGBI)'? With woodpigeons, gundogs, and firearms featuring ever more strongly on the agenda and an explosion of interest and activity in courses and wetland conservation, it seemed that the association's path was clear, name change or not.

But in May 1973 another of those events occurred which changed yet again the course of the association's history. For over two years a Government working party had been considering whether, in the interests of maintaining both public safety and law and order, any further changes needed to be made to firearms law. Against a background of growing criminal use of firearms and the new controls on shotguns which had been introduced in 1967, Home Office officials and the police had considered various options for strengthening the law and finally they published their findings in the form of a consultative document, 'The Control of Firearms in Great Britain'.

The 1973 Green Paper, as it immediately became known, struck the shooting community and the gun trade like an Exocet missile. Its proposals were hugely restrictive and, if translated into law, could have wiped out large areas of the sport and its associated activities. Shotguns would have been licensed in the same way as rifles and pistols, with full territorial conditions upon their use, while the semi-automatic and pump-action guns used by wildfowlers and pigeon shooters would have been prohibited altogether. New collections of firearms would have been banned and swingeing restrictions would have been placed on firearms dealers, air weapons, antique firearms and young shots.

John Anderton received his copy of the Green Paper, read through it and immediately contacted Peter Turner. He then visited Turner's house in Birmingham overnight and the two of them spent the following day analysing exactly what effect the Government's proposals would

The top table in shirtsleeve order at the 1973 AGM. Left to right: Lord Arbuthnott, John Anderton, Jeffery Harrison, Peter Turner

The WAGBI stand at the 1973 CLA Game Fair at Abercairny

have and preparing the bones of a response. Joining them was another key figure, a chief inspector from West Yorkshire Constabulary with an encyclopaedic knowledge of firearms law who had already written a book on firearms controls. Colin Greenwood provided the technical detail which supplemented Turner's legal knowledge and Anderton's political skills. The three of them worked through the document, trying to find the dangers and how they could effectively be dealt with, and came up with a twelve page summary, on the basis of which they dispatched a request for the Home Secretary, Robert Carr MP, to receive a WAGBI delegation under the leadership of John Farr MP.

'Although a small number of the proposals may have a marginal effect in reducing armed crime, the majority of them will only impose unnecessary and oppressive restrictions on those who obtain their recreation with firearms, without materially affecting their criminal use,' they commented. WAGBI went on to mount a robust defence of semi-automatic and pump-action shotguns and firearms collecting, and voiced its strong opposition to conditions on shotgun certificates, territorial restrictions, 'good reason' requirements for shotguns and other infringements on the personal liberty of shooters.

The Green Paper, said WAGBI, was based upon a fundamental misconception of the problem and on unreliable statistics. If its recommendations became law they would interfere very seriously with legitimate sport without in any way contributing to a reduction in armed crime. The association protested that the working party which had written the document comprised only the police and the Home Office, with no representation from shooting sports, and that only seven weeks had been allowed for public consultation.

At least that latter hurdle was overcome and, largely as a result of WAGBI representation, the Home Office extended the consultation period. Thus at its July meeting, the management committee convened in a council of war. Its first business was to greet the association's new president elect, the Viscount of Arbuthnott, an active cross-bench peer and a vice chairman of the Scottish Nature Conservancy Council who had tremendously impressed Anderton at their first meeting and who had expressed his clear wish to be associated with the grass roots of shooting. Anderton and Turner then briefed the assembled management committee members. Numerous meetings of the Long Room Committee had been held and together with the other shooting bodies it had been decided that the best course of action would be to exert heavy pressure on the Government to withdraw the Green Paper and set up a standing committee with representation from knowledgeable experts in the sporting use of firearms and the gun trade. Anderton commented that this was 'the toughest battle which WAGBI has ever taken on. If it failed then there would be little or no reason for continuing as an association.'

Strategy and tactics were discussed. There was an urgent need for public relations, for the briefing of legal counsel and for an individual letter to every single WAGBI member, the first time such an action had been considered since February 1949 when the then three hundred odd members had been individually balloted on whether WAGBI should continue as an independent organisation. Above all there was a need for money. Anderton took a deep breath and asked for £2,500 to be drawn from the reserves. The management committee responded by authorising expenditure of £5,000.

At the annual general meeting which followed immediately after the Committee had concluded its business there was fighting talk over the green paper. Lord Arbuthnott lauded the responsible approach which WAGBI took towards its business and was duly elected, a telegram was sent from the meeting to Robert Carr MP and a vote of appreciation to the firearms subcommittee was tabled by Fred Pearson of the Fenland WA although a proposal to change the name to 'WAGBI – The Shooting and Conservation Association' tabled by Jeff Harrison was quickly withdrawn under what *Shooting Times* referred to as a 'rattle of musketry' from the membership. *Shooting Times*, though, responded brilliantly to the campaign to defeat the Green Paper, as did *The Field*. Other organisations such as the BFSS weighed in too, and the Gun Trade Association published a series of stark advertisements in the shooting press with the net result that the shooters in their masses reached for pen and paper and bombarded the Home Office with impassioned responses to what were increasingly looking like a set of ill-considered proposals. Judging by the sheer number of letters received by MPs and officials it was reckoned at the time to be the largest lobby on any one topic since the war.

By mid September the Government had taken a drubbing in by-elections at Ely and Ripon and the following month it received both barrels in a heated debate on firearms control in the Upper House tabled by Lord Swansea. Anderton and the other shooting representatives sitting in the public gallery listened with satisfaction as Home Office Minister Viscount Colville admitted the Green Paper had been too sweeping and confirmed that the Government was prepared to make concessions. Shotguns would not after all be placed under Section 1 controls, there would be no limits on the numbers of shotguns held or any territorial conditions, and more significantly the Government signalled its support for the Long Room Committee's idea of a standing advisory committee on firearms comprising representatives of the Home Office, the police and sporting shooting.

When the Queen's Speech was published at the State Opening of Parliament that autumn, there was no mention of any future Firearms Bill: the campaign had been a success. However, the cost in human and financial resources had been tremendous. John Anderton had had to delegate virtually all his other work to Barry Bailey in order to deal with firearms matters and by the end of the summer the entire staff was physically and mentally exhausted. After one particularly tough string of meetings Anderton had written a personal note to John Ruxton apologising for the fact that he was burnt out. 'Since arriving in my office at 10.15 I have failed to do anything of any merit, so have decided to go home and remain there until such time as I have recouped some energy and can see, think and hear straight.' The net cost of the exercise, after donations received, was £1,676, and the annual accounts recorded a deficit of over £2,000 on the year.

Victory over the Green Paper had also accentuated the shortcomings in WAGBI's structure and the management committee realised that it was necessary to appoint a financial administrator, to increase the woodpigeon secretary's work to full-time and to strengthen WAGBI's representation in the regions. Reaction from the membership more than justified these decisions, for the September recruitment figure of nine hundred and seventy-seven was exceptional, pushing the total number of members up to twenty-eight thousand.

Chapter 7
A ROOF OVER OUR HEADS

teady growth of the staff at headquarters highlighted a growing problem, that of office space and accommodation. On 7 January 1974 Colin Barwell joined the staff. Barwell had retired from the RAF with the rank of Squadron Leader after service in South Africa and the Middle East and had gone into civilian life as manager of Southampton airport. The professionalism which he brought to financial control and administration was much needed but, like everybody else, he required office space from which to work, and the offices in Watergate Street, Chester, were already bursting at the seams.

Discussions had been held with WAGBI's landlord, who had a vacant second floor flat and a cellar which could be added to the present suite of accommodation. There was thus the opportunity of terminating the existing lease, which still had four years to run, and entering into a new fully repairing twenty-year lease for increased office accommodation. It was an attractive proposition, but a full structural survey would be required and the management committee took the cautious approach, deciding first to establish what alternative properties might be available. Anderton conducted a full assessment of future accommodation needs, using as his baseline the regulations

John Anderton (right) with Colin Barwell, who lent great stability to BASC's finance and administration

laid down by the Offices, Shops and Railway Premises Act 1963. He also allowed for an increase both in membership and the staff to service it. Quickly he concluded that even with the flat and the cellar, the present building would only be attractive for a maximum of five more years. Clearly WAGBI would have to think about moving, and investigations so far had yielded very little suitable alternative property.

What about a freehold purchase? Peter Turner pointed out that a building which was wholly owned by the association would give security and at the same time enable a large sum of money

John Anderton in his office at WAGBI's headquarters at Watergate Street, Chester

to be raised on a mortgage in case of an emergency. However, buying a property would require a major fund raising effort and another management committee member, Sir Alastair 'Buster' Graesser questioned whether this was the right moment to appeal to the membership for what would inevitably be a very large sum of money.

Despite the obvious risks, Anderton kept his ear close to the ground and in July he reported that he, Colin Barwell and Buster Graesser had visited a property which looked promising. The former water mill at Rossett, seven miles south of Chester, had been fully converted to good quality office accommodation just four years previously and indeed had won a Welsh Heritage Year award in 1973 for outstanding renovation work. Now its owners, Mitaim Holdings, had fallen on hard times and had to dispose of the mill house plus two acres of land and a dilapidated stable block immediately to the rear. There could hardly have been a more suitable place at which to base WAGBI's operation. Ducks paddled and quacked on the millpond in front of the delightful yet imposing office building, while the greensward beyond kindled thoughts of conservation courses and gundog events. As to location, while north Wales might not have seemed the obvious choice for the headquarters of a national organisation with an increasingly active parliamentary lobby, Anderton had his roots firmly in the north-west. He argued that, geographically speaking, Rossett was pretty much at the centre of the United Kingdom, and provided you drew a line from Londonderry to Kent and from Caithness to Cornwall he was probably about right, though it doesn't always seem like that to those living in the populous south-east of England.

Management committee members were asked for their thoughts. Turner, who had at the outset been fully in favour of purchase, now urged caution, pointing out that the market for office rents was stagnant and that there was plenty of space available for the asking. Others put forward the view that what was needed was not so much a rented office as a permanent home for the association, with a museum, a meeting room and a library – which already had books to fill its shelves, thanks to a bequest from Turner's predecessor, the association's former legal adviser John Gow, who had instructed that his extensive collection of sporting books and papers was to be given to WAGBI upon his death. A figure of £85,000 was being asked for the property, but Anderton was well aware of the precarious financial situation in which the vendors found themselves and reckoned that £70,000 would probably be accepted, or possibly less if the property remained unsold for a few months more. In addition, further funds would be required to pay off the two remaining years of the current lease, to purchase essential office equipment and to cover legal and professional fees and possible redundancy payments to those staff who might not be prepared to move from Chester.

The site at Rossett was quickly recognised as a perfect home in which WAGBI could settle and as a base for future expansion

Marford Mill was built in 1791 as a water mill. It was converted to prestige office accommodation and won a Welsh Heritage Year award in 1973. Three years later in 1976 it was bought by WAGBI as the association's new national headquarters

All depended upon the success or otherwise of the proposed membership appeal. An appeal letter was drafted and tested on a selected number of members. In it, the mill was described in glowing terms as a place which had all the facilities which WAGBI could want for, as somewhere to which members could come for weekend courses, 'a suitable nerve centre of the very future of shooting and conservation'. The letter boldly underlined the opportunity which now existed: 'This is the right time, for never again will the property market be as depressed as now.' Gifts or loans were invited from the entire membership, with Anderton personally topping and tailing the letters to those 10% of members who were regarded as the core of WAGBI's supporters. It was not a good time to ask for money, though. The economy was in a dire state, there was increasing unemployment and across the country there sounded the painful creak of tightening belts. Membership fees had only just been raised and, to cap it all, in November 1975 the BFSS launched its own fighting fund to raise £250,000 in order to challenge the latest anti-coursing Bill before Parliament.

On 1 February 1976 the committee met at Mitaim House, as the property at Rossett was called, to decide whether or not to proceed with negotiations for the mill, the land and the derelict buildings. With only one member voting against the purchase, the management was given a clear mandate to proceed and within two days their offer of £65,000 was accepted and a deal struck, subject to survey. Peter Turner set about dealing with the necessary legal documentation while opinions were canvassed as to what the building might be called. Mitaim House was obviously no longer an appropriate title, a much better one being Marford Mill, the name by which the building had been known from the time that it was built in 1791 up until its conversion. Local views were sought, and the proposal to rename the building Marford Mill was found to be universally popular.

There remained just the small matter of finance. Luckily the landlords of the existing headquarters building were prepared for WAGBI to relinquish its lease a year early with a cash settlement in lieu of dilapidations, while the vendors of Marford Mill, George Maxwell Developments Ltd, were keen to dispose of the furniture, carpets and fittings, all of them less than four years old and in exceptionally good order, so a deal was struck and for an extra £1,100 the property came carpeted and furnished. So much for the proposed expenditure. On the income front, things were not quite so rosy. The appeal had 'crawled painfully, somewhat in the right direction' and had reached something under £25,000, with twenty-two affiliated clubs having donated or lent money, so collecting boxes were brought out at the Game Fair, a spate of clay shoots and a special draw was organised and full coverage was sought in the sporting press. Revitalising the appeal had an immediate effect but, nevertheless, it still looked as though a mortgage would be needed and arrangements were made to borrow £30,000 over five years. All was now set for the purchase to be concluded and it just remained for the managing trustees to signify their approval. This they did at a special meeting convened at the CLA Game Fair at Glanusk Park. Formal possession of the new headquarters building was obtained on 4 October 1976 and the move from Chester took place two weeks later. All but four of the staff were prepared to move to Rossett and in the case of those who had to incur extra expense as a result of a longer journey to work, Anderton saw to it that they received an appropriate travelling allowance on top of their normal earnings.

Mary Anderton and Barry Bailey draw the winning ticket for the Holland & Holland gun draw in 1975

Marford Mill belonged to WAGBI and the sense of elation amongst the staff and the management committee was huge. The purchase had been a gamble, but good intelligence and canny negotiation had resulted in a remarkable deal for the association, and the members responded accordingly. Within months the extra publicity and a stunningly successful draw sent the appeal fund soaring to nearly £63,000. Borrowings were paid off and it was not long before Anderton had his eyes on the derelict stable block behind the mill as a site for further expansion.

The mid 1970s were a nervous time for the field sports community. Labour was back in power and was threatening its traditional targets of hunting and coursing, whilst the accession of Britain to the EEC under the Government of Edward Heath in 1973 had opened yet another regulatory tier within which shooting could be sniped at. Nor had the spectre of further controls on firearms fully receded, for whilst the Green Paper had been seen off, police associations still nursed hopes of stricter shotgun laws. Those within the larger sporting organisations started to look objectively at the structures of and interrelationships between the representative bodies which had grown up and developed over the years and wondered if there was not some room for reform, reorganisation or streamlining. Those within the smaller ones sought shelter.

One of the latter was the Gamekeepers' Association which, with just eight hundred and fifty members, was struggling to survive. In 1973 its secretary, Pat Gouldsbury, was not far off retirement and there was no cash available for a suitable replacement to be found. The matter had been discussed with the association's president, Lord Walpole, and at the Gamekeepers' Association AGM in July of that year the principle of amalgamation with another body was first mooted. WAGBI was the obvious choice, for 10% of the GKA's membership were also WAGBI members. By 1974, agreement in principle had been reached regarding a merger with no cost or liability upon WAGBI, which would in turn set up a gamekeeping committee and start providing services to keepers, including a special category of membership. Lord Arbuthnott signalled his approval, though he stressed that the 'keepers should not be rushed into a decision, and on 27 July 1974 at their AGM held at the Stratfield Saye Game Fair, the Gamekeepers agreed to a merger. WAGBI sealed the marriage at an extraordinary general meeting of its own in September and the union became effective from 1 January 1975. Pat Gouldsbury, who was also a member of WAGBI's management committee, would continue to look after the gamekeepers' employment register and deal with employment matters.

Among the first activities which reflected the new involvement in gamekeeping matters was the publication of a guide in the WAGBI magazine to those predatory mammals which could legally be controlled. These at that time included pine martens, otters, badgers, hedgehogs and wild cats. Phil Drabble, writing in the *Birmingham Evening Mail*, rounded upon the two associations for what he called their 'spine-chilling shotgun marriage', claiming that the article was a 'complete guide for decimating almost everything but pheasants while staying within the law'. He added that it would 'drive the wedge even deeper between conservationists and sporting men'. WAGBI responded by saying that the guide was simply to point out to members what they could and could not do if troubled by a particular predator.

Negotiations between WAGBI and the GKA had taken time and had required a good deal of careful footwork, but they had what was an essentially quite straightforward end in sight. Far more complex were those which resulted, a year later, in the creation of a new organisation to represent the interests of seven million hunters across Europe.

Although set up initially as an economic community of nations, the EEC was by the mid 1970s assuming competence in environmental matters too, and in 1976 officials of the German hunters' association, the Deutsch Jagdschutz-Verband (DJV) discovered that two biology graduates were writing a draft report on bird protection for the European Commission. The Germans called their friends in the Dutch hunting association, the Koninklijke Nederlandse Jagersvereniging (KNJV) and invited them for a meeting in Frankfurt. It was clear that the biologists concerned knew little about hunting and cared less, and that their draft, if it were to be turned into a binding Directive, would have very serious consequences.

Future European legislation on bird protection was foreshadowed at the Heiligenhafen IWRB meeting in 1974. Left to right *George Atkinson-Willes, IWRB; Anthor Gandarsson, Iceland; Hugh Boyd, Canada; John Anderton*

Before long, the jungle drums were beating around Europe, and in Britain both WAGBI and the BFSS were alerted. For more than ten years, since that first International Waterfowl Research Bureau (IWRB) conference in St Andrews in 1963, WAGBI had been actively involved in wildfowl conservation at a European level, however, the personalities with which it had dealt were by no means anti-hunting. Though they might argue over such matters as season length and shooting at night, many of the IWRB representatives were either practising hunters or had hunted in the past and the common goal of wildfowl conservation was far more important to them than any minor ideological differences over sport shooting. Subsequent IWRB meetings had taken place in Iran, where in 1971 the Ramsar Convention on Wetlands of International Importance had been signed on behalf of the UK Government by John Anderton, and at Heiligenhafen on the Baltic coast of Germany in 1974. John Swift and Jeffery Harrison had attended that particular gathering and Harrison sensed at the time that international legislation might be forthcoming in the not too distant future.

For several years Anderton had played an active role in the International Council for Game and Wildlife Conservation, better known by its French title, the Conseil International de la Chasse (CIC), a grouping of hunting interests which he hoped could be developed into an international lobbying organisation with sufficient teeth to address the growing threat of legislation at a European level. He had also explored contacts with several of the national hunting bodies, including the KNJV and Danmarks Jaegervorbund, the Danish hunting association, whilst also spreading his wings across the Atlantic through visits to the Texas-based organisation Game Conservation International (Gamecoin). However, it became clear to him that the CIC, which at the time was a meeting point for mostly francophone trophy hunters, had neither the will nor the capability to become involved in the hand-to-hand combat which he realised would be necessary if hunting were to be defended against the worst excesses of European bureaucracy.

Now the danger was all too evident. On 9 March 1977 the BFSS convened a meeting at the Cavalry Club in London for representatives of hunting associations from around Europe. With paintings and mementoes of famous cavalry engagements adorning the walls around him, Gustav Rønholt, President of the Danish hunters, was struck by the parallels between the situation faced by a small and ill-equipped band of hunters girding their loins to attack a formidable enemy in Brussels, and the Light Brigade's legendary charge upon the superior Russian guns at Balaclava. He reflected further on the fact that whilst the Light Brigade had, through its action, established forever its heroic reputation, a rather large number of its soldiers had died in the process. Those present agreed that the existing arrangements for the representation of hunting in Europe were unsatisfactory and that a new umbrella grouping was required, so the delegates from eight of the nine EEC member states decided to form the provisional executive for a federation of hunting associations, the Fédération des Associations de Chasse de l'UE (FACE). The ninth nation, France, preferred to stick with the CIC for the time being, although it joined FACE shortly afterwards. Agreement was further cemented at a black tie reception and dinner in the House of Lords, hosted by the Duke of Beaufort, and the leaders of Europe's hunting associations departed ready to work alongside one another in a new partnership. More than one of them commented on the fact that, only a few decades earlier, several of those same individuals had been trying to kill each other on the battlefields of Europe or the seas surrounding them.

John Anderton explored a range of links with international hunting organisations. In 1975 he visited Game Conservation International (Gamecoin) in the US

September saw the establishment of a FACE General Assembly, with the Earl of Mansfield appointed president and Wim Verhoeven as the federation's first secretary general. A budget of 2,200,000 Belgian francs (€ 55,000) was adopted and accommodation was found in Brussels at the offices of COPA, the association of European farming organisations. For most of the other EEC member states there was no particular difficulty in nominating the one national representative to sit on the FACE Board, since most other countries had only one national hunting association. That was not the case in Britain, where a number of organisations existed. Which of them was to bear Britain's torch in Europe? Was it to be the BFSS, WAGBI, or perhaps one of the other smaller bodies which should represent the UK in the corridors of Brussels and Strasbourg? Obviously there was potential here for inter-association rivalry on a grand scale but, all credit to those involved, a solution was found. Rather than appointing one single organisation to lead the UK delegation, a national body, FACE UK, was created, on which all the British sporting associations, large and small, could be represented in order that their collective voices could be heard at FACE headquarters.

Meanwhile John Swift immersed himself in the technicalities of the draft EEC Directive on the Conservation of Wild Birds. Immediately he saw the dangers for UK shooting traditions, for the Directive proposed restrictions on the sale of migratory birds, the shooting of female black grouse and capercaillie – then still a quarry species in Scotland – and a ban on the use of multi-shot shotguns. There were also concerns over trapping, night shooting and that old favourite, punt gunning. Swift visited the rapporteur in Strasbourg to present the UK's views and ended up spending thirty-six hours in discussions with both the rapporteur and the other national delegations, talking about the implications for UK shooting.

The principal threat, Swift quickly realised, was not from anti-hunters, but from the other European hunting representatives who simply did not understand the problems and the sporting traditions of the UK. In its haste to create a set of uniform regulations applicable to the entire territory of Europe, the EEC was in danger of overlooking the marked regional differences which existed between the different member states. For example, in the Netherlands there were only a few thousand rooks left, in less than ten rookeries, so in its first draft Directive, the Commission proposed to ban the shooting of rooks throughout Europe. This was despite the fact that rooks were a huntable species in the UK and one which caused significant agricultural damage. The hunters quickly realised the danger of the Commission's 'divide and rule' approach, and countered by asking whether, just because there were no more salmon in the polluted Rhine, fishing for salmon was now to be banned in Scotland? Commission officials took the point and thought again about the rook.

Swift prepared papers on the traditions of hunting in Britain, sending them both to other European hunting delegates and to the UK Department of Environment officials, at the same time as inviting key Europeans to come to Britain and see the situation there at first hand. In the end it was punt gunning and night shooting which remained the final sticking points, with the EEC wanting to ban all shooting from half an hour after sunset to half an hour before sunrise, a restriction which would have had devastating consequences for wildfowling and which would also have impacted on gamekeeping and pest control. Despite bitter argument between the French and the Italians on the one hand and the British on the other, the Birds Directive was eventually agreed and adopted in 1979. It was not all that might have been hoped for, but so far as Europe's hunters were concerned, it ended up a good deal better than it had started out.

Europe was not only involving itself in environmental matters. In the early 1970s there was a growing view that a mandatory shooting test for those who wished to possess firearms and hunt game was not far off. Barry Bailey had said as much to the WAGBI management committee in 1973, and the resulting discussion had set the association thinking about a voluntary shotgun proficiency scheme. Now the Council of Europe, attracted by the German hunting licence or *Jagdschein*, floated the suggestion that all member states within the Council should have similar mandatory licences, together with the training and testing programmes that would go along with them. When the matter was raised in the FACE family, the UK immediately found itself in a rather small minority, for only it, along with the Irish Republic and Greece, did not require its sport shooters to hold a hunting licence. This was largely an accident of history, resulting from the fact that unlike most of continental Europe, the British Isles had not experienced a revolution in the nineteenth century and neither had they been occupied by Napoleon or subsumed within the tentacles of his legal code. Instead, Britain and Ireland had developed their own arrangements to ensure wise use of quarry and the safety both of hunters, and the public. However, the historical rationale behind Britain's hunting legislation now cut little ice with her European partners.

Training and testing became subjects of detailed and serious discussion within WAGBI, and it was decided that, like it or not, the association had to move forward with a voluntary scheme, for if it did not, then there could soon be formal legislation from Europe. The Government was sounded out, and there was found to be support for a voluntary training programme – though not a mandatory one – so priority was given to shotgun shooting competence and safe handling. Within FACE UK a voluntary examinations committee was formed, though it decided to confine its function to defining how the structure of a voluntary examination, which might in due course become mandatory, could be implemented. It even went so far as to produce a format for the putative manual for sport shooting, covering ethics, natural history, conduct, weapons, marsh, moor and field, game bird management, conservation and shooting skill. Examination was to be by multiple choice question, with four questions selected from each chapter within the manual, to a maximum of fifty. In addition, there would be a practical shotgun shooting test, with qualified examiners and examination centres.

Eventually the process stalled. While Europe still called for mandatory training and testing, the UK Government, at the instigation of the British shooting organisations, made a statement to the effect that in its opinion, hunting standards in the UK were excellent and that, moreover, the cost of introducing tests was unjustified. The Irish delegate was more direct. He said that his Government couldn't get the Irish to take a b****y driving test, let alone a hunting one. Furthermore, the bar was open and that's where he was heading. He left the chamber and the other delegations followed. Nothing further was heard of that initiative.

Perhaps it was the result of wrestling with the problems of sporting representation within Europe that the question of how best to ensure the continuation of field sports at home in Britain returned time and time again to the mind of John Anderton. Constantly he mulled over the issues in his own head and discussed them with others: the destruction of habitat which was resulting from the intensification of agriculture; pollution which was blighting rivers, lakes and marshes; the growing militancy of an anti-field sports lobby whose activists had, in just a couple of decades, managed to swing opinion within Parliament and influential bodies such as the RSPCA; the threat to the private ownership and use of sporting firearms; and as he saw it, the biggest threat of all, namely the huge majority of sportsmen and women who were not prepared to join any organisation. Eventually he concluded that a top level meeting was needed which would sketch out a proper structure, with various organisations each looking after their own sector and with a single 'umbrella' body overseeing the whole.

The 'Diamond Plan' as it became known, was not a WAGBI initiative but a personal one conceived by Anderton himself. In August 1977 he set out his proposals in a *Shooting Times* article entitled 'Frankly Speaking'. In it, he pointed out that there currently existed some thirty organisations purporting to look after the interests of hunting, shooting, fishing, coursing and falconry. 'It is time we faced the facts and look at them objectively,' he said.

'With certain notable exceptions there is scant communication between societies, the incidence of one sport knocking another is too frequent, and is done in the mistaken belief that to deflect the spotlight elsewhere means "my sport can creep away unharmed". It is a thoroughly irresponsible practice which only benefits one's opponent.

'All too often, when one sport is attacked the attitude of people involved in a different sport is "let them fight the threat on their own, my sport is not involved, so it does not concern me". This is not only the attitude of many individuals but some associations.

'Too many individuals contribute nothing to any society, but take out a lot. Indeed, many sportsmen, so-called, consider they are the elite of the countryside with a God-given right to do as they please. This also shows in the attitude of some organisations.

'Not enough is done in the field of adult education, or of the young whose opinion is created in school by those who have little or no sympathy with field sports. Insufficient emphasis is placed on high standards of sportsmanship, etiquette, consideration for others and of the quarry we pursue, eg, some commercial shoots take out far too much in the making of a fast buck.'

He proposed an all-embracing Council for Field Sports with responsibility for public relations and political representation, sitting above three separate representative bodies, one each for hunting with hounds and coursing, shooting and falconry, and angling. Funded by these three bodies, via the Council, would be a conservation and research foundation.

'It makes sense to sink differences, jealousies and long-established misconceptions,' continued Anderton. 'Sport is an aspect of leisure, and leisure administration today is a profession. Unlike sailing, football and the like, field sports really are threatened. It is time that governing bodies took the future of their sports a deal more seriously. They carry an immense responsibility.'

Reaction to the article was immediate. Some congratulated Anderton and supported his every word, while others doubted the practicalities of what was proposed. In an assessment of the defence of field sports in Parliament, Marcus Kimball MP spoke of the individual enthusiasm which drove the defence of field sports at Westminster and commented: 'The idea of superimposing a Council above the whole range of Country Sports Organisations could well blunt this enthusiasm and would certainly reduce the effectiveness of any Parliamentary activity. Any such re-organisation can only be justified if it is accompanied by a review of each Society's functions and the payment of one Countryside subscription, allocated between the Societies according to each individual's enjoyment of, or love of, each sport – a simple computer operation.'

Notwithstanding the cooler reaction than that which he had hoped for, the idea of a council within which the different sporting bodies could sit as equals, talk face-to-face in order to settle their differences and plan for the future together still gripped Anderton. He discussed it with WAGBI's patron, HRH The Duke of Edinburgh who thoroughly approved. Not only that, but Prince Philip also suggested that the perfect chairman for such a council might be Lord Porchester, HM The Queen's racing manager and a highly respected figure in the world of country sports and activities. HRH suggested that Anderton should pop round to see Lord Porchester

John Anderton, Lord Arbuthnott and Richard Bream at the 1977 Leicestershire Wildfowlers' Association dinner. The LWA was a staunch supporter and the first club to adopt the rule that all its members automatically became members of WAGBI

at his London home in Cadogan Square, which Anderton did right away. By the time he got there, Porchester had already received a telephone call from Prince Philip, and naturally he was delighted to agree to chair a series of meetings at which the proposal could be explored. All the field sports organisations were invited and none declined.

It was in 1978 that the first meeting was held at the Cavalry and Guards Club, and the proposal was that there should be created a federation of sporting associations which would prevent conflict through rivalry, promote the political defence of field sports and consider the matter of charitable status. Lord Porchester suggested that it be called the Country Sports Federation, but the title did not appeal to the angling bodies, which the BFSS considered essential to the success of the venture. A second meeting was therefore held on 1 June 1978, this time at Anderton's own Naval and Military Club, at which Lord Porchester suggested an alternative title which was supported by all parties, the Standing Conference on Countryside Sports. The name stuck, and the SCCS continues to this day as a highly respected forum in which issues of concern to field sports and the countryside are discussed, debated and even resolved. Currently over eighty organisations and private members attend the twice-yearly Conference meetings.

Chapter 8
FROM WAGBI TO BASC

*I*n spreading its wings to embrace the increasingly complex politics of field sports at national and international level, WAGBI could not for a moment ignore the desperate need to deal with the demands of its grass roots supporters, the wildfowlers, in the further-flung parts of the United Kingdom. The management committee was well aware that the association was still failing to make much of an impact in Scotland and resolved to do something about the matter. The lack of membership strength and organisation north of the border was to a considerable extent an accident of legislation and the management committee knew this full well. While in England and Wales the Crown controlled all sporting access to the foreshore, thus obliging the wildfowler who wished to gain access below the high water mark to be a member of WAGBI or one of its affiliated clubs, there exists in Scotland an historic right of public recreation on the foreshore, which includes the right to shoot. Thus anyone could shoot the foreshore provided they were able to gain access to it via a public right of way or by the consent of the neighbouring landowner, and in consequence there was no real need for the Scottish fowler to join any club or association. Public shooting rights on the Scottish foreshore could only be extinguished – and thus brought under central control – through the creation of local or national nature reserves such as that at Caerlaverock on the Solway.

So not only was there a dearth of Scottish fowling clubs, but WAGBI members in Scotland were also spread fairly thinly on the ground, which was a little ironic given the huge importance of Scotland as a destination for sporting visitors from south of the border. In 1973 the management committee decided that a serious effort had to be made to address the lack of representation in Scotland and a meeting was convened at the Isle of Skye Hotel, Perth, in October of that year at which hand-picked WAGBI members from all over Scotland were invited to discuss the proposal to appoint a regional officer. Recruitment commenced shortly afterwards and of the fifty-eight applicants, eight were selected for interview. Meanwhile, since funding for a development officer had already been secured from the Sports Council in England, an approach was made to the Scottish Sports Council in the hope that it would provide support for a WAGBI man to be put on the road in Scotland. Barry Bailey was despatched northwards and visited the Scottish Sports Council, whilst calling also on the Scottish Solway WA and the Caerlaverock NNR Panel. It was not long before the appointment of a full-time Scottish representative was made, the job being given to Gerald Haine who in April 1974 was introduced to the management committee as the association's first development officer, Scotland. Guided by Arthur Cadman, Haine toured his new bailiwick, visiting all the main wildfowling areas including the Firth of Tay, the Black Isle, the Cromarty Firth and Munlochy Bay. A further meeting was held at the Isle of Skye Hotel, where representatives of such Scottish fowling clubs and joint councils as did exist agreed to set up a Scottish committee under the chairmanship of George Taylor. The meeting was a great success, much goodwill was generated and Scotland was divided for administrative purposes into twelve regions. Headquarters did its best to support the new developments in Scotland, and the following July the management committee met in Stirling, but by and large Haine was allowed simply to get on with the job without any real support, direction or supervision. It was not long before he got fed up with this and in October 1975 he resigned. Anderton accepted that he had been let loose without sufficient training or guidance and pledged not to make the same mistake again. Haine was replaced the following year by David Cant who, unlike his predecessor, spent a period at head office learning about the association and understanding the way it worked before getting to grips with Scottish issues. Before long, membership activities in Scotland were being organised, such as a highly successful wildfowling course at Kingseat, near Dunfermline. David Cant introduced the course and spoke on the history of wildfowling, to be followed by Arthur Cadman and Eric Begbie, secretary of the Eden Wildfowlers, who helped arrange morning flight on Loch Fitty for the course participants. A further boost for WAGBI in Scotland came with the organisation of the Highland Field Sports Fair in August 1978 at Dochfour, Inverness and the Tayside Field Sports Fair the following year at Errol Park, near Perth. These popular fairs were to become regular events in the association's Scottish calendar. Initially WAGBI had no formal Scottish office, but that was remedied in January 1979 when it agreed to lease premises at the estate office at Boquhan, Kippen, near Stirling, providing for the first time a real base for Scottish activities.

John Richards (right) with Arthur Cadman, a staunch WAGBI and BASC supporter who particularly assisted the association with its development in Scotland

Since its formation, WAGBI had also enjoyed a considerable measure of support across the Irish Sea. In the early years, the association's writ ran across the entire island of Ireland, though since the postwar renaissance it had focussed exclusively upon the six counties which remained part of the United Kingdom. By the mid 1970s the growing political tensions within the province were starting to have a serious impact upon sporting shooting, and in particular upon the private ownership of firearms. The RUC was actively trying to reduce the number of sporting guns, firearm certificates were becoming increasingly difficult to obtain and the strain was showing within the beleaguered fowling clubs of Northern Ireland. All of them operated their own conservation schemes, with the Strangford Lough WA leading the way with its own conservation centre, but the clubs needed support from their national body. As with Scotland, the solution seemed to be to put a man on the ground within the province, and so the matter was broached with the Sports Council of Northern Ireland.

In 1976 John Richards and Colin Barwell visited the Sports Council NI in order to discuss possible future funding, however, the situation contained an added complexity in that grant aid was already being given to a home-grown organisation, the Ulster Game and Wildlife Society. The UGWS had begun in 1925 as a wildfowl, game and fisheries organisation. At the time, it was more of a protection society than a sporting one, and after the original body folded it was reconstituted in 1948, forming clubs to encourage conservation, vermin control and game rearing programmes. However, by the mid 1970s the organisation was slipping into the doldrums, for it had enjoyed considerable influence at Stormont and had suffered badly when the Stormont Parliament was suspended. Some within the UGWS felt that the best way forward for shooting in the province was to merge with WAGBI, however others wished still to maintain their independence and thus local opinion was divided. Agreement with WAGBI was reached, though, on the formation of a local joint advisory group which could advise on the work programme of a future development officer.

Nearly two years passed before further approaches were made to the Sports Council NI, which made it clear that a favourable response to WAGBI's request for funding would be forthcoming if a joint application were to be made with the UGWS. Further negotiations ensued, whereupon the UGWS met and decided that they could not sustain the financial commitment which would be involved in appointing a development officer for the Province, and they therefore withdrew any objection to an application being made by WAGBI. The matter was still a sensitive one, though, and Tommy Wightman, the Northern Ireland representative on WAGBI's management committee, invited the Society's honorary secretary, Gordon McCloud to meet the committee at Marford Mill. He did so in September 1978, and told WAGBI that his colleagues back in Northern Ireland would support joint working, contact and co-operation within the Province. For its part, WAGBI said that it in no way intended to be a 'big brother', but that it wanted to extend its full co-operation in Northern Ireland and avoid any potential conflict. This was exactly the message that the Sports Council NI wished to hear, and the following month it agreed to offer funding to the value of £3,000 for the coming year to enable the employment of a development officer for Northern Ireland, whose job description and terms of reference were to be jointly discussed and finalised.

Once more, WAGBI was extending its sphere of operations in line with the continued growth in membership which it was enjoying. Once more, the cracks were beginning to show. When it had re-established itself in the 1950s, the association had been run by a small group of volunteers. Enthusiastic and committed amateurs gave their time and their experience to run the association's day-to-day activities, driving things on under Anderton's leadership: one day they might be meeting and lobbying Government officials while the next they would be rolling up their own sleeves to organise duck and goose rearing or to wield a bow saw or billhook at Boarstall decoy. Those involved paid their own expenses and saw to it that there was always a large measure of fun in the proceedings. Indeed they often arranged WAGBI activities to suit themselves – a meeting might be fixed around a morning flight or some other shooting opportunity, and many were the hours spent by WAGBI officers on the Medway saltings – conveniently close to London – at the instigation of that arch-enthusiast Jeffery Harrison.

By the late 1970s things had changed. Membership had reached 45,000 and new members were joining at a rate of more than 8,000 per annum. The workload was quite simply too heavy even for the most enthusiastic of amateurs to contemplate, and the full-time staff was growing year by year. In 1978 the membership records and data were computerised, using ICL 1501 data capture equipment and microfiche readers – regarded at the time as the most advanced technology on the market. WAGBI was now a fully professional organisation, but what had not kept pace with the changes was the association's organisational structure. Still the management committee endeavoured to involve itself in the minutiae of the association's business, frequently tripping over the professional staff in the process.

In March 1978 matters were brought to a head when Anderton received letters of resignation from John Richards, Denis Graham-Hogg and John Bond, who had been appointed just two years previously as events secretary. Anderton was devastated. In a letter to the chairman, Bill Bailey, he wrote: 'What I have been fighting so hard over is lost. Have we over-reached ourselves? Should we revert to what WAGBI was formed for originally and give up all pretence that we are THE shooting organisation in the UK?'

He was particularly depressed about the threatened break-up of the young, hard-working team of professionals which he had laboured so hard to assemble. In contrast to what was then the norm within voluntary organisations, especially those in the field sports sector, Anderton had sought to recruit graduates, 'young people with fire in their bellies, not retired service people with a pension and a private income'. He feared that if such people were lost to WAGBI then the tempo would slow, original thinking and, most importantly, staff motivation would be lost.

The crisis triggered a special meeting of the management committee at which the breakdown of confidence and trust between the committee and the staff was debated in full. Members of the committee recognised that it was simply not possible for them to run Marford Mill on the basis of the occasional committee meeting. Either they had to let the staff manage the association's daily affairs or they had to meet much more frequently – an impossible task.

WAGBI's chairman, Bill Bailey, a dedicated and able Essex wildfowler with a commercial management background who had tried hard to bring modern business thinking to his chair-manship, recognised that his own relationship with Anderton had reached breaking point. While on the one hand he infuriated the director by his constant intervention in daily activities, he was likewise irritated by Anderton's constant complaints about the impact of his heavy workload upon his personal life. There were faults on both sides and both men knew it.

Hard talking ensued, and by the end of a long meeting, agreement had been reached on the establishment of a broad-based finance and general purposes committee on which the director and heads of departments would sit – albeit as non-voting members. Meanwhile the manage-ment committee would focus its attention on broader matters of policy rather than trying to manage the staff. Salary structures were to be reviewed in line with those set by the Sports Council, proper job specifications were to be introduced, and there was even discussion about the introduction of postal voting for seats on the management committee – though this latter pro-posal was a sight too radical for some, and it was several years more before it was finally imple-mented. Bill Bailey's chairmanship, which had been called into question, was reaffirmed and he agreed to stand for the chair of the association once more at the forthcoming annual general meeting, though he stressed that the next twelve months would be his final year. The three staff resignation letters remained for a time in Anderton's in-tray, but were eventually withdrawn.

The first of September 1978 promised the dawning of another wildfowling season and among the many who were out on the marsh at first light that day was Jeffery Harrison. He was a truly remarkable shot and along with another WAGBI stalwart, 'Jimper' Sutton, Harrison enjoyed a wonderful morning flight, shooting no fewer than five right-and-lefts including his first at shoveler, but tragedy struck later that day when Harrison collapsed and died suddenly at home, surrounded by his family. His contribution to WAGBI and to wildfowl conservation had been immeasurable and his departure left a gaping void. He was a big man in every sense of the word and it was often said by Anderton that 'a day with Jeff was as full as a year', for in his

Whither WAGBI? In this celebrated photograph, Jeffery Harrison (left) and John Ruxton (right) appear to have sharply differing opinions about the association's future direction

company there was never a dull moment. His practical understanding and technical knowledge of wildfowl had kick-started WAGBI's goose and duck rearing and releasing programmes and his own sportsman-naturalist's ethic had played a major part in framing the association's whole conservation philosophy. In the international sphere he had set up the first duck wing surveys in order to better understand the mysteries of wildfowl migration and he had played a pivotal role in a string of crucial international conferences. Harrison's own personal monument, the Sevenoaks Wildfowl Reserve, which had been created from a collection of barren Kentish gravel workings, was to continue and develop with the support both of his widow, Pamela Harrison and of WAGBI. A memorial trust was established to fund the running and staffing of the reserve, but the association's conservation mantle now fell on the shoulders of Harrison's protégé, John Swift.

As the new director of conservation and research, Swift's first job was to address an offer which had been made by the Nature Conservancy Council to fund, to the tune of £10,000 over three years, a survey of conservation management undertaken by wildfowling clubs around the country. Clearly this would require the appointment of a new member of staff, and after some three hundred and fifty applications had been received and sifted through, the job was given to a new biology graduate from the University of Wales Institute of Science and Technology. Tony Laws was not a Welshman, though, but a native of Suffolk whose father had been a wildfowler on the Alde, and who had plenty of practical experience as a rough shooter. Originally his job had been to go out around the country and develop new conservation projects, but as the NCC grant crystallised, his task transformed into the identification of baseline information about the existing shooting and conservation interests of the wildfowling clubs, for it was recognised that only when the present state of play was known could any meaningful new conservation programme be developed. It is hard to overstate the long-term importance to wildfowling of Laws's work. It was to underpin the securing of shooting across prime conservation sites for decades to come, and it still forms the bedrock beneath BASC's work with wildfowling clubs to this day.

Laws was very quickly joined by another new member of staff. John Harradine, who took up his post on 1 October. Harradine had studied wildlife and fisheries management at Edinburgh before going on to take his doctorate in the conservation impact of rural rat control. While Laws set about surveying and recording the clubs' conservation activities, Harradine's task was to assist wildfowling clubs to secure their tenure of coastal wetland sites which were important for nature conservation by developing management plans and so enabling them to obtain Crown leases. However, very quickly Harradine picked up the duck wing survey which had been lying dormant since Jeff Harrison's death. This important work not only increased understanding of wildfowl migration, but had the added benefit of enabling wildfowlers to get directly involved in waterfowl biology. The survey quickly achieved popularity and it soon became evident that Harradine's real strengths lay in research. Since Swift urgently needed more statistical data on the membership and its shooting activities, Harradine was directed into a research role. As for the provision of land management advice, this task was ultimately given to another new recruit to the team, land agent Anthony Holliday.

But the young conservation and research department still had its biggest task to come. It was quite obvious as the 1970s drew to a close that the 1954 Protection of Birds Act was getting very long in the tooth. International conventions such as the Ramsar Convention on Wetlands, the Council of Europe's Berne Convention and the Bonn Convention on migratory species signalled that conservation needed to be driven by the protection of habitats, not merely wildlife species. In 1979 the EEC Birds Directive came into force, setting the overall parameters for wild bird protection across Europe. In Britain, this was the trigger that set in train what was to result in the Wildlife and Countryside Act 1981.

In the late summer of 1979 the Government issued a string of consultation papers on countryside matters, such as public footpaths, species protection, habitat conservation and moorland conservation. Parliament was told that while most of the requirements of the new EEC Directive were met by existing UK legislation, there were deficiencies, and that these would be addressed in a forthcoming Wildlife and Countryside Bill. Field sports had endured a worrying few years of constant sniping under the Labour Government of Jim Callaghan, and the minister responsible under the new Conservative administration, Environment Under Secretary Hector Monro MP, was anxious to allay their fears that traditional countryside activities were again under threat. A countryman and sportsman himself, Monro reassuringly told *The Field*: 'Field sports have an absolute right to continue. There will be nothing restrictive in the Bill.'

Not everybody was convinced by these blandishments. Sporting, farming and landowning organisations alike clamoured to have their say in the new proposals, the parliamentary time slot for a Bill came and went, and the legislative process stalled for a further twelve months. During this time, Anderton, as a member of the advisory committee on the Protection of Birds for England and Wales and Arthur Cadman, a member of the equivalent committee in Scotland, both worked hard in closed session during the crucial planning phase of the Bill. Both Anderton and Swift held further meetings with ministers and with Department of Environment officials in London. Swift also gave evidence to the All-Party Conservation Committee of both Houses of

Parliament. In September 1980 a further government paper was issued, and it became evident that the proposed Wildlife and Countryside Bill would affect most of those who either lived on the land, managed it or took their recreation there. It was going to involve some pretty far-reaching stuff. So far as shooting was concerned, the sea ducks were to be protected, along with the whimbrel, stock dove and the sawbill ducks; magazine capacity of semi-automatic shotguns was to be restricted; and restrictions were to be placed on certain methods of killing, including the use of self-locking snares. At the end of November the Bill itself was published, signalling the start of bitter confrontation with the bird protection lobby over the traditional targets of night shooting, the February foreshore season and the shooting of shore waders, all of which the RSPB wanted to see prohibited.

During the Bill's final stages the normally calm and placid atmosphere of the House of Lords was rent by what amounted to hand-to-hand combat. Night shooting and the February season were saved, but Anderton and Swift watched in horror as, after protracted and muddled debate, Peers divided in favour of amendments which would prohibit all Sunday shooting and protect the redshank, curlew, jack snipe and bartailed godwit. Confusion reigned in the Lords' chamber as the arcane process of deciding upon the various amendments rolled out, with some peers not knowing which way they should be voting. The result, so far as WAGBI was concerned, was disaster. The Sunday shooting ban was later reversed in the House of Commons thanks to a further government amendment, but the loss of the curlew and redshank from the quarry list was a severe blow to the wildfowlers who argued, with justification, that there was no good conservation reason why these two species, for generations the traditional quarry of the foreshore gunner, should have been protected.

Perhaps it was the sheer breadth and complexity of the campaign fought over the Wildlife and Countryside Bill, coupled with the continuing unease over the possibility of further firearms legislation which reawoke the calls for WAGBI to embrace, clearly and unambiguously, every aspect of sporting shooting. Perhaps the old arguments for changing the familiar WAGBI name had never gone away in the first place. Either way, the first few weeks of 1981 saw, launched within the principal sporting magazines, a fresh debate on the concept of a national shooting association.

'For its part WAGBI has grown into one of the largest, most efficient and robust of all field sports organisations, and is unused to standing on the touch-lines,' commented *The Field* in its editorial of 14 January. 'It is unfortunate that for so long it has handicapped itself with a name which represents only part of its work. That it reflects origins rather than present status is not realised by all, and it should be. Probably its members shoot more gamebirds now than wildfowl. And there are no doubts about its ability to serve members' needs across the whole shooting spectrum.'

In his 'New Year's Thought' in *Shooting Times*, Tony Jackson followed a similar theme, arguing for a powerful all-embracing shooting organisation which could speak with authority at every level. He wrote:

'WAGBI are at the cross-roads. It is decision time, I believe that they are sufficiently well-organised, have the capability and knowledge plus the organisational ability justly to claim to act on behalf of all sections of the shooting community. But...and it is a big but...they can no longer continue under the title of the Wildfowlers Association of Great Britain and Ireland.

'Yes, I know and have heard umpteen times the argument for retaining the title WAGBI. It is readily recognised, both at home and abroad and one should not destroy or cast aside a name and seventy-two years of proud history at the stroke of a pen. I agree. The title should most certainly not be lost nor the specialised representation of fowlers' interests but the title WAGBI has an Achilles heel. The game shot, probably a syndicate man and no worse for that, cannot identify with an organisation which, while desperately trying to convince him that they represent the interests of all shooting men still, by their title, are apparently partisan in their outlook.

'What I am really talking about is the NSA – the National Shooting Association. An organisation based on the present WAGBI structure and capable of dealing with the interests of all shooting men, whether they shoot with a smooth bore gun at duck, pigeon or rabbits or with a rifled bore at deer.'

Jackson's proposal was taken up enthusiastically by *Shooting Times* readers, the response being positive and almost overwhelming. Support came in the shape of letters, telephone calls and articles from influential contributors. It came from the game shooters, from the rough shooters, even from the wildfowlers. Naturally the debate was joined as eagerly inside Marford Mill as out of it, for Anderton had long been an advocate of a title for the association which embraced all that he hoped and dreamed that WAGBI could aspire to. He found an ally in Major General David Lloyd Owen, who had taken the chair of the association after working for eighteen months as an

David Lloyd Owen with John Anderton at Bowood in 1979. Lloyd Owen was a chairman of great leadership who opened the way to the founding of the Campaign for Country Sports

enthusiastic and highly successful membership recruiter. Lloyd Owen was every inch a gentleman of the old school. Unlike virtually all previous WAGBI chairmen, he had a sporting background not in wildfowling but beagling and game shooting, moreover his breathtaking war service working behind enemy lines in North Africa with the Long Range Desert Group, which he later went on to command, indicated that he was a man of action and a decision maker. Lloyd Owen became involved with WAGBI at the time of the 1973 Green Paper, when he had been so impressed with the association's efforts that he had written to Anderton and offered his support. Both director and chairman knew that the time for a name change was now or never.

Anderton allowed the correspondence in the shooting press to run for two months before responding with the news that at the annual general meeting in June, a resolution would be placed before the membership to change the name of the association to 'The Shooting Association (for Conservation and Shooting in the Field)'. He reassured members that the old WAGBI name would not be forgotten, and expressed the view that had Stanley Duncan lived, he would have been in total agreement and delighted with what was now proposed.

He concluded: 'We hope that the shooting community in general and our membership in particular will see the wisdom of the proposed change and will grant it full support since the whole future of their sport is bound up with development of a large, strong, efficient and wholly representative organisation which will care for all who shoot irrespective of their backgrounds, or the branch of the sport they follow.'

On Saturday 6 June 1981 the annual general meeting, held at Eaton Hall, home of the Duke of Westminster, was attended by one hundred and two members and presided over by the Viscount of Arbuthnott. In the course of the debate it became clear that what was needed was a title which reflected both WAGBI's shooting and conservation credentials, but which also flagged up its role as a national organisation for all shooters. Thus the rather clumsy offering on the order paper was scrapped and in its place, Lloyd Owen proposed from the chair that it should be replaced with the title which is now so familiar, 'The British Association for Shooting and Conservation'. The resolution was put to the meeting and was carried by eighty-five votes to seventeen. BASC was born.

Lloyd Owen assured members that the change would not mean that the association would make any less effort in the future on behalf of wildfowlers, nor that their contribution would be forgotten. They would always, he said, play a leading part in the association's policies and efforts. However, he continued, the new title would reflect the role that the association had developed in recent years of safeguarding the interests of all shooting sportsmen – wildfowlers, rough shooters, game shooters, gamekeepers or stalkers. He added that with 51,500 members including 333 affiliated clubs, 182 game shooting syndicates and 47 group supporter organisations, the association was one of the largest shooting organisations in Europe. BASC, he pledged, would continue to safeguard and champion the interests of all who are involved in shooting.

At the conclusion of the meeting, Hector Monro MP, now Minister for Sport, applauded the decision to change the name, saying that it could only lead to a better understanding of the excellent work the association was undertaking at present and thus lead to a well-deserved increase in membership support.

Tony Jackson, a committed supporter of the name change campaign, left the meeting deeply satisfied. He found sympathy with those who had spoken passionately in favour of the old WAGBI title, but argued that it was time to look forward, not back. He was reassured by the undertaking given by Lloyd Owen that the importance of the wildfowling clubs would always be recognised, and looked forward to some really hard, tough strategic thinking:

> 'The Association holds, in my view, a very good hand, but the cards have to be played with care and expertise. The assets are several: a professional, dedicated staff working from an attractive, large headquarters which is now owned by the BASC; a wide-spread, loyal club network; a sound membership base on which to expand, an international reputation and, best of all, goodwill.
>
> 'One of the first tasks will be to mount an effective PR campaign to "sell" the new title and policy. It will not be easy but BASC is here to stay, a fact which we must now recognise.'

It was only by a whisker that Jackson's final sentence remained true, for on Friday 8 January 1982 BASC very nearly disappeared completely in a puff of smoke. On a cold, snowy day a faulty central heating boiler malfunctioned, overheating the flue and setting light to the timber beams which ran close to it. The male staff were enjoying a quiet lunch break in the rest room when John Richards burst in and said that the building was on fire. Everybody thought he was pulling their leg, whereupon Richards went out to check again, returning promptly with the news that yes, fire had indeed broken out. A prompt evacuation followed. The fire caused significant damage to the rear of the building, but quick action by firefighters, who ripped off roofing slates to get to the seat of the fire as the snow fell around them, saved Marford Mill. Irreplaceable archive material was, however, destroyed, and it was by a miracle that the old WAGBI minute books themselves were saved. Had it not been for the efforts of the Wrexham Fire Brigade that winter's day, this history of BASC might never have been written.

Marford Mill had a lucky escape from destruction by fire in January 1982

Wrexham Fire Brigade
damps down the blaze,
which started in a faulty
central heating boiler

The Mill survived, but
precious archive material
was damaged or destroyed

The WAGBI 4 Bore

Visitors to Marford Mill rarely fail to be impressed by the magnificent WAGBI 4 bore, which was bequeathed to the association in 1969 by Beris Harcourt-Wood, a former member of the WAGBI executive committee. The gun was built by Tolley, one of the great names in traditional wildfowling guns, and was acquired by Harcourt-Wood from Frank Southgate RBA (1872-1916), the consummate wildlife artist and wildfowler from Wells, Norfolk who, according to Hugh Pollard 'used gun and pencil with equal accuracy'. Harcourt-Wood used the gun for many years along the north Norfolk coast, especially around the Holkham gap, Wolferton, Dersingham and Snettisham, where his fame as an accurate shot quickly spread. Some thirty years before Harcourt-Wood's death, he lost the sight of his right eye whilst undergoing an operation. After this the gun was restocked with a full cross-over stock to enable him to continue shooting with his left eye. The double 4 bore gun weighs 28 lb and measures nearly 5 feet in length. Unusually for a shotgun it is fitted with two leaf sights.

The WAGBI 4 bore, bequeathed to the association by Beris Harcourt-Wood

Like many other large bore wildfowling guns of its era, the 4 bore is a back-action hammergun with rotary underlever. Note the unusual additon of two leaf sights

The gun was fitted with a cross-over stock after its owner lost the sight of his right eye

Chapter 9
PRIDE...AND A FALL

*J*ohn Anderton had long cherished the notion of creating a full-time public relations department. He fully understood that now the name of the association reflected its wider aspirations in the world of shooting, BASC needed to reach out to a huge new audience of game shooters, deer stalkers, airgunners and others who had not previously regarded themselves as potential members of what was ostensibly a wildfowling association. Even more important was the need to take to an increasingly urban population the wider message of shooting and its importance to wildlife habitats and the landscape and economy of the countryside.

Over the years a succession of people with experience of the world of journalism and the media had been invited to join the management committee or to offer their expertise in other ways. A few had provided some useful advice but none had stayed the course. Now a more professional approach was needed. Clearly a new staff member with both media experience and a knowledge of shooting and the countryside was what was required, but meanwhile Anderton

BASC appeared for the first time in its new livery at the Tatton Park Game Fair in 1982

wanted to lose no time in promoting the new BASC, so he brought in a PR consultancy, Agripress. Its proprietors, the genial Max Reader and Ray Grater had particularly strong connections with the agricultural media and were able to open up new lines of communication with farmers, a community which whilst eagerly involved in shooting was almost totally oblivious of the need to join a shooting association of any sort. When eventually the new PR man arrived at Marford Mill, he too came from a background in the farming industry. Having trained in agricultural economics, I had spent five years building up the publicity department of farm machinery manufacturers Bentall Simplex of Maldon, Essex. But when I was not sitting in my office, I was out wildfowling on the Blackwater estuary or hunting with the Colchester Garrison beagles, so when I arrived at Marford Mill on – appropriately enough for an organisation which still clung tenaciously to its wildfowling roots – 1 September 1982, I brought with me both a knowledge of the communications industry and a passion for field sports.

There was a huge job to be done, but I quickly found that the message of shooting and the countryside was one which the media actually wanted to hear and this made it far easier and more exciting to sell than the grain dryers and animal feed mills which I had been used to promoting. Amongst the first tasks was the publication of the National Shooting Survey, a detailed study which had been set up in 1979 by John Harradine and which sought basic information about the nature of sporting shooting in Britain. By means of a sample survey, Harradine had over three years amassed a huge amount of knowledge about how many people went shooting, who they were and what they shot. It was the first time that such a detailed appraisal had been carried out and it attracted much interest from the national media, TV and radio journalists, many of whom were very surprised indeed that the overwhelming majority of shooters were neither ruddy-cheeked farmers nor tweeded peers of the realm. For the very first time, shooting was starting to stick its head above the parapet, break down the old stereotypes and bring to the general public a wider understanding of who sporting shooters were and what they did.

The National Shooting Survey featured on everything from Radio 4's *Today* programme to the newly launched TVam breakfast channel, and was covered in the broadsheet press as well as the countryside, sporting and farming magazines. It demonstrated what today is so blindingly obvious, namely that when field sports make the effort to provide genuinely interesting information about themselves, people will listen. Very soon, BASC was setting up a network of regional PR volunteers, shooters with a background in journalism or broadcasting who could help co-ordinate publicity at a local level. Media training courses were arranged for senior staff members, a small PR steering committee was set up and the tired and dated range of promotional material, most of it still carrying the WAGBI logo, was upgraded and redesigned. A suite of new recruitment advertising was designed and a colour brochure illustrating the work of the association was produced and dispatched to the movers and shakers in conservation, politics and the media. *Shooting & Conservation*, BASC's quarterly magazine, was given a face-lift and enlarged in size, colour was introduced inside as well as on the front cover and new, interesting feature material was brought into the publication.

Meanwhile the PR department set about the bread-and-butter work of promoting the burgeoning number of events, courses, shows and activities which BASC was now organising. Of course there were the old favourites, the Gamekeepers' Fair and the BASC Safari, but new events were also being introduced by John Richards and his inventive development team. Among them was the BASC roadshow, a form of indoor country sports fair staged during the winter months when the holding of a traditional outdoor country show was impossible. Trade stands, allied associations, local shooting club exhibits and BASC's own information and educational stands were brought together to entice the shooting public through the doors, and what a hit these events proved to be from the very start. The first, at Dorking Halls, Dorking, Surrey, in February 1983, attracted a crowd of nearly seven hundred, an attendance which stunned and delighted Richards and his colleagues.

Marford Mill in the early 1980s was very definitely an exciting place at which to be, with its own unique atmosphere in which elements of change and tradition were blended together. Modern management practices, cutting edge biology, research-based marketing and regular staff meetings mingled with corduroy trousers, the reek of wet Labrador and the smell of gun oil, while above on the quarter deck John Anderton presided over everything like a benign admiral, always expecting his ratings and junior officers to work hard but to play hard too. Most nights saw the lamps burning late at the mill, but there was generally some flexibility in the daily schedule, especially if the chance of an evening flight or a precious game shooting invitation was in the offing.

Beneath Anderton were the two Johns – Swift and Richards – plus Colin Barwell. Swift's team comprised conservation officer Tony Laws, who focussed on the issues arising out of the management of sensitive conservation sites by wildfowling clubs. This involved the survey and evaluation of sites, the drawing up of management plans and liaison with the conservation bodies. John Harradine provided sorely-needed research into all aspects of sporting shooting, ensuring that hard fact was available to back up BASC's arguments and points of view. Anthony Holliday, as a qualified land agent, provided professional land management services to clubs and other membership groups, but in due course he left BASC to return to his core profession. The nascent international programme brought in a range of expertise to deal with the European conservation issues which were now driving British legislation.

WAGBI and BASC stalwarts gathered to present John Anderton with a painting to mark his 25th year of service with the association in 1982

BASC's conservation and research team: John Harradine, Tony Laws and Peter Mayhew at the 1986 Wildfowling Conference

Richards' camp consisted of David Leathart, whose large estate car was permanently filled with show stands, gundog training gear, exhibition boards and all the other paraphernalia which kept him, as events officer, almost permanently on the road during the summer months. A graduate of the Hampshire College of Agriculture, Leathart had spent eighteen months as a keeper on the Duke of Northumberland's Alnwick estate and had joined WAGBI in 1979. When he was not setting up, manning or dismantling one gundog event or roadshow, he was organising the next. Gerry Turner, a former school teacher, was BASC's education officer, who was responsible for preparing the growing library of codes of practice, organising courses and, most importantly, setting up and running the BASC Proficiency Award Scheme, a comprehensive course of instruction on sporting shotgun shooting. Jean Skinner, John Richards' long-suffering secretary, meanwhile dealt out a bewildering range of advice in response to members' enquiries.

The administrative side of BASC was handled by the cool and unflappable Colin Barwell, who managed both the accounts department and Tom Cave's membership team and dealt with issues such as employment matters, pensions, insurance and the motor fleet.

Events Officer David Leathart and Education Officer Gerry Turner ran BASC's shows, exhibitions and training courses in the early 1980s

Although life at Marford Mill could in no sense be described as routine, there was undoubtedly a certain annual rhythm to the activity there. During the winter there were the roadshows, followed by club AGMs, while the conservation department kept a weather eye on the thermometer – all hands being called to battle stations if the mercury dipped for long enough to precipitate the threat of a cold weather ban on wildfowling. With spring came the start of the outdoor events season, always kicked off by the Gamekeepers' Fair at Packington Park, Meriden. Courses, gundog competitions, clay shoots, country fairs and of course the annual general meeting in June, in those days normally a fairly small and sedate though nevertheless important event. Summer culminated in the CLA Game Fair, by far and away the most important show of the year. Every member of staff was on duty, plus a host of regular volunteers who lived on site in what came to be known as 'the gipsy encampment'. Each had his or her own special task. Bill Morris, husband of Jean Morris, John Anderton's personal assistant, was a key figure in the setting-up and dismantling of the site while horticulturalist Fred Barrett provided the flowers and pot plants. Indeed, he was even involved in breeding a WAGBI rose. By the 1980s the BASC enclosure was impressively organised with great efficiency and perhaps lacked the element of piracy which existed at earlier Game Fairs, when raiding parties would go out in the night to 'liberate' fence posts and railings which would be seen the following morning installed around the WAGBI site and painted green. On one notable occasion the 'gipsies' took things just a little too far for the Game Fair director, General Geoffrey Armitage, whose stentorian voice crackled over the public address system the following morning with the order from HQ: 'Will Commander Anderton report to Game Fair Control. Immediately.'

Membership recruitment was a hugely important task at the Game Fair, and by the early 1980s the association's appeal to a much wider audience than merely the coastal wildfowler led to enormous numbers of members joining each year. Over one thousand new members at a Game Fair was not unusual, and at Stowe in 1981 and again at Tatton Park the following year, the first Game Fair at which BASC appeared in its new colours, eleven hundred new members were signed up. Considerable attention was paid to corporate identity, and alongside the livery of green and white appeared the new logo, depicting the head of a pheasant within that of a goose and that of a dog, a reference to the new all-embracing association. Alongside it, rather lamely positioned on the four sides of a cross, were the initials BASC. The logo was the result of a competition launched amongst the membership, which attracted over two hundred entries, but it was not universally popular, and there were mutterings of plagiarism when attention was drawn to the similarity between it and the logo used at the time by Pedigree Petfoods. However, Anderton was not budging. The logo stayed, and it has survived the test of time even though it has since been through a number of transformations. Its introduction did at least have one immediate effect, that of converting overnight all existing WAGBI membership items into collectors' pieces. Car radiator badges, blazer badges, buttons and even windscreen stickers bearing the familiar old red and white 'flying goose' roundel were quickly bought up and examples now change hands for sums which would have had the WAGBI stalwarts of twenty-five years ago reeling with disbelief.

Nothing encapsulated more entirely the 'family spirit' of WAGBI than the band of helpers who annually attended the CLA Game Fair. This group was taken at Bowood in 1979

One of John Richards' ambitions was to create more shooting opportunity for the membership and, perhaps even more importantly, to enable those with an interest in one branch of shooting to experience a different aspect of the sport. In developing the Sporting Invitation Draw, he was able to broaden the sporting horizons of large numbers of shooters whilst at the same time raising money for the association. The concept was simple: BASC members offered the opportunity for a day or two's shooting to a guest, and the opportunities were placed in a draw with tickets for sale to the entire membership through the magazine *Shooting and Conservation*. What really set the Sporting Invitation Draw alight, however, was the offer from Tony Arnold, a BASC member living in California, to host a US duck hunting trip for a lucky British shooter. With an all-expenses-paid waterfowling holiday in the offing, the draw was guaranteed a huge take-up amongst the membership and it became an overnight success.

Margaret Thatcher went to the country in a general election in 1983. Field sports, and especially the hunting world, were greatly worried about the possibility of another Labour government which would bring with it the inevitability of further attacks on hound sports. Anderton was also exercised by the need for a united front within the countryside and went to considerable lengths to appear on the same platform alongside senior BFSS figures at public meetings. When the Co-Operative Wholesale Society banned hunting with hounds across its extensive farms, it was BASC which sent out forms to each of its members and raised a mighty petition against the decision. Now, with elections in the air, the senior management at BASC decided that it was time to respond to the growing clamour in the sporting press for hunters and shooters to act together in unison. Although BASC chairman David Lloyd Owen had taken considerable personal pains to keep both the BFSS and the Game Conservancy fully informed, relations with the BFSS had inevitably become tense while the new demarcation lines between the two organisations settled down after the change of title, indeed, as Lloyd Owen himself put it some years afterwards: 'One thing was clear, that the relationship between BFSS and ourselves was thoroughly bad.' But in 1982 something happened which opened up the possibility for a new relationship between Marford Mill and the BFSS headquarters at Kennington Road, the like of which could not have been envisaged before – or possibly after. In May of that year Marcus Kimball retired as BFSS chairman and was replaced by Stephen Hastings. Hastings was Member of Parliament for Mid Bedfordshire, a joint master of the Fitzwilliam Hunt and, more importantly a personal friend of David Lloyd Owen. The two men had met in September 1942 while preparing with the SAS for the big raids on Barce, Tobruk and Benghazi prior to El Alamein. The two of them had immediately hit it off and had kept in touch ever since.

In November 1982 the two chairmen exchanged letters which acknowledged that BASC should take the lead on all shooting matters, and the way was open for a joint campaign. Writing in the Spring 1983 edition of *Shooting and Conservation*, Anderton commented on the need for all field sports to work much more closely together. 'To achieve and maintain all that we value, country sports must bury their differences and close ranks, be they fox, hare or stag hunters, stalkers, coursing folk, those who shoot as well as those who fish or are falconers and all who support them. We are all in this together. Let no one doubt it for a moment.

'This long sought after change of attitudes, now more than ever apparent, will explain the rapid growth of trust between the BASC and BFSS. These two Associations have jointly formed the Campaign for Country Sports, which has responsibility for co-ordinating all activities associated with the forthcoming General Election.'

The new entente soon drew in the other country sports representative bodies, and developed form and substance. A chairman for the Campaign for Country Sports (CCS) was chosen in the

Keep politics out of country sports! BASC members demonstrate in Nottinghamshire against county council attacks on hunting, one of many demonstrations with which BASC was involved as part of the Campaign for Country Sports

person of former Conservative Chief Whip Sir Humphrey Atkins, and the campaign toured the country, raising the spirits and enthusiasm of the sporting community. With the glow of the Falklands victory behind her and with disarray in the Labour ranks, the result of the general election was never seriously in doubt, but the campaign carried on, still drawing large audiences even after the election was over. In the autumn at a rally in Leicester's De Montfort Hall, Anderton spoke alongside Max Hastings, Leicestershire mineworkers' leader Jack Jones, Peter Tombleson of the National Anglers' Council and Sir Humphrey. To an audience of eight hundred, cheered by a slick cabaret routine from the girls of the Cottesmore Hunt, Anderton emphasised that field sports had to put their house in order and exercise strong internal discipline. He also warned of the growing threats to shooting from Brussels, with the hint of problems for game rearing and shooting over areas of special protection.

Sir Humphrey followed with a reaffirmation of the aims of the campaign: 'All we seek is that we can continue to have the right to take part in the traditional sports of the countryside.' The CCS would, he said, continue because following Labour's defeat the opponents of country sports were now hard at work among the other political groups at Westminster. 'For the Campaign to rest on its laurels would be to court disaster.'

As a rallying point for country sportsmen, the CCS was both refreshing and very effective. Nothing before had been seen like it, and it marked a sea change in relations between the two biggest field sports organisations. For a while, it seemed as though here at last was the over-arching body which Anderton had envisaged six years before in his 'Diamond Plan', a body which would co-ordinate and marry the strengths of its individual partners, but would not usurp their authority or deny them their own freedom of action. In time, however, the CCS started to drift and the old rivalries started to reassert themselves. A joint working party was set up under Lord Vestey to look into how field sports organisations could work together in the future, and as a result the CCS was given a constitution and was transmogrified into the Council for Country Sports, but with memories of the general election fading into the blue horizon and a Conservative government comfortably installed once more at Westminster, the Council and its supporters did exactly what Humphrey Atkins had warned them not to. No longer was Labour a credible party of government; country sports breathed a sigh of relief and slipped into a golden slumber. One wonders whether the 2004 Hunting Act would have been passed if, twenty years previously, they had made greater efforts to alter political opinion among Labour's new elite as it dragged its party back towards electability.

Such things had not even been thought of during the summer of 1983, for there were other, more celebratory issues on BASC's agenda. It was the association's seventy-fifth anniversary, and the occasion was marked in a memorable way with a visit by none other than the patron, HRH the Duke of Edinburgh. Although he had been formally associated with WAGBI since 1968, he had never before visited the organisation's headquarters, and a great deal of planning went into ensuring that the tour of Marford Mill went like clockwork. Touching down out of a grey and drizzly sky at 10.25 on 3 June from a Wessex helicopter of the Queen's Flight, Prince Philip was greeted by the Vice Lieutenant of Clwyd and former WAGBI Council member Sir Alastair Graesser, together with the Viscount of Arbuthnott, David Lloyd Owen and John Anderton. A tour of all the departments in the Mill followed, the tour taking a full hour during which Prince Philip discussed with members of staff the details of their work. Then, before a bevy of press photographers and TV cameras, he unveiled a commemorative plaque in the reception area.

Also in reception was the magnificent set of six 'Wildfowl and Wader' guns built by Holland & Holland specially to commemorate BASC's anniversary. These exquisite guns, the brainchild of Holland & Holland's managing director Malcolm Lyell, a close friend of Anderton's and a staunch supporter of BASC, had been embellished with drawings by the young Rodger McPhail, then at the start of his meteoric rise to the front rank of Britain's sporting artists, and engraved by master craftsman Ken Preater. The six guns, a pair each of perfectly matched 12 bore game guns, 20 bore game guns and 12 bore three inch magnum wildfowling guns, were housed in a superbly built cabinet and Prince Philip had the opportunity to meet both the artist and the engraver. Before a buffet lunch, held in a marquee on the headquarters site, Prince Philip was presented with a specially bound copy of John Humphreys' new book *Stanley Duncan, Wildfowler* and the new painting by Rodger McPhail *Shooting Impressions*, and introduced to Council members and their wives.

Finally, at 1.00pm the royal party took their leave of council, officers and staff, leaving everybody back at the Mill with a host of memories. The day had gone faultlessly, without the slightest hitch – if you discount the unfortunate incident outside the front gate of Marford Mill. For as the stream of traffic passed by on the Chester to Wrexham road, one unfortunate driver happened to look to his left at the moment Prince Philip walked across the tarmac towards the front doors of the building. His jaw dropped so far that he failed to notice that the car in front of him had stopped and, with a loud bang, he crashed into it…right at the feet of the Chief Constable of North Wales in his full dress uniform.

There was a new confidence within BASC. Its ever-growing schedule of events coupled with a bold approach to PR and promotion was spreading the association's message ever wider amongst the shooting community and reaching entirely new audiences. BASC was starting to be heard within the farming community thanks to a carefully cultivated interest in shooting by *Farmers Weekly* and *Farming News*, whose rough shooting and wildfowling editor, Don Taylor, became a keen BASC member. At the same time, BASC turned its attention to another branch of shooting which had hitherto been totally ignored by the field shooting associations, that of air rifle shooting. With the demise in 1983 of the National Air Rifle and Pistol Association, airgunners were now seeking an association to represent their interests, and while the National Smallbore Rifle Association expressed a willingness to take on the administration of paper target shooting competitions, BASC's Gerry Turner saw a natural link between the competitive air rifle field target shooters, the airgun live quarry hunters and the broader church of field shooting. It was recognised by the BASC development team that air rifle shooting was the entry point to shooting sports for thousands of people, and while many of them went on to enjoy shooting with shotguns or cartridge rifles, others continued to enjoy using air rifles for hunting live quarry such as rabbits and other small pests, or for shooting at artificial field targets.

'Airgunners can't afford not to be represented!' wrote Turner in *Airgun World*. 'History shows that people who don't form a common front are always the first to be picked off when the going gets rough.' He set up BASC's first sporting air rifle course in Warwickshire in March 1984, and quickly got to work developing a code of practice for air rifle shooting in the field. Regular articles in *Airgun World* followed with the enthusiastic support of the editor, Paul Dobson. 'Back in the late seventies airgunners had no one to defend them against the threat of further legislation,' said Dobson. 'Today we have a powerful association that is ready to stand up for airgunners if the powers that be attempt to impose further restrictions on our sport.' Membership was opened to airgun hunters, while field target shooting clubs – whose members did not shoot at live quarry – were offered a fast-track option to register with the association.

Developments such as this helped to spread the BASC message among large numbers of shooters whose orbit had not hitherto been touched by the association, and they joined in their thousands. Recruitment records tumbled. The all-time record recruitment figure of 1982 was beaten the following year by an astonishing margin of 18% when no fewer than 12,970 new members joined. BASC was on a roll.

What Marford Mill failed to spot, though, were the warning rumbles which issued from amongst the most faithful core of its supporters, the body of men around whom the association had been born and through whose efforts it had emerged in the 1950s to become Britain's premier country shooting organisation – the wildfowling clubs. Fowlers were disgruntled and dissatisfied. The loss of the redshank and curlew from the quarry list in 1981 had generated deep resentment, while some of the more fiercely local wildfowlers still harboured a smouldering anger over the loss of 'free' foreshore wildfowling which they regarded as having been 'taken over' by WAGBI following the Crown foreshore agreement. To make matters worse, the 1982 wildfowling season was curtailed by a severe weather order which was signed by Environment Secretary Michael Heseltine a few days before Christmas, when thousands of fowlers were eagerly looking forward to a few precious days of holiday sport on the foreshore. This provoked huge wrath from the fowling clubs, and especially from those in the south west of England where the weather conditions were relatively mild. Why had BASC not argued in favour of a regional order which would have enabled them to continue fowling? Why had it argued in favour of a ban at all? And why was the publicity surrounding the ban so utterly abysmal? Wildfowlers felt that they were no longer at the centre of the organisation that they had founded and nurtured – their organisation. They felt betrayed. From around the coast came minor tremors and the deep, ominous sound of seismic trembling. Then, at the annual general meeting on 9 June 1984, came the eruption. It should not have been hard to predict that there were going to be fireworks, for the two principal resolutions for discussion, one from John Fuller and David Gray of South Essex WA calling for the reinstatement of a national non-scientific duck ringing scheme; and the other, from John Seago of Suffolk, calling for postal voting for all resolutions at the AGM, had been duly tabled and support for them canvassed around the East Coast clubs throughout the spring. What shocked Anderton and the others within the BASC hierarchy was the arrival of coachloads of wildfowlers at the Duke of Westminster's Eaton Hall, Chester, where the meeting was due to be held. For many of the two hundred and eleven who attended there was standing room only – the number present was four times that which would normally be expected at an AGM and not enough seats had been arranged. Battle was joined almost immediately, with demands for the accounts to be broken down to show the expenditure 'of every last pound', for an investigative committee to scrutinise the workings of the firearms committee and for the minutes of BASC Council meetings to be disclosed.

Fuller and Gray's resolution was fiercely debated. The old WAGBI duck ringing scheme, which had been stopped in 1980, had been popular with the clubs. It had provided them with details of the fate of birds that they themselves had reared, and had given the average club member the chance to participate in a practical way in a national conservation programme. The fact that the rings provided no fresh data of any scientific importance was irrelevant to the fowlers. Neither did they care that there were good reasons why the whole emphasis of BASC's conservation activity had shifted from duck rearing to habitat conservation. Their argument was simple: wildfowlers wanted to rear, ring and release ducks. More importantly, they were angered that the old-fashioned down-to-earth WAGBI that they had fashioned and loved had apparently vanished, to be replaced by an organisation run by technocrats who stalked the corridors of

All those in favour... A worried John Anderton threads his way through the packed and troubled AGM of 1984

Whitehall and Brussels, not the creeks and saltings of some lonely estuary. An attempt by the top table to water down the resolution only made matters worse, and it was passed intact. The second resolution did not fare quite as well. While the democratic principles behind it were self evident, it was recognised that postal voting for AGM resolutions would deny the opportunity for full debate and would force questions to be reduced to a level of simplicity that would make it much easier for extreme measures to be passed. It was defeated by 124 votes to 57, with 12 abstentions. Sitting next to John Swift at the top table was the Duke of Wesminster, who leaned over and asked, as the missiles flew about the room: 'Are your meetings always like this?' David Lloyd Owen, the staid military man, refused to take points from the floor, cut short the discussion at 'any other business', and the AGM dissolved in bitter recrimination. Jonathan Young of *Shooting Times* wrote:

> 'WAGBI became BASC because the old organisation was based on a wildfowling club struc-
> ture which limited its appeal and made it too cumbersome to respond quickly to the threats
> from an increasingly professional opposition. Now the association has over 60,000 members
> to give it authority and has efficient research and publicity teams which can quickly counter
> any attack with hard scientific facts.
>
> 'Unfortunately much of this scientific work is not understood by many members. Though
> the facts are available they are often indigestible. So, although it is essential, the scientific
> work's value cannot be appreciated by many members and they would prefer the BASC to
> concentrate on providing member services – such as the duck ringing scheme – the value of
> which are obvious.
>
> 'But if the BASC HQ does follow that latter course, it will no longer have the resources to
> undertake the scientific research that now protects our sport. And it is the BASC staff who
> will be blamed if our interests are damaged.'

In a reflective article, Tony Jackson commented that the esoteric issues related to Brussels, scientific research and the mysteries of Whitehall upon which BASC now concentrated, passed the average wildfowler by, not through any inability to understand the points under discussion, but through parochial indifference. 'The righteous may raise their hands in horror at such lack of enthusiasm for the higher planes of sporting understanding, but these lads know what they want – simply to pursue fowl as their fathers did in the knowledge that their sport will be protected by an organisation devoted to and understanding of their aims. Here lies the rub – a lack of confidence in BASC and its apparent inability to identify with wildfowling.'

The stormy AGM became the subject of furious debate in the *Shooting Times*. Some of the criticism levelled at BASC headquarters was fair – clearly it should have listened much more closely to the wildfowling clubs which still remained by far the most influential sector within its overall membership. Other observations were less reasonable. Particularly stinging was the contention that the staff had no practical knowledge of or interest in foreshore wildfowling, that their habitat was the committee chamber, the office and the laboratory, not the marsh; that in place of 'mud on their boots' they had 'cigar ash on their shoes'. For those of us at Marford Mill who had spent our formative years on the Dee, the Solway or, in my case, the Ouse Washes and the Blackwater estuary, this suggestion cut deep.

BASC headquarters was dazed, shocked and demoralised, and a big post mortem followed. For the conservation team, there was no alternative but to refocus its activities upon duck ringing and rearing, but it did not stop its work on SSSIs, for Laws and Swift knew full well that if they didn't get that right, then wildfowling on key wetlands would simply disappear. Tensions grew between the conservation and the development departments and there was more agony to follow. After the AGM came the Game Fair at Broadlands, where, on the Friday evening, John Anderton was woken up shortly before midnight with the news that all the helpers in the 'gipsy encampment' were hitching up their wagons and pulling out. Anderton pulled on his silk dressing gown and came down to the site in his Volvo. Lighting a cigarette, he spoke to the campers, who had been infuriated by a misunderstanding over a bottle of wine which had been allegedly purloined from the hospitality area, poured oil on troubled waters and urged them all to pull together. The BASC Game Fair site was saved.

However, it was now the gun trade that was spitting blood. An over-ambitious programme launched by the BASC sales department had booked large tented shops at county shows and field sports events throughout the summer, with the object of making money for the association by selling a wide range of sporting paraphernalia. Quite apart from the fundamental trading errors it had made – booking its marquee at events which were unsuitable or where there was minimal field sports interest, and accepting hopeless sites – it had failed to appreciate the offence which would be taken by those of its trade members who now saw their representative body in open competition with them on the show circuit. With the Game Fair over, it was realised that the ill-conceived sales adventure was starting to incur heavy losses, and the remaining bookings for the BASC sales marquee were hastily pruned. Many shows still demanded cancellation fees, however, and the ignominious retreat cost the association some £20,000. Anderton vowed that in future, BASC would restrict its sales effort to membership items, the sale of which could not be seen as competition by its much-needed trade members.

When normal life resumed at the end of the summer, BASC realised that it had to mend fences with the wildfowlers, and in particular to bridge the gulf of understanding which existed over the strategic issues of wildfowling policy within Marford Mill. The Council meeting on 20 September saw some tough talking, and at the end of it David Lloyd Owen announced measures to improve communications between members, management and staff, including a string of regional membership meetings with fowling clubs, a further schedule of winter roadshows and an enhanced show programme for 1985. Council had also given further consideration to the idea of introducing more democracy into BASC's decision making process and plans were revealed for a postal ballot for the election of council members. Outright opposition to mandatory shooting tests was reaffirmed, as was a commitment to seek reinstatement of brent goose, curlew, redshank and stock dove to the quarry list.

After the disastrous 1984 AGM, BASC set about restoring the confidence of its wildfowling members. Here Ian Odin, chairman of Chichester Harbour WA; Philip Hawes, Pagham Harbour WA; and Martin Cole, chairman of the Three Harbours Joint Council; invite questions from members to John Swift, Jack Carter and Tony Laws

BASC returned to its wildfowling roots at an exhibition organised by the Essex Joint Council of Wildfowling Clubs at Colchester Castle museum in 1984. At the right of the group is Neil Yates and beside him are past WAGBI chairman Bill Bailey and Essex Joint Council chairman Malcolm Lawson. On the left is Sqn Ldr Mike Townsend

A new Wildfowling Liaison Committee was decided upon to provide a formal channel of communication from the fowling clubs to BASC council, and it was announced that a national wildfowling conference would be staged early in 1985, to which all the affiliated fowling clubs would be invited and where policy and strategy for the future defence of wildfowling would be discussed frankly and openly.

It was recognised that the job of communication with members at local level had to be taken up a gear, and the proposal was put forward that a regional officer should be appointed, to be based not at headquarters but out in the country amongst the members themselves. The idea met with the support of the council, which decided that not one, but two regional officers should be taken on. No sooner had the decision been announced and the first steps taken to recruit suitable candidates, however, than another familiar face departed. John Richards had become increasingly frustrated that the association was, in his eyes, devoting too much time and effort to purist conservation work and not enough to defending shooting and promoting the sport. He felt that the development of BASC's firearms work, encouragement of young people into the sport and the finding of new shooting opportunity for existing members should be given more attention. He also felt that there were those in the wider political world in which BASC operated who were manipulating the organisation in an attempt to control the shooting lobby, and in August

1984, after twelve years with the association, he tendered his resignation. His departure was greeted with shock by the wildfowlers, but John Anderton paid tribute to him in *Shooting Times*: 'John has not only made a massive contribution to the fortunes and welfare of the association, but has immersed himself in it, commencing in the "deep end", from which he has never vacated. The BASC is, and will remain, very heavily in his debt.'

Chapter 10
REBUILDING

ornerstone of BASC's determined campaign to win back the hearts and minds of its core supporters, the wildfowlers, was the holding of the first national wildfowling conference at the De Vere Hotel, Coventry, on 19 January 1985. The event was the largest gathering of wildfowling members that the association had ever organised in its entire history, and no aspect of planning was left to chance. Sponsorship was provided by *Shooting Times* and Eley, clubs from all over Britain were invited, and no fewer than fifty-three local wildfowling associations were represented, their delegates coming from as far afield as Devon and Westmorland. Wildfowling conferences these days run to a fairly predictable formula, but back in 1985 the idea of discussing a series of highly technical and potentially alarming subjects with all the big hitters of the wildfowling world gathered together under a single roof – and in a way which would enable them to participate fully in the proceedings – was quite a scary one for those involved, and a great deal of thought was given to the arrangements for the big day. The crowded agenda for the event was divided into four themes: legislation and political action, wildfowling opportunity, education and training, and PR and local communications. John Ruxton provided the event with a surefooted chairmanship and it turned out to be a huge success.

Graham Howe makes sure his voice is heard at the BASC Wildfowling Conference

First up were the issues which were generating the most heat – erosion of the quarry list, mandatory testing, shooting over sites with high nature conservation status and the hard weather ban. Graham Howe of the North-West Joint Council spoke for everybody when he said of the loss of wader shooting: 'We've always lost, and we need a victory. The curlew and redshank were our Dunkirk. There is no conservation reason why they should not be shot.' Unanimous opposition to mandatory shooting tests was registered, and a double 8 bore load of BB was fired across the bows of the NCC by the fowlers, who warned that its policy towards wildfowling clubs operating over SSSIs had to be simple, fair and uniform across the country. Heavy criticism was levelled at the arrangements for severe weather wildfowling bans – one of which, ironically, was in operation as delegates took their seats in the conference hall. 'As soon as we get any snow – and we've been praying for hard weather – there's a ban. Wildfowl can look after themselves, they can fly south,' said Kevin Thatcher of Wells WA.

As the subject matter turned to wildfowling opportunity, Tony Laws took the lectern and spoke both of the growing competition for wetland which existed between wildfowling clubs and conservation bodies, and of how BASC was helping clubs design management plans which would demonstrate their good stewardship of important sites. But delegates warned that more was needed. Fowlers had to buy land, not simply lease it, said David Gray of South Essex WA, who argued that BASC should be establishing a land purchase fund to which fowlers could have access. Various suggestions were made as to the way in which such a venture might be financed, including a levy on shotgun cartridge sales and a siphoning of revenue from the Game Licence. Neither suggestion seemed sufficiently convincing, but it mattered not, for the seed had been sown and although it was not fully to germinate for a while yet, the concept of a land purchase fund had fired the wildfowling membership, the BASC council and the staff alike.

Closing the conference, John Ruxton gave a pledge to the wildfowlers that they would never again be forgotten, that BASC would be more robust in defending their interests and that it would act in future as the pressure group for shooting men. 'With that sort of attitude, backed up by the solidarity shown at Coventry,' reported Jonathan Young in *Shooting Times*, 'there is little doubt that we can all work together to get back what we have lost and ensure that no further encroachments are made on our sport.'

That first wildfowling conference was an undoubted success, and the national conference became a fixture in the wildfowling calendar. In its second year, 1986, it remained in Coventry, but it was not long before it started to move around the country, hosted by local wildfowling clubs or joint councils, though always with the administrative backup of Marford Mill.

With the applause of the Coventry delegates still ringing in its ears, a mightily relieved BASC staff set about the next phase of its fight back and appointed the association's first two regional officers. Each of them was to have a slightly different task, for Marford Mill was conscious that there were two very different jobs to be done in the regions. In the East of England there were already lots of members and a large number of affiliated clubs, and thus servicing the demands of a thriving membership network with a large wildfowling component was the primary concern. In the south-west of England, however, while BASC membership was spread more thinly on the ground, police firearms licensing statistics indicated that there was a particularly high concentration of firearm and shotgun ownership. Whoever was to take on this area would have new member recruitment very much on his agenda.

Both regions were large – in practical terms too large for singlehanded regional officers to manage – but even so, John Dryden and David Myles started work early in 1985. Dryden, forty-three, had started shooting at fourteen and was a keen rough shooter, game shooter and

The Wildfowling Conference, originally held to rebuild relationships with the wildfowling clubs, became a regular national forum for wildfowlers

John Swift (left) with Sir Hector Monro, John Ruxton and Professor Norman Seymour at the Wildfowling Conference

wildfowler. He was also an experienced deer stalker and wrote the regular 'Talking Stalking' column for the new country sports broadsheet newspaper *Shooting News*. Based in Somerset, he would be responsible for the whole of the south and south-west of England, from Berkshire to Cornwall. The fifty-year-old David Myles had thirty years of experience in rough shooting, game shooting and wildfowling, stalked in Caithness and had an interest in natural history, particularly ornithology. He was also

South West regional officer John Dryden on his appointment in 1985

an experienced and active beekeeper. His territory was to extend from Nottinghamshire and Lincolnshire in the north to the River Thames in the south, taking in Buckinghamshire, Bedfordshire, Northamptonshire and all stations east. Both men had a huge job to do, but they set to it with a will, and for the first time, BASC could rely on a full-time staff member to organise and arrange the local events its members demanded and, equally as important, to represent the needs of shooters at county hall and local authority level.

David Myles, one of the first two regional officers appointed by BASC

David Lloyd Owen (right) receives a retirement presentation from Lord Arbuthnott at the 1985 AGM

A new breeze was blowing through Marford Mill too, and in April 1985 John Swift, who as Director of Conservation and Research had expanded and extended the role of his department, was appointed Executive Director. In addition to his existing portfolio he now assumed responsibility for political representation, services to members, field events and education, although Anderton remained head of the association's full-time staff. At thirty-six years of age, Swift was married with two children and was actively involved in a rough shooting syndicate on the borders of Cheshire and North Wales. He was also a keen deer stalker.

WAGBI had taken an interest in deer for some years. During the course of the Parliamentary debates in the late 1970s which had eventually resulted in the Deer Act 1980, the association had been much exercised over the question of night shooting. While some had argued for a total prohibition of all shooting at night in order to exercise better control over the growing problem of deer poaching, WAGBI was acutely conscious of the need to protect traditional moonlight flighting of ducks and geese. Equally, though, it was aware that a substantial number of members were actively involved in deer stalking, and John Harradine's national shooting survey confirmed that there were indeed some 3,500 stalkers already in membership, with many more clamouring to join. A small group of enthusiasts on BASC council argued convincingly that BASC should do more to represent the interests of its deer stalking members through the setting up of a committee and the establishment of a specialist department, and council member Peter Keyser, a sporting art dealer and a keen stalker, was asked by David Lloyd Owen to go ahead and draw together a number of senior and influential figures from the deer world to form BASC's first deer committee. The British Deer Society was invited to maintain a presence on the committee and among the early members were Jeffrey Bale, Bill Grant and Arthur Cadman. A professional forester and former deputy surveyor of the New Forest, Cadman had written the Forestry Commission's first official leaflet on fallow deer and had been at the forefront of new scientific and humane forms of deer management.

Not only were deer numbers in England growing steadily, but attitudes towards them were changing. No longer were roe deer seen as vermin to be wiped out by means of indiscriminate drives with shotguns, as they had been as recently as the early 1960s, for with the introduction from continental Europe both of age and sex selection based on practical deer counts and of ethical control with centre fire rifles, there had come an appreciation that deer were a uniquely sporting quarry which were to be regarded with respect. No longer was the term 'deer stalking' confined to the pursuit of red deer on the Scottish hill, and an enthusiasm for lowland stalking in England was being kindled amongst a much wider section of the shooting community. Enthusiasm was there, for sure, but what in many cases was lacking was deer stalking opportunity.

Late in 1984 BASC was able to change all that when it was presented with the chance to take a lease on the stalking rights at Spadeadam Forest in Cumbria. Situated close to the Northumberland border in the massive Kielder Forest complex, Spadeadam was described as being pretty close to the stalker's idea of heaven, with undulating valleys and plantations of young pine and sitka spruce, all of which had been established with deer control in mind. The forest was well managed by head forester Gordon McReddie, and offered an annual cull of sixty roe does and forty bucks, providing excellent opportunities for BASC members to enjoy some challenging stalking. The project was masterminded by Bill Grant OBE, a Lake District stalker and a member of the new BASC deer committee, and administered by Jean Skinner from Marford Mill. Stalking would be by permit only at a three hourly rate of £18, and Gordon would accompany all those hunting the area for the first time as well, of course, as any novices. Spadeadam was a ground-breaking project and the first of a number of stalking schemes which eventually came to be operated by BASC in the north of England, East Anglia and Scotland.

The idea of formal stalking courses to educate budding new BASC stalkers had originated with events held by Ronnie Rose at Eskdalemuir, but the BASC deer committee quickly saw Spadeadam as the ideal venue for training the keen and enthusiastic new generation of stalkers, and the association's first stalking course was held there in June 1985. Twenty members attended to hear lectures by Bale, McReddie and his Forestry Commission colleague John Cubby. They spent an evening watching deer and the following day undertook practical stalking training. The course was hailed as a great success and was repeated the following year. BASC also joined together with the British Deer Society to create a new Deer Stalker's Code, designed to set down in writing the principles of humane and responsible deer management and the legislation underlying it. Much of what the code said still applies today.

Back on the marsh, things were not going altogether as planned. While Part 1 of the Wildlife and Countryside Act – the bit which protected the curlew and redshank – had generated all the heat and excitement, it was Part 2 – which dealt with countryside conservation – that was now starting to cause serious problems for wildfowling. The threat centred around the many Sites of Special Scientific Interest which were now being renotified by the Nature Conservancy Council and over which, according to the new legislation, occupiers had to obtain NCC consent in order to undertake 'potentially damaging operations' such as shooting. Some 67% of the land shot over by wildfowling clubs had SSSI status and wildfowlers were suddenly faced with the prospect of applying to the Government for permission to go fowling over marshes which they and their forefathers had shot for decades. To make matters worse, the EC Birds Directive now envisaged a string of internationally designated sites – Special Protection Areas or SPAs – where even tighter control would be exerted to ensure that hunting would not jeopardise nature conservation. Early on in the process, Swift had a series of discussions with the NCC, which was taking a particularly cautious line in its method of establishing the criteria for what was to be allowed, or otherwise, within protected sites. The wording of the European Directive was vague, but it seemed pretty clear to BASC that the NCC was asking shooters to sign up to more than the law actually demanded. Discussions became increasingly fractious and eventually BASC put its foot down, telling the NCC that there was absolutely no requirement within the 1981 Act for it to restrict shooting in the way that was being proposed: in short, it was acting illegally. Swift wrote to Leo Batten, the NCC officer in charge of SSSI policy at the time, saying to him that if the NCC was to continue on its present course, then BASC would have no option but to state publicly that the council was breaking the law. Swift waited for a response, but when none came, Marford Mill went ahead and lit the blue touch paper by issuing a sharply worded press release. The anticipated political explosion duly occurred. Swift was at a dinner party when the telephone rang, with a very agitated Lord Arbuthnott at the other end asking what on earth BASC thought it was doing.

Arbuthnott was both president of BASC and chairman of the Scottish NCC, so once the nature of the problem had been explained to him, he found himself in a unique position to bring all parties around the discussion table. NCC had been deeply stung by the accusation that it had been acting beyond its lawful powers, but in the end, BASC was proved right. The council's policy was altered to recognise wildfowling as a legitimate activity over SSSIs, thereby allowing a formal policy of co-operation to be put in place, and in due course the two bodies agreed and signed a joint statement of common interest and co-operation. The newly appointed chairman of NCC, William Wilkinson, a former RSPB council member, a powerful figure in the society and a strong advocate of site protection, held a series of meetings with BASC and gradually a working accommodation was reached. Work on SSSIs now assumed an even greater importance

Peter Fox joined BASC to undertake research on the relationship between shooting and wildfowl disturbance

within the conservation team at Marford Mill, and a new conservation officer was appointed. Peter Mayhew, who had joined BASC straight from his zoology degree at Glasgow University, took on much of this extra workload under the guidance of Tony Laws who in 1982 had become senior conservation officer. Mayhew went on to receive a PhD for his work on the feeding ecology and behaviour of the wigeon. A second conservation officer, Peter Fox, also joined BASC as a result of a joint project with the Wildfowl Trust and RSPB on the effects on wildfowl and waders of disturbance by shooting. Fox ran a series of experimental case studies, and when Mayhew left to join the RSPB, Fox took over his work.

Security of tenure for shooters in general and wildfowlers in particular was the watchword of the day. While some clubs battled with the new wildlife and countryside legislation to secure their consents to shoot over important wildlife sites, others saw cherished chunks of marshland slip out of their hands and into those of conservation bodies such as the RSPB, the Wildfowl Trust and the county naturalists' trusts. There was a growing realisation that freehold purchase was the only way in which wildfowlers could guarantee security of their shooting in the long term. However, with a few notable exceptions, wildfowling clubs simply did not have the financial muscle to buy land. Most fowlers paid a basic subscription which barely covered the BASC capitation fee, leaving just a few bob in the kitty at the end of the year to buy the farmers from whom they cadged their shooting rights a bottle of whisky at Christmas. In 1985 Old Hall Marshes came onto the market. A traditional sporting estate on the north shore of the Blackwater estuary in Essex, the property had been owned by a well known sporting landowner, Brigadier Colvin, and during the back end of the year, when the fleets rose with the autumn rains, spilling out across the permanent grassland which lay behind the sea wall, the marshes were alive with clouds of teal and wigeon. Up to fifteen thousand birds overwintered there in a good season, providing some of the finest duck shooting to be had anywhere. While the sport behind the sea wall was enjoyed by Colvin and his guests, who shot no more than six times a year, local wildfowlers from the Tollesbury and Colchester clubs had access to the saltings and foreshore by leave of the estate and in return for their sport helped the keeper, Ken Salmon, patrol the marshes to discourage poachers. David Gray and John Fuller of the South Essex WA, who had masterminded the purchase of Bridgemarsh Island back in 1963, tried in vain to put together, through the Essex Joint Council of Wildfowling Clubs, a proposal whereby shareholders could buy into a corporate ownership venture and secure the future of the marshes for wildfowling. However, the purchase price of three-quarters of a million pounds was simply too large and there were not enough takers prepared to put their money up front and buy the shares which Gray was offering: the Old Hall estate was purchased by the RSPB. Much ill feeling and indignation amongst the Essex wildfowling fraternity was engendered when the inevitable happened and the local fowlers were stopped by the new owners from shooting their old haunts. There was much talk of piracy, and some of the Mersea gunners hinted darkly that they would carry on shooting anyway, accessing the saltings by boat and making a quick seaborne getaway if spotted by the warden. But Gray and Fuller appreciated that piracy and poaching was no way to ensure the future of wildfowling in Essex or anywhere else for that matter. The only serious way of maintaining local fowling rights and preventing a similar loss of shooting opportunity in other parts of the country was to ensure that wildfowling clubs could compete financially with the RSPB.

Together, and drawing inspiration from the thriving US shooting and conservation body Ducks Unlimited (DU) they formulated a proposal for a dedicated fund which could be used to secure land for shooting and conservation in the UK. A resolution was placed before the BASC annual general meeting in 1986 and this led to the creation of the Wildlife Habitat Trust (WHT). The Trust, administered by BASC, was financially separate from the association, and it was enthusiastically supported with donations and other fund raising by the wildfowlers, who quickly realised that they would be its principal beneficiaries. A year later, the trust advanced its first loan, enabling the purchase of sixteen acres of freshwater marsh within the Rockland Broad SSSI by Norwich and District WA. In 1988 Kent wildfowlers were supported by the WHT in their purchase of one hundred and eighty-four acres of land at Cliffe and Cooling Marshes, a purchase which was especially noteworthy insofar as it also received financial support from the Government itself. This fact caused ripples in the House of Commons when a parliamentary question enquired what the NCC thought that it was doing in funding 'the gunmen of Kent'. By 1989 Little Oakley and Lytham St Anne clubs were able to make land purchases with the trust's help, and suddenly the WHT was on a roll.

BASC looked at ways of building up the trust's resources and hit upon the idea of selling an annual stamp to supporters. The 'duck stamp' had long been used in the United States to raise revenue for wildfowl conservation and direct links had already been established between BASC and DU, which was interested in working up a duck stamp programme in Europe. DU's Matt Conolly came to Britain and spoke to wildfowlers, whipping up interest in a stamp project and prompting Tony Laws to head for the States to see if a deal could be struck. It was not long before a three-year contract was agreed, with DU underwriting the production of the stamp, including both the artwork and the printing. Of vital importance to the project, however, were the wealthy American duck stamp collectors. Like philatelists interested in securing first day covers, they were interested in the 'first of nation' stamp, that is to say the first duck stamp issued by each nation State. It was clear that the big bucks would be going to whoever produced Britain's first duck stamp, and it was equally clear that the WHT was not alone, for the Wildfowl Trust had also latched onto the duck stamp concept. Eventually it became a race to see who would get their stamp published first and claim the lucrative American market. Laws went all out to demonstrate that only the WHT stamp was the authentic product of UK waterfowl hunters, and he got Ministerial endorsement for the project to back him up.

BASC won the race, and on 24 July 1991 the first UK hunter's habitat stamp was unveiled, bearing a picture by Rodger McPhail of pintail over the lighthouse at Sutton Bridge, a landmark of major significance in the history of British wildfowling. Even the launch party, though, was thwarted by potential disaster, for just as the Environment Minister Tony Baldry MP got up to make his speech to the assembled guests at the Naval and Military Club, Piccadilly, a bomb alert was sounded and the entire building had to be evacuated. Eventually the launch took place at the RAF Club just a few doors down the street. A second and rather less formal party was held afterwards at the Game Fair and soon thousands of British wildfowlers and shooters were buying the £5 habitat stamp. The Wildlife Habitat (Conservation) Stamp Trust (WHCST) was established in 1992 to run the UK Habitat Conservation Stamp programme and act as the WHT's commercial arm. The Wildlife Habitat Charitable Trust (WHCT) was also established in 1992 to take advantage of the benefits of charitable status, and to expand the WHT operation, providing increased support for the conservation of wildlife and habitats through the provision of grants. An important feature of the habitat stamp was that a proportion of the revenue raised was channelled by Wetlands International into projects in other parts of the western Palearctic flyway down which Britain's migratory waterfowl travelled. Funding by the UK of wildfowl conservation in the Baltic states – which were only just emerging from the Soviet Union – was unique in its time, and the groundbreaking work which the WHT, Wetlands International and FACE did was to help in rolling out duck stamp agreements in Sweden, Denmark, Italy and Ireland.

In the past, most people had come into the sport of shooting by way of a local or family connection. Perhaps a shooting father or uncle would introduce his son or nephew into the sport, or perhaps a potential recruit would express an interest to the captain or gamekeeper of an existing shoot in their district and go on to take part as a beater, then as a pigeon shooter and perhaps as a gun on beaters' days. Of course lots of shooters still get involved in exactly the same way today, but in the 1980s the social make-up of sport was changing fast, and BASC recognised that the old tried-and-tested routes into shooting simply were not available to many of those who were clamouring to take part in a sport which was still hide-bound by tradition and mystique. There was a need, not just for advice and printed codes of practice, but for a practical course of instruction designed to guide the novice into shooting.

Among the architects of the proposed new shooting course was Lincolnshire school teacher Robin Marshall-Ball, one of whose pupils had suffered a devastating shooting accident. As a result of this, Marshall-Ball had devised a shotgun shooting course with a strong emphasis on gun safety and had written about it in *Shooting* magazine. The article came to the attention of BASC and John Anderton invited Marshall-Ball to Marford Mill to see what the association might learn from his experiences. In 1983, after months of experimentation and discussion, Gerry Turner launched

Jack Charlton lent his support to BASC's recruitment drive in 1985

BASC's Proficiency Award Scheme. Open to all members over the age of fourteen, the PAS offered a ten-week course, one evening a week, with lectures covering subjects such as shotguns and cartridges, gun safety, quarry identification, game shooting, rough shooting, wildfowling, gundogs, gamekeeping and the relationship between shooting and conservation. The textbook for the PAS was written by Turner, with support from every BASC department and the genuine interest and approval from the association's patron, HRH The Duke of Edinburgh, who contributed a personal foreword. *The Handbook of Shooting – The Sporting Shotgun* was published by Pelham Books and remains, suitably revised and updated, popular today.

Of course it was not possible for one person to deliver courses in all parts of the country, throughout the year. Turner realised that the only way in which demand would be met was for him to train up a countrywide team of Honorary Regional Education Development Officers, who would in turn gather local groups of instructors from amongst the experienced shooters in their own districts to deliver the PAS lectures. Thus not only did the PAS serve the vital function of bringing keen novices of all ages into shooting, but it also engaged a complete new generation of volunteers into the work of BASC. It was a brilliant and highly successful concept.

Of course the PAS had its detractors, principally those who still believed that BASC's secret desire was to pave the way for a mandatory shooting test such as existed in continental Europe, which it would go on to administer on behalf of the state. That was certainly not Turner's intention. He was totally committed to voluntary education and training, but he also saw the PAS as a means of raising standards in shooting. Initially there were only a handful of HREDOs, but slowly the number grew, and by 1985 a total of twenty-six regional helpers had been recruited and forty-seven courses had been run, helping hundreds of new shooters to gain a foothold. The PAS was an imaginative scheme, but it never really achieved the lift-off which BASC had hoped for, largely because it rested on the shoulders of volunteers and required a huge input of headquarters time and administration to ensure that standards were maintained. Even so, PAS courses continued to be run for many more years and the lessons they taught BASC's education and training department led on to the exploration of new avenues of shooting instruction and programmes of education for young shots and eventually women shooters. There are many shooters who are active in the field today that owe their grounding to the PAS, and several HREDOs went on to serve BASC loyally in a variety of other capacities.

It was not only shooters who were finding it hard to get into the fast-growing sport. Young gamekeepers had always found it difficult to get their first foot on the ladder. BASC thus came up with two new schemes to assist them. The Gamekeeper Youth Placement Scheme provided boys between fourteen and seventeen with the opportunity to work alongside an experienced professional keeper during the school holidays, ideally living-in with the keeper for a week, helping with the work and getting a taste for the various tasks to be done at other times of the year. The cost was £50, and the scheme represented a good way for people of school age to find out if they were suited to a career in keepering. The scheme was masterminded by David Leathart, who recruited twenty-five keepers prepared to assist. For those who wanted to take their interest a step further, Leathart developed the concept of a twelve-month working placement, with would-be keepers joining a BASC Trainee Gamekeeper Register, whereupon BASC would endeavour to place them on suitable estates. Several trainees were found working placements, but again, the complexity of administration eventually caused the scheme to founder. Today, the legislation surrounding employment and child protection would make such schemes impossible, but in the mid 1980s they represented genuine attempts by BASC to further the lot of the gamekeeping profession.

BASC's education and training programmes were starting to be noticed in high places, and in September 1986 the Minister for Sport, Dick Tracey MP, visited Marford Mill to cement the decision by the Sports Council to recognise the association as a sporting shooting governing body and to increase levels of funding for its education and training and air weapons safety programmes. During his visit, the Minister, a former British Field Sports Society PR officer, was shown the work of the association and had the chance to discuss the future of training in sporting shooting in depth with BASC's chairman, Simon Cussons, and with Anderton, Swift and Colin Barwell. It was an important visit, and one which set the seal on BASC's relations with the Department of the Environment over training matters.

Chapter 11
FIREFIGHT

*A*t the same time as it set up its new Regional team in early 1985, BASC appointed its first firearms officer. Since publication of the 1973 Green Paper, Anderton had become acutely aware of the potentially devastating impact which the further ratcheting up of controls over legal ownership of firearms might have upon shooting sports. Although the Government had not pursued the proposals which the Green Paper had aired, ten years down the line the principles behind them were being pressed with increasing vigour by police spokesmen and the threat of swingeing new controls over shotguns was growing. At AGMs and wildfowling conferences alike, demands for BASC to devote more of its resources to firearms matters were regularly made, one of the strongest campaigners being Colin Greenwood, now retired from West Yorkshire Police with the rank of superintendent and turned firearms consultant. Greenwood, though a member and supporter of BASC, was never afraid to be openly critical when he thought that the association was slacking, and his editorship of *Guns Review* provided him with a platform from which he was able to prod Marford Mill into action. The war against shotgun ownership was hotting up, he warned, and as BASC's first firearms officer, Brian Hughes was to find himself in the front line.

Hughes had spent much of his working life in Africa. Originally an officer in the British South Africa Police in what was then the colony of Southern Rhodesia, Hughes had gone on to work in the field of African wildlife management, initiating the programme by which game animals – which carried much greater immunity to tropical diseases than imported European livestock – were ranched for meat. As a professional hunter he had naturally gained experience with a wide range of firearms, and had in fact shot virtually everything from a .177 air rifle to a .600 nitro express. As the embers of Empire finally died, Hughes, on his departure from government service in Africa, had opted for the traditional passage home by ocean liner. A patient, methodical man with a policeman's eye for detail, he was the natural person to develop BASC's nascent firearms department.

Within a couple of months of Hughes's arrival at Marford Mill, there was the sniff of a renewed campaign by the anti-gun lobby. Local authority police committees, briefed by senior police officers, were lobbying the

Brian Hughes joined BASC in 1985 as the association's first firearms officer

Home Office and mounting an effective campaign on TV and in the press to discredit shotguns. Their aim was to have shotguns licensed in the same way as rifles and pistols, which were subject to Section 1 of the Firearms Act 1968. Such a development would require applicants for certificates to demonstrate good reason for possession of each and every shotgun and at the same time subject shotguns to tight new security controls. The police also wanted to see a total ban on semi-automatic and pump-action shotguns and terrifying TV footage of the effects of such weapons at close range was released and broadcast.

Hughes immersed himself in the statistics and pointed out what the effects of such changes to the legislation would be, countering the claims that shotguns stolen from legitimate owners were widely used in crime. If obligatory security requirements were imposed upon shotguns, he said, then it would result in the police having to visit and report on some 800,000 homes in addition to the 160,000 homes it currently visited in order to inspect firearms. The burden of work placed on an already overstretched police service would be tremendous and it would create unnecessary friction between the police and shooters, many of whom did not like the idea of having policemen tramp about their homes. Hughes added that the cost of the exercise would be enormous, and that in all probability it would be passed on to shooters in the form of heavy increases in firearms fees. 'Why attack shooters instead of the criminals who use firearms against the community? There is a real enemy,' said Hughes.

In 1985 Douglas Hurd MP took over from Leon Brittan MP as Home Secretary and addressed the Standing Conference on Countryside Sports. He made it clear that he accepted that the imposition of full 'Section 1' controls on shotguns would not be justified 'in terms of commitment of police resources and the likely reduction in armed crime'. However, he warned that he was considering making it a condition of possessing a shotgun that it was stored securely when not in use.

The war of words continued for a further two years, and police calls for tougher controls on firearms were redoubled after a fatal shooting during an attempted wages snatch at a London abbatoir, but on 19 August 1987 the dam broke. At lunchtime that summer's day in the quiet Berkshire town of Hungerford, twenty-seven-year-old Michael Ryan, armed with a self-loading assault rifle and a pistol, shot dead sixteen people, including his mother, and wounded fourteen others before killing himself. It was at the time the worst mass murder in British history, and the political repercussions unleashed shock waves which were to have a huge impact upon shooting sports. Hurd immediately announced an urgent review of firearms law, to include a ban on semi-automatic weapons, limits on the amount of ammunition which could be stored in the home and restrictions on the number of weapons which could be held on a certificate. His proposals, however, were vague and imprecise, and BASC pressed the Home Office for clarification, pointing out that a ban on self-loading rifles would affect professional deer stalkers and gamekeepers and cause major interference with legitimate sporting shooting. In a press statement, Anderton said that it would be impossible for self-loading shotguns, widely used for training and clay pigeon shooting, to be treated like rifles. He did, however, welcome a proposal to raise the sentences for those convicted of carrying firearms in crime. 'The reduction in armed crime must be tackled by increasing the likelihood of criminals being caught and the severity of penalties handed down by the Courts,' he said.

Within hours of the Hungerford tragedy itself, the telephone lines to Marford Mill were jammed by members worried about the impact upon their own shotgun or firearms ownership of the likely government reaction. In addition to his normal caseload of members' enquiries, which were in any event piled up high upon his desk, Hughes now faced an endless series of phone calls, some of them lasting up to forty-five minutes. When one call finished, there would be another member waiting his turn, but in the short term there was in fact very little advice which could be given. There was not even any clear picture as to how many self-loading weapons – both shotguns and rifles – there were in legal ownership, and one of Hughes's first actions was to meet the Gun Trade Association and make an assessment of the number of guns which might have to be modified in some way. Very soon he was spending one or two days a week in London at meetings with the British Shooting Sports Council and other bodies, for it was essential for him to keep his finger on the pulse of what was happening. It was an exhausting period, but the rest of the staff at Marford Mill lent their full support. Colin Shedden, John Harradine and John Swift all shouldered a share of the burden, while Jean Skinner was a tower of strength, keeping some semblance of normality within the firearms department. Meanwhile John Anderton was always there to discuss and advise. Hughes tried to keep them all in the picture to ensure that the best collective decisions could be taken.

The Government's position was gradually becoming clear. Speaking at a Police Superintendents' Association conference in Torquay on 22 September, Hurd outlined proposals to ban private possession of 'high powered' self-loading rifles, and bring all semi-automatic and pump-action shotguns 'which have a greater fire capacity than traditional single and double barreled shotguns' under at least the same control as those for rifles and pistols. Hughes joined a six-man BSSC delegation at a meeting with Home Office Minister Douglas Hogg on 30 October, at which the Minister confirmed that the proposals on self-loading firearms were not aimed at .22 rifles and pistols, and that neither were single shot or bolt action centre fire rifles at risk. He also indicated that he was prepared to discuss limitations on the capacity of magazine shotguns so that they could continue to be retained on a shotgun certificate. However, the Government seemed set on a security condition for shotguns. During November there was a round of consultation with the shooting and countryside organisations, but it was painfully obvious from the body language of the Ministers and civil servants concerned that the Government was not going to listen to anything which it did not want to hear. Its mind was made up. In December it issued a Firearms White Paper, followed swiftly by a Bill.

BASC Council met to discuss the imminent legislation and resolved to fight. 'The time for negotiations is over,' said the association's chairman, Simon Cussons. 'Now is the time for action.' He warned the membership to be ready for a campaign against the Bill, particularly those aspects of it which threatened the possession and use of magazine shotguns. Around the country the message went out in the form of regional press releases; individual members, shooting syndicates and clubs were encouraged to meet their MPs and of course the winter round of BASC roadshows became platforms for opposition to the Bill. The event in Ipswich on 19 February attracted hundreds of members to the town's Corn Exchange, where Swift spoke of his serious concerns over the likely impact of the legislation on shotguns.

As with other campaigns on firearms issues, the parliamentary legwork devolved onto a small group of individuals from within the British Shooting Sports Council, backed by a House of Commons team under BSSC vice chairman Sir Hector Monro MP and his lieutenant Jerry Wiggin MP. BASC, in the shape of Hughes and his colleagues, were actively briefing MPs and, as the Bill progressed through the parliamentary process, peers. The Lords, from their more detached and objective standpoint, were particularly skilled at rubbing off some of the hard edges of the Government's proposals and one success which was achieved was the 'estate rifle' clause which enabled non-certificate holders to use a rifle whilst shooting as guests of private occupiers of land. Hughes and Fred Silvester, former Conservative MP for Manchester Withington and a political consultant engaged by BASC, met Lady Saltoun of Abernethy to discuss the matter and suggest a possible wording, and she responded by recommending the suggestion to Home Office Minister Lord Ferrers. Hughes and his colleagues from the BSSC also pressed successfully for the establishment of a long sought after Firearms Consultative Committee which would provide expert advice to the Home Secretary. Together the parliamentary team whipped up considerable support from the Conservative and Ulster Unionist benches and the Government accepted that shotguns with magazine capacities not exceeding two shots could remain on a shotgun certificate and that there would be a welcome, if modest, compensation scheme to owners of self-loading centre fire rifles, but no other substantial concessions were wrung from the Home Secretary.

During an angry and ill-tempered all-night sitting of Parliament, debate on the Bill was guillotined by the Government and the legislation was passed in May 1988. As Swift had predicted, while the headlines focussed on the prohibition of self-loading rifles, especially assault rifles of the type Ryan had used, the real impact of the new law was felt by hundreds of thousands of shotgun owners, who were now faced with the cost of installing steel security cabinets and of having their magazine shotguns modified. Inevitably, as police firearms licensing authorities and shooters alike tried to get their heads around the new regulations, the volume of enquiries to the BASC firearms department from members applying for new certificates, renewing their old ones or just simply trying to stay within the law started to spiral upwards. However, the rapidly increasing case load of members' firearms queries did at least provide Hughes with a rich seam of up-to-date evidence on the administration of firearms law to take to the meetings of the newly established Firearms Consultative Committee, to which he was appointed as one of its founder members.

More staff, as ever, demanded more space in which to work and Marford Mill was by now almost bursting at the seams. Offices had been divided up with portable panels and every cupboard appeared to be occupied by someone. Anderton had long cherished the idea of developing the redundant stable block behind the Mill, and at long last he got his wish. The derelict structure itself was in a poor state of repair and had to be virtually rebuilt from the ground upwards, but the vision of a suite of offices plus a large central meeting room-cum-lecture theatre was to be realised, whilst added to the design was a caretaker's cottage and a secure armoury. Building work had got underway during the summer of 1986, and by the following year the new complex was complete. Generation of finance for the project had gone ahead in tandem with the development, and by 1988 over £110,000 had been raised, thanks to a number of substantial individual donations. There was still some £180,000 to be found, however, and as part of the fundraising effort BASC held an eightieth anniversary ball in a marquee at the Mill. With a live band and disco, the evening was a tremendous success which brought in a useful contribution towards the funds needed to clear the building cost.

It was not only at Marford Mill that BASC was investing in bricks and mortar. Since his appointment, David Cant, BASC's director development (Scotland) had moved the association's Scottish headquarters repeatedly around the Scottish countryside, basing his work wherever he was living at the time. Effectively BASC Scotland was operating out of a suitcase. However, the Scottish membership was growing and Cant had established a number of successful country sports fairs which were popular with local members. He had also set up a sporting art competition and a very successful sealed bid sporting auction which in its first year offered red, roe and sika stalking, ptarmigan, grouse, duck, partridge and pheasant shooting and salmon fishing, all of it donated by Scottish BASC members. Now it was time to bring a little more permanence to BASC's operation in Scotland, and after a search for potential properties, an old cottage and redundant steading were found at Trochry, near Dunkeld. BASC supporters and various local

In January 1986 the stable block behind Marford Mill lay derelict…
…but by the following summer, building work to create new office accommodation, a meeting room and lecture theatre, plus a caretaker's cottage and armoury was well underway

associations were encouraged and cajoled into donating funds to secure its purchase and conversion. This was achieved, the steadings becoming BASC's first permanent Scottish centre and the
cottage becoming office accommodation. The Trochry office was opened by Lord Arbuthnott in
November 1987. By and large, affairs in Scotland continued at a placid and peaceful pace, with
much of Cant's energies being devoted to the running of the BASC fairs. But there was one trou-
bling blot on the face of Scottish sport which threatened to bring shooting into serious disrepute.

Populations of grey geese were increasing and reaching a level where they were starting to
impinge upon agriculture. A few smart operators had seen the opportunity of making a quick
profit by offering paying guns the promise of shooting large numbers of geese.
Commercialisation of goose shooting grew rapidly. After all, communications between Scotland
and the south had never been better, more people wanted to shoot wildfowl and the wildfowling
clubs in England had waiting lists. Goose guides sprang up overnight and there was no shortage
of small hotels willing to accommodate the visiting shooters. Once the cash was handed over, the
pressure was on for the guides and hotels to deliver, and it is hardly surprising that under such
pressure the rules were broken. Soon there were reports of barrages of shots being fired at birds
in excess of one hundred yards away, on some occasions from illegal unrestricted semi-automatics.
One correspondent to *Shooting Times* commented: 'These lunatics make the so-called marsh
cowboys seem like saints.'

John Humphreys, writing in the same magazine commented: 'Some of the black deeds would
make your hair stand on end and they reflect disastrously on the sport of shooting.' He wrote of
southerners and continentals – mostly Italians – being systematically overcharged by hotels,
farmers and middle men, then left in a likely field and told to get on with it, and of a bag of nine-
ty-two geese shot in one day, the corpses left to rot in a ditch. It became a regular practice for
disreputable goose guides to move their clients over the course of a week to a succession of
different fields in which they knew perfectly well the guns would not stand an earthly chance of
getting a shot. Then, the day before their departure, the guests would, as if by magic, find themselves at last in the 'right place' – where of course the geese had been feeding all along – and get
some shooting. Next week the procedure would be repeated for the next party. Good, responsible
guides found their reputations tarnished by association and both they and the shooters demanded
that BASC take some action.

Goose shooting was the subject of a discussion during a Scottish sub-meeting at the 1986
Wildfowling Conference, whereupon BASC brought together the goose guides and thrashed out
a code of practice for guides, hotels and shooters alike. Voluntary bag limits were agreed, together
with time limits for shooting, limits on the numbers of guns and the cessation of artificial
feeding. The support of other organisations was canvassed, and the code was supported by the
National Farmers Union (Scotland), the Scottish Landowners' Federation, Scottish Natural
Heritage and the Scottish police forces. Standards had at last been set, and by and large the code
of practice worked. Guides knew what was expected of them and while some continued to flout
the rules, most abided by them and a running wound in the side of shooting sports was effectively staunched.

In Northern Ireland, as in Scotland, BASC's working base was achieving a much more
satisfactory state of permanence. In May 1986 Michael McMeekin had been appointed part-
time regional officer, and the following year that position had been extended to a full-time capacity. McMeekin, who had been brought up shooting and fishing with his father and uncle around
Glenwherry, Co Antrim, was operating out of a portacabin, but the search for more
suitable office accommodation was on, and the opening of a new BASC NI office in the

courtyard of Galgorm Castle, Ballymena, in May 1988 was a major milestone in the association's activities in the province. Galgorm's owner, the Hon Christopher Brooke, gave the venture his utmost support and the new office suite was fitted out with the latest equipment, including an answering machine, fax machine and word processor. Performing the opening ceremony was Lord Lyell, Minister responsible for agriculture in Northern Ireland, who spoke of Government recognition that farmers needed to find alternative uses for their land and that shooting was one such potential use. In his speech, Lord Lyell commented that sound leadership and reliable advice on shooting and conservation would be required, and referred to the warm relationship which now existed between BASC and the Forest Service of Northern Ireland. Lord Lyell went on to present the first eighteen Proficiency Award Scheme certificates and badges to have been gained in the province, the results of a successful course organised in the South Down area by Michael McAteer.

Mike McMeekin was appointed BASC's regional officer for Northern Ireland in 1986

Smiles from regional officer Mike McMeekin as Lord Lyell (right) opens the new BASC Northern Ireland centre at Galgorm Castle in 1988

BASC had been instrumental in the success of an open day at Seskinore, Co. Tyrone, which over two years had grown into a fully fledged country fair, attracting an attendance of nine thousand in March 1988. Now McMeekin was to set about developing a BASC Country Sports Fair in the two hundred and forty acre grounds of Galgorm Castle itself, bringing together working gundog events and competitions, clay shooting, fishing, ferrets, falconry and all the familiar country fair attractions. Included also for the first time in Northern Ireland were trials of new game cover crops which would be on show to local farmers and landowners interested in developing their own shoots. McMeekin's appointment, the establishment of the new Country Sports Fair and, in particular, the setting up of permanent office accommodation represented a huge step forward for BASC's activities in Northern Ireland, where the association had a membership of two thousand, together with thirty-five affiliated clubs.

Attending the Galgorm opening was John Anderton, the trip to Ballymena being one of his very last official engagements on behalf of BASC, for in June 1988 he was to retire. After thirty-one years in the director's seat, Anderton left the association which he had built up from a small group of enthusiastic amateurs with a following that numbered barely a few hundred to an internationally respected organisation with a membership that hovered on one hundred thousand. He had forged the all-important links between shooting sports and the conservation movement and seen BASC develop in a myriad of ways which would have been inconceivable in the mid 1950s. A fully staffed education and training department set the standards for shooting and ran courses all over the UK, the conservation and land management team, backed up by an in-house research department ensured that sportsmen had somewhere to shoot and something to shoot at, while the firearms department tried its hardest to see that they had something to shoot with. Moreover, from a small body which struggled to cater for the needs of coastal wildfowlers,

A staff meeting in the library at Marford Mill in the late 1980s

Anderton's creation had spread its wings – as he always hoped that it would – to oversee every aspect of sporting shooting, and it had a new name which reflected that fact. Anderton never allowed anybody to forget that when he took over WAGBI the association consisted of two suitcases. When he left it, there was a fully owned national headquarters with a newly opened office suite and meeting room annexe, office headquarters in Scotland and Northern Ireland and a developing string of regional offices elsewhere across the UK.

With his rugged, weather-beaten face, piercing blue eyes and that famous vice-like handshake, he was capable of inspiring effort, efficiency and, above all, loyalty, to a degree that is not often met today. Coupled with this extraordinary talent was an intellect which was capable of sizing something or someone up in a moment and then getting the most out of it. But for the space of a few years in the 1950s, the fortunes of WAGBI and BASC had been tied up with the dreams and visions of two men. Now the second of these was to depart, and there was a huge gap to be filled.

John Swift, director and chief executive of BASC since 1988

Naturally BASC Council members had debated amongst each other long and hard the best way of recruiting a new chief executive. Was it to be an outsider, someone who could bring in fresh ideas together, perhaps, with the experience of running another major organisation or business? Or was it to be the promotion from within of someone who knew and understood the sometimes finely balanced issues surrounding BASC and its activities, someone who had a grasp of the politics of shooting and conservation, but who also understood the very special sensitivities of working with volunteers. After months of consideration, Simon Cussons, himself the former managing director of a major national company, had been convinced by the latter. John Swift had been executive director since 1984. He knew BASC's business inside out and had the intellect to steer the association forward into new territories. Just as Anderton had done in the 1950s, he had bridged the divide between the shooters and the science-based conservation movement, to which he could speak with knowledge and authority. Most importantly he had proved himself a formidable negotiator with the power brokers in Whitehall and Brussels. Council approved the appointment of Swift as director designate.

Before his final curtain call at the 1988 annual general meeting, Anderton wrote a stiffly worded letter to his successor, warning him against unseemly gifts, 'wingdings' and sumptuous dinners upon his retirement. The most he wanted was to break open a few bottles of plonk with the staff at Marford Mill. Swift replied: 'If you think you are going to be able to escape on the strength of a few bottles of vin ordinaire, you have misjudged the affections of your friends. All will be well – lie back and enjoy it.'

The AGM itself was a curious union of two halves, for during the business part of the meeting there was the by now almost traditional fractious debate, fuelled of course by the setbacks suffered as a result of the Firearms (Amendment) Act 1988, during which Colin Greenwood called for a third of BASC's resources to be devoted to firearms matters. Then the mood of the meeting changed. John Anderton took the stand to bid farewell to the members, after which he moved into John Swift's seat to the accompaniment of a long and emotional standing ovation. Swift in turn moved into the empty director's chair, and the handover was complete. And while there were indeed several bottles of plonk cracked open and shared between Anderton and the staff, there was of course, as Swift had intimated, much more besides. That autumn, on 7 November at the Army and Navy Club in Pall Mall, Lord Arbuthnott hosted a dinner for Anderton's retirement. Present was HRH The Duke of Edinburgh plus all the senior figures of the shooting and conservation world with whom Anderton had worked, collaborated and sparred over a quarter of a century: Lord Swansea of the British Shooting Sports Council, Sir Derek Barber of the Countryside Commission, Sir Hector Monro MP, Sir Stephen Hastings of the BFSS, William Wilkinson and Max Nicholson of the Nature Conservancy Council and of course many more. It was in every respect a glittering occasion and one worthy of a man who had been WAGBI and BASC's guiding star for so many years.

Chapter 12
BIG BAGS AND BIG BANGS

By converting the redundant stable block behind Marford Mill into a brand new office suite and lecture hall, John Anderton had ensured that BASC would have room in which to breathe and expand its operation into the future. There is no doubt that the investment was a sound one, but in making it, Anderton had spent all of BASC's reserves. As the Duke of Westminster arrived at the Mill on 15 December 1988 to officially open the building and unveil a plaque outside the lecture hall which had been named after him, Barclays Bank was in the process of converting the association's £150,000 bridging loan into a medium term mortgage. That was in addition to the chunky overdraft. For the next couple of years, BASC's finances did not emerge from the red.

Barclays were understanding, however, and appreciated the cyclical nature of BASC's income, which peaked in the autumn when members renewed their subscriptions at the beginning of the shooting season and went through a long, lean period in spring and early summer. At the 1989 annual general meeting Simon Cussons had handed over the chair to John Ruxton, but Cussons was still lending his considerable business and financial expertise to the Executive and Finance Committee in an effort to rebuild the association's resources. He pointed out to the committee that BASC's income was essentially fixed: it could do its best to recruit more members, but unlike a commercial company it could not easily diversify and find new income streams. It must therefore, insisted Cussons, control its expenditure in such a way as to move back towards a break-even position. Income in 1990 was dismal. Shows and draws had been affected by the general economic downturn and the Game Fair at Margam Park, Port Talbot, had produced a very poor cash return which was not helped either by the event's marginal location or the excruciatingly hot weather. Swift was determined to get BASC back into a position of financial security, but things were still looking bleak and, perhaps rashly, he promised that when the finances stayed in the black all year round and there were healthy reserves in the bank once more, he would dance a jig in the car park. Alec Rogers, who had taken over as director of administration upon the retirement of Colin Barwell, carried out a full review of costs, the Executive and Finance Committee anxiously studied the figures at successive meetings, and by early 1991 BASC's new head of finance, Henry Wilson, felt comfortable with the level of loss contained within the audit. In general terms, Cussons was right about the nature of BASC's income, but even he hadn't allowed for the windfall which arrived in the shape of a bequest from Edward Banks, a longstanding and devoted member from Somerset who bequeathed his estate to BASC upon his death. Anderton had been aware of Banks's intentions for some years, but the £200,000 which the legacy produced allowed the loan on the new building to be paid off and enabled the setting up of a new political lobbying operation through Advocacy, the public affairs consultancy run by Fred Silvester who had done so much to help during the Hungerford campaign. It would be easy to surmise that BASC was simply baled out of a hole by the generosity of one benefactor, but although the Banks bequest was hugely important, it would not have solved the association's money problems if it had not been matched by hard focus upon controlling expenditure, financial prudence and good accounting practice. This important lesson was not to be lost upon the management, which went on to build up reserves of £100,000 by the mid 1990s. Banks received his due recognition in the form of the suitably inscribed portrait of himself and his pack of Welsh springer spaniels which hangs today in the Duke of Westminster lecture hall, though in reality his memorial is the building itself and all that goes on within it. Swift was to be reminded of his terpsichorean promise, and he danced his jig in the car park outside Marford Mill.

Money was behind another malaise of the late 1980s and early 1990s. Big city bonuses, the huge explosion of corporate money and the 'yuppie' culture of the Thatcher years had encouraged conspicuous excess in a number of quarters. BMW and Mercedes dealers made a mint, as did champagne merchants and purveyors of all manner of luxury goods. Among the other beneficiaries of the 'big bang', however, were the commercial game shoots. Commercialism in shooting was not new, but the growth in corporate days brought with it a phenomenon which many game shooters found disturbing – that of big bags. Letters started appearing in the sporting press deploring what was happening within game shooting and the rumour mill lurched into action with tales of how obscenely large numbers of pheasants were being shot and the unwanted carcasses buried. Feelings were running high. Nervously the great and the good within the shooting world discussed the subject and decided that something had to be done. But what? With the animal rights movement growing in strength and political sophistication it would be madness to draw attention to obvious and blatant bad practice which could instantly be latched upon to the detriment of shooting. Regulation had to be from within. BASC had already developed and published codes of practice which set standards for various branches of shooting and at the council meeting in September 1988 Michael Fenwick, chairman of the association's game shooting committee, proposed a code of practice for the organisers of game shoots, specifically designed to maintain standards within the sport. Such a code would clearly require agreement with both the BFSS and the Game Conservancy, and it was suggested that a meeting should be held to discuss the matter of commercial game shooting. The meeting with the two other organisations took place early in 1989 and resulted in a joint call for a gathering of commercial shoot proprietors and sporting agents to allow them to put their house in order.

Joint discussions on a code of practice continued but it was not until September that the first draft was submitted by the Game Conservancy. When the text appeared, BASC was not satisfied with the guidance it offered because, in the opinion of the association, it was not firm enough to meet the concerns which were being voiced increasingly within the sporting press and more especially within BASC's own membership. Colin Shedden was commissioned to prepare an internal report examining the whole subject, taking into account the guidelines on Farming for Game which had been produced by the Farming and Wildlife Advisory Group. By May 1990, using the research which had been carried out, John Dryden and a small working party had reached what it regarded as a final draft of its *Guidance for Game and Inland Duck Shooting*, which was sent for consideration by the BFSS and Game Conservancy. Much of what the guidelines said was unexceptional – release dates, stocking rates in release pens, retrieval of wounded and dead game, topping-up – but there was one crucial difference to what the Game Conservancy had proposed: BASC had mentioned the unmentionable. Numbers.

The manner in which it did so was hardly outrageous by today's standards: 'Provided that the correct number of birds have been released before the start of the season, the drives are shot as recommended during the day and rested properly, and the rules of sportsmanship and respect for game are observed, the question of bag numbers should regulate itself. The vast majority of

BASC opens its eastern regional office at West Stow, near Bury St Edmunds, Suffolk

members, however, will enjoy the sport and company that a one-to-two-hundred bird day can produce for six to eight guns, and in many instances a good deal less than that. More and more of our members are coming to the view that a five-hundred bird day is more than enough for any party of guns,' said the guidance.

The result was like a cartoon by H M Bateman. Shock waves reverberated around the upper echelons of game shooting and, not for the first time, the cultural differences which lay entrenched within the shooting world were laid bare for all to see. On one side of the debate stood the field sports establishment, conscious of the enormous value which game shooting provided to rural landowners and managers, and not a few of whose members enjoyed the odd rather large day themselves. On the other stood a mass-market organisation of rough shooters, wildfowlers and syndicate game shooters, most of whom would regard as truly exceptional a day's shooting which resulted in a bag that reached three figures. The row would probably not have been so bad had not *The Times* managed to get hold of the story that, alone among the shooting organisations, BASC was suggesting an upper limit of five hundred birds on a day's game shooting. Once the figure was out in the open, however, *Shooting Times* mischievously ran it in bold type on the magazine's front cover. BASC, it was implied, was proposing bag limits for game shooting.

If the controversy over the concerns which had initiated the guidance was robust, then that which followed its publication was furious. BASC was pilloried for going it alone. Perhaps it had misread the signals or, more likely, failed to take sufficient influential game shooters with it in the course of its deliberations, but it stuck to its guns. 'The numbers issue in game shooting is a nettle that has to be grasped,' said Swift, deploring the controversy which had been stirred up in the sporting press. 'Read the guidelines and code carefully' urged Jack Carter, a member of the working party which had produced the document. 'The figures were suggestions based on members' views, and provisions are made for greater levels of stocking and shooting provided there is no damage to habitat and that management is sound.'

Slowly the controversy died down. However, relations with the BFSS and the Game Conservancy had been damaged, as had those with *Shooting Times*. Indeed, at a meeting with the magazine's editor, Jonathan Young, sharp words were exchanged. Gone was the cosy relationship which had existed in the past, when WAGBI could rely implicitly upon its friends at the 'Shooter' to support the association's line through thick and thin. Now the sporting press was becoming just as sceptical and investigative as any other branch of the media. For his part, Young accused BASC of being obsessed with secrecy and of being slow and flat-footed when it came to meeting his own tight weekly deadlines.

While the five hundred bird limit was buried like those mythical pheasants on a big-bag day, the issue of how to deal with excess and bad practice was not, and the work which was done by all three organisations went on to become refined within the Code of Good Shooting Practice Committee of the mid 1990s, which drew in a much wider range of countryside bodies and which produced the code that has become the accepted 'gold standard' of game shooting. And curiously, when figures were finally produced to guide shoot managers on the size of the bag which they should aim for on a driven day, they were not a million miles from those which BASC had envisaged fifteen years earlier.

Democracy within the governance of BASC had made great strides since the retirement of John Anderton. In the early 1980s the council was still essentially a hand-picked body of supporters, often people whom Anderton had met in the course of his activities; people who he thought might be useful to the association in some way and who had expressed a willingness – or had been persuaded – to help. Election to council was pretty much a formality which could be dealt with at the next annual general meeting, since meetings were only attended by a small number of the faithful that would support pretty much any proposition that was put before them by the management. If there was any glitch, then a potential candidate could in any case be co-opted after the meeting and all would be well. The same was true of the appointment of chairmen, who were elected at the AGM by the membership. Faced with a vacancy caused by the retirement of an incumbent chairman and presented with a candidate who had been groomed by Anderton, the members at the AGM unfailingly did the decent thing. Indeed, the assumption that a particular individual would 'take the chair' after the AGM was quite blatant. For example, when in 1970 John Wardell stepped down as chairman at the annual meeting which was held that year in Norwich, the name of his successor, John Ruxton, was already printed on the menu card for the celebratory dinner on the evening after the meeting.

Growth in membership during the 1980s brought pressure to bear upon cosy arrangements such as these, and while Anderton at first resisted the calls for democracy, he could not continue doing so for ever. The 1984 meeting, with its demand for postal voting for all resolutions at AGM, was something of a watershed in the governance of BASC, and it caused Council to devote much time and effort into the bringing of more membership participation into the association's decision-making process. Postal voting was, in 1984, fiercely resisted by the Council and ultimately defeated on the floor of the meeting, but as always, the issues were brought away and considered in the cool light of day, then acted upon. Council decided that postal voting for resolutions was not the right approach, for many of the issues involved were of such complexity that they could not adequately be decided by means of a simple 'yes' or 'no' on a voting slip by those who had not been exposed to the full debate. Instead Council was attracted to the idea of electing its own members by postal ballot, so that those who were called upon to deliberate over the management of BASC would be much more directly accountable to the membership. Council put the proposal for postal elections to the AGM, it was approved and thereafter as members retired from council, their replacements were decided by full postal ballot. By the mid 1990s, the entire council comprised of members who had been directly elected by the membership.

Postal voting threw up a further issue, that of electing a chairman. With the membership of council now being decided by postal ballot, it was clearly inappropriate for the chairman to continue being elected by a show of hands at the AGM. What would happen if, for instance, a democratically elected council found it impossible to work with a chairman foisted upon them by a cosy clique attending the AGM? To avoid the possibility of a mis-match between council and the chair, a further rule change was approved, allowing council to elect a chairman from amongst its own number. In time, a short council meeting was instituted upon the conclusion of the AGM to elect the chairman and vice chairman, together with the chairmen – and ultimately chairwomen – of the various advisory committees. The process of democratisation was a long and sometimes tortuous one, but there is no doubt that it placed the association in a much stronger political position when dealing with government, statutory agencies and indeed those within the field sports world itself.

Graham Sugget joined council in 1987, one of the first tranche of members to be elected under the new postal voting provisions. Suggett was principal of Warwickshire College of Agriculture at Moreton Morrell, and was to become a staunch supporter of the association who later served as chairman. Naturally he took an interest in getting young people involved in shooting, conservation and land management and indeed the students at Warwickshire College were actively engaged in the management of the shoot on the college farm. In September 1988 he raised the whole question of what more BASC could do for young people. There was a junior category within membership, but not a lot else, and Suggett pointed out that the younger element within the farming community, and especially students at agricultural colleges such as his own, had a natural affinity with BASC and all it stood for. He suggested that the association should have a presence at the Royal Show, Britain's premier agricultural show at Stoneleigh, Warwickshire, and that it should develop a category of membership suitable for the seventeen to twenty-three-year-old age group.

BASC did not at the time have a full-time education officer, but that was remedied in 1990 with the appointment of Stella Rees and Suggett was given the task of liaising between council and the new education department. Stella's principal task was to be that of developing BASC's expansion into the school and youth area, with the aim of developing a junior section. It was not simply a matter of encouraging school children to take a more informed interest in shooting and the countryside, for there was also a keener edge to the involvement of young people. In the aftermath of the 1988 Firearms Amendment Act, the police had taken an increasingly tough line over the granting of shotgun certificates to those under the age of fifteen. Although the law provided no lower age limit for the holding of a certificate, young people of eleven and twelve were being refused certificates purely on grounds of age, while other would-be young shooters were being dealt with in an entirely inappropriate manner, such as being asked to attend interviews at police stations. This was something which concerned the association greatly, for its bottom line was to enable young people actively to take part in shooting sports. Around the country it took an interest in such cases and in April 1990 appeals were lodged in Chelmsford and St Albans against the refusal of the Essex and Hertfordshire forces to grant certificates to young people of good character. Pressure on the police paid off, appeals were allowed and the message started to filter around the firearms licensing departments that young applicants could not simply be dismissed on grounds of their age.

Matters were taken a step further in 1992 when Alan Milburn MP launched a campaign to alter the legislation and restrict by law the possession and use of shotguns by the young. Eleven-year-old Duncan Sinclair-Wills appeared on behalf of BASC in the press and on television. Despite extreme pressure he conducted himself admirably and played a valuable role in resisting the pressure for a change in the law. He received a special award from the association at the 1993 annual general meeting.

Meanwhile, however, Stella Rees was designing and developing a formal programme for BASC juniors. It was named 'Young Shots', and had its own badge and logo. More importantly, it had a whole lot of exciting activities. Courses, clay shooting instruction sessions, training days, visits to gamekeepers and even full-blown weekend camps were held under the Young Shots banner and, naturally, those who had attended Young Shots events found themselves at a distinct advantage when it came to their applying for a shotgun certificate. The launch at the Game Fair 1991 was a big success, and before long Stella was working on a teacher pack for schools which would include a dossier of factual information about shooting and the countryside plus BASC's new video *An Eye for the Country* which featured Norfolk teacher and BASC member Martin

At every game fair or country show, BASC staff took a major part in the drive to increase membership. Colin Shedden signs up a new recruit

Sylvester. He was to become one of the first members of the new education and training committee. Young Shots was, and is, a huge success story. It has brought thousands of young people into shooting, and while some of them would, through family connections, probably have got involved anyway, many others have taken up the sport who would never have done so had it not been for the BASC scheme. Most importantly for the future of shooting, all those who have attended BASC's Young Shots events have been given a thorough grounding in the basics of safety, responsibility and respect for quarry and the countryside.

Despite their fundamental importance in the success and prosperity of game shooting, little had been done to further the lot of gamekeepers since the amalgamation in 1973 with the Gamekeepers' Association. BASC had, through the Gamekeepers Welfare Trust, which it had inherited along with the association itself, made some cash grants to distressed keepers or their families, while two gamekeeper

BASC president Lord Lichfield, chairman Graham Suggett and John Swift at the BASC Gamekeepers' Fair

youth placement schemes were operated by David Leathart while he was with the association. Otherwise the interests of gamekeepers within BASC sat in the doldrums. This was to change as a result of the work of Ian Grindy. Head keeper for Sir John Moores, founder of Littlewoods, at Halsall in Lancashire, Grindy and a small group of his friends were in the habit of travelling around the country at the end of each season to gamekeepers' days on each others' estates. Towards the end of the 1984 season the group was setting the world to rights in the lodge at Tulchan when the talk turned to the representation of the gamekeeping profession. Widely regarded as traditional guardians of the countryside, the keepers themselves realised that, with the considerable power which they wielded within the shooting industry, they had the capability of playing a central role in the promotion of game shooting. Already the moorland gamekeepers were starting to get their own group together, and now the low ground keepers were impatient to follow suit.

Grindy was at the time writing a regular column for *Shooting Times* and this had given him both a wide circle of contacts within the profession and, most importantly, considerable influence. He was therefore the natural focus around which the stirring of political interest amongst gamekeepers was to coalesce, and he decided that a new body needed to be formed, preferably within one of the major organisations. Initially he approached the Game Conservancy but, mindful of the political nature of what he was proposing, they felt that such a group within their ranks could conflict with the organisation's charitable status, so Grindy went instead to BASC. Swift could see the writing on the wall. He was conscious of the position of gamekeeping in relation to the developing political fortunes of shooting and had noticed in particular how issues such as illegal poisoning were increasingly grabbing the media spotlight. He was keen to harness the enthusiasm of such an influential group so, early in 1989 Grindy was invited to join BASC's game shooting committee. By September of that year, a separate gamekeepers' working group had been set up. It was not yet a full-blown committee, but at least the keepers had a base from which to work. Among the early members to join were David Clark, Don Ford, Walter Cole, Brian Mitchell, David Whitby and Derek Vaines, while Grindy's own employer backed him to the hilt by allowing him the time in which to work on behalf of the gamekeeping profession, travelling around the country, visiting other keepers and speaking at the inevitable string of meetings.

Among the first things which the working group did, with the help and support of John Harradine of BASC's research department, was to initiate a gamekeeper survey to determine exactly the extent to which game shooting in general and gamekeeping in particular managed the countryside. The results were impressive. A huge proportion of the British landscape was found to be under the direct influence of gamekeepers, while no less than 80% of Sites of Special Scientific Interest were also under their control. The information, which was extremely valuable to BASC, established the keepers as a major force within the association. BASC's gamekeeper membership started to climb and in 1990 Grindy was elected to BASC council.

During the course of that year, dismay within the gamekeeping profession following the public controversy over publication of BASC's *Guidance for Game and Inland Duck Shooting* nearly upset the applecart altogether. Grindy and the other members of the working group sought a meeting with the association's chairman and vice chairman, John Ruxton and Peter Misselbrook. John Swift and Michael Fenwick, chairman of the game shooting committee, also attended the meeting, which was held at Halsall. Feelings amongst the keepers were running high. They felt overlooked and poorly catered for by the association and some of them wanted to quit altogether and form their own separate body. Grindy, however, felt that the position was not irretrievable and suggested the immediate setting up of a gamekeepers committee within BASC, with himself in the chair. The committee would co-operate with the executive and finance committee to see how gamekeeper services and communications with the profession could be improved, there would be a regular newsletter exclusively for gamekeeper members and, most importantly, BASC's executive would look at employing an experienced gamekeeper to staff and run a game and gamekeeping department as soon as possible.

Every part of the country was to be represented on the new gamekeepers committee, together with special delegates to cover game farming, commercial game shooting and gundog work. Although there were two resignations from the working group, most gamekeepers supported the idea and immediately Grindy set to work building up his committee. By the end of 1992 gamekeeper membership within BASC was showing a 23% growth. Backing for the keepers was provided by Lord Guernsey, who offered to host a gathering at Packington Park, near Coventry, and this event snowballed into an annual spring conference with visiting speakers and its own clay shoot. Gamekeepers had well and truly established themselves as a major force within BASC, a force which rivalled in its level of influence that of the wildfowling clubs themselves, and one which was prepared to flex its muscles. Eventually, in February 1993 after much advertising and readvertising, and after many interviews, Stewart Scull, former head keeper to the Earl of Bradford at Weston Park, joined the staff at Marford Mill to develop BASC's new game and gamekeeping department. It was a high water mark for gamekeeping within the association.

NICK RIDLEY

BASC's Young Shots programme has been one of the association's most successful – and arguably most important – activities of recent years

Clouds were gathering, however, over another vitally important group within the membership of BASC, the pigeon shooters. Prompted by the German Green party, the European Commission was taking a close look at its own legislation, and in 1990 it informed the British Government that the Wildlife and Countryside Act 1981 did not comply with the framework laid down by the European Birds Directive. Specifically, by freely allowing the shooting of 'pest' species – such as the woodpigeon – at any time of the year, Britain was in breach of Article 9 of the Directive. The Department of the Environment called a meeting of interested organisations and, on 17 September, Environment Minister David Trippier MP announced that in order to satisfy Europe's demands he intended to issue a series of general licences permitting the shooting of woodpigeons and other pests, and that these licences would include a close season from 1 March to 30 November. BASC reacted instantly, condemning the proposal which would have devastating implications for some 350,000 British pigeon shooters, not to mention the farmers whose crops they protected. Swift immediately assembled an action group comprising BASC, BFSS and the Game Conservancy, also bringing on board Ian Grindy to advise on the implications for gamekeeping and professional pigeon shooter and *Shooting Times* correspondent John Batley. BASC, meanwhile, had sought expert legal advice from specialists in European law and, armed with the knowledge which the lawyers had provided, were convinced that a close season was not required.

During the course of the autumn, a formidable campaign was mounted. Aided by a series of articles in *Shooting Times*, coverage in the national press and radio, mass meetings of members in Warwickshire and at the Scottish centre at Trochry and a detailed briefing to all affiliated clubs and syndicates, the association started to exert serious pressure on the Government. Letters poured in from members to MPs and to the minister himself and before long Trippier was wondering what a hornets' nest he had stumbled into. The shooters' case was greatly aided by intelligence from Yves Lecocq, director general of FACE in Brussels, who indicated that Europe was in any case looking at the possibility of amending the Directive, and on 15 November Environment Secretary Chris Patten announced to Parliament that he was dropping his proposals. It was a significant victory, but one which had only been won through close understanding of the complex European legislation, harnessing of all the available expertise, joint working with allied organisations and, crucially, massive lobbying support from the membership. Realising the lack of detailed knowledge which existed about woodpigeons and pigeon shooting, John Harradine and John Batley instigated a programme of research which was to pay dividends as political debate about pigeon and corvid shooting rumbled on and when, two years later, the Government finally introduced its open general licences for pest bird species, there was no mention of close seasons.

Chapter 13

TO MERGE, OR TO DEVOLVE?

*A*fter more than ten years in power, Margaret Thatcher's Conservative Government was, by 1990, faltering badly at the opinion polls. Field sports had always regarded themselves as being relatively safe in the hands of the Conservatives and much – some would say too much – of their combined effort as election time approached had traditionally been spent in ensuring that friendly blue hands were there to greet them once the polls closed. But with Thatcher ousted as party leader and her successor, John Major, beset on all sides by his political opponents, it was clear to the management of BASC that there was a need to address the possibility of a change of government.

The Council for Country Sports, by now a loose federation comprising a large number of country sports organisations, was clearly lacking in political edge. While the CCS had sufficed back in 1982, BASC was no longer happy with its performance or direction and felt that, if it was going to survive, it at least needed a formal constitution. BASC's vice chairman Peter Misselbrook, an astute Scottish lawyer with a fresh and lively turn of mind, agreed to chair a working party to consider an alternative form of governance for the CCS, but his recommendations for a smaller, more focussed and closer knit organisation did not find favour with the other parties. As ever, at the heart of the problem were the cultural differences between BASC and the BFSS, together with the inevitable competition between the two organisations for shooting membership. This competition was regarded within BASC council as obvious and understandable, if undesirable, and although a number of attempts were made to address the problem, it was deep rooted and was never satisfactorily solved.

As the 1992 general election approached, BASC threw its weight behind the CCS common front which was designed to defend all field sports but principally hunting with hounds, the activity which was regarded as being at the greatest risk. At the same time, however, BASC ran its own parallel campaign specifically on shooting and conservation issues. Already it had dipped its toe into the party conferences by running occasional fringe meetings and now, with conservation, agriculture and land use issues featuring strongly in the media, it was decided that the association should have a presence at all three major party conferences. Particularly successful was the fringe meeting at the Labour conference in 1991, the feedback from which had indicated that shooting was not currently an issue amongst Labour MPs. Their concern was rather to do their best to get BASC to distance itself from hound sports. In this they failed, with BASC making it quite clear that that while it was a shooting and conservation body, it would nevertheless support hunting in line with its commitment to the CCS.

The relationship between BASC and Labour had troubled those at the BFSS's Kennington Road headquarters who feared, understandably enough, that the Labour party's traditional opposition to hunting with hounds could one day lead to an anti-hunting Bill being given government backing. Suspicion over BASC's links with Labour was not new, indeed John Anderton had, back in WAGBI days, been challenged by the BFSS with being a closet socialist whose objective was to support the nationalisation of land and sporting rights in order that the typical WAGBI members could be allowed shooting opportunities they had never previously dreamed of. Whilst that particular suggestion had been nothing short of ludicrous, BASC nevertheless had large numbers of Labour supporters amongst its membership, especially in the north of England, and when it was approached with a view to giving its support to canvassing for the Conservatives prior to the 1992 general election, it declined, reaffirmed its political non-alignment and pointed out that its support or otherwise for individual candidates would be judged not by the colour of the rosette which they happened to be wearing, but their attitude towards field sports. Over twelve hundred letters were written to election candidates by BASC members in an effort to obtain their personal commitment to field sports, especially shooting, and the results were co-ordinated by Marford Mill in order that the bulk of the membership could be given guidance on their voting intentions. In the event of another attempt to ban hunting, BASC council agreed that it would fight any Bill on the grounds of freedom of choice. There was no question of any deal with the anti-hunters: council recognised that the animal rights movement was just as violently opposed to shooting as it was to hunting with hounds. They had every reason to do so, for on 25 January 1991 the Animal Liberation Front had fire-bombed Marford Mill, destroying a portacabin behind the main office complex and prompting a full security review.

Firefighters attended Marford Mill on 25 January 1991 to extinguish a blazing portacabin following an arson attack. Responsibility was later claimed by the Animal Liberation Front

GRAHAM DOWNING

BASC chairman Peter Misselbrook (right) with Mrs Marie Anne Zarina, Counsellor of the Embassy of Latvia, at the CLA Game Fair, Cornbury Park in 1994. Mrs Zarina visited the BASC stand to support a donation by the Wildlife Habitat Trust toward wildfowl conservation at Lake Engure in Latvia, an important breeding site for pochard, tufted duck and shoveler

Confounding the pollsters, John Major won the 1992 election and installed another Conservative Government. This may have been a relief to many in the field sports world, but it only postponed yet again the matter of tackling the perennial problem of what to do with the CCS, which was still the formal basis for co-operation between the major campaigning field sports groups. Misselbrook, now BASC chairman, revisited the review which he had chaired and insisted that the body needed a non-partisan chairman, an independent secretariat and sufficient funds with which to mount any political campaign. He agreed to pay BASC's £8,000 share of the CCS election campaign costs, but advised that unless there was movement on reform or that a future policy for such movement could be agreed between the chairmen of BASC and BFSS, this cash would be the last to come from Marford Mill's coffers.

In May 1992, however, there was a new development in the continuing relationship between the two organisations, for Misselbrook was approached by the Earl Peel with the suggestion that BASC and BFSS might merge together into a single body. This proposal was backed by a discussion paper from Bill Andrewes, chairman of the Campaign for Hunting. Conversations between the two parties, and especially between Misselbrook and the incoming chairman of the BFSS, Charles Goodson-Wickes, continued over the next two years. At Kennington Road chief executives came and went and eventually whispers started to spread of a possible amalgamation. Initially the idea had some appeal, but by early 1995 negotiations foundered over the transfer of the Society's financial liabilities to BASC, which was itself only just emerging from years of debt and which had needed to work very hard indeed in order to get its books straight. Council debated the matter of co-operation and convergence in its entirety on 15 March 1995. It considered a series of options, ranging from the status quo, through various partnerships within such bodies as a revitalised CCS or FACE UK, right through to merger in one of a number of different ways, concluding that whilst co-operation and joint lobbying was essential, it was opposed to the creation of a single merged organisation and its associated transfer of undertakings. So far as BASC council was concerned, merger was off the menu.

Misselbrook immediately gave co-operation a high strategic priority and to underline this, Stewart Scull joined the joint working party on hunting and shooting convened by the Masters of Fox Hounds Association and the Game Conservancy while BASC's new head of communications, Robin Peel, co-ordinated a joint lobbying campaign with the BFSS over the anti-hunting Private Member's Bill introduced by John McFall MP. Three months later, the new BFSS chief executive, Robin Hanbury-Tenison, visited Marford Mill with the news that the Society was going to form a broad 'Countryside Alliance' of rural interests and launch a shooting initiative, which would include a fund raising exercise. Swift received a message from Lord Stockton, inviting BASC to become part of this initiative which was to be known as the Campaign for Shooting.

Swift set out BASC's stall on its external relationships at the 1995 AGM. 'BASC stands four square with other country sports,' he said. 'It will support joint lobbying initiatives to combat the threats to any country sport and will work actively towards common goals of joint co-operation.' This was not sufficient for one member who was in attendance: Richard Tice called for the merger debate to be reopened and for a national referendum to be held. A letter arrived from his solicitors seeking access to BASC's entire membership list and the opportunity to place advertisements in the association's magazine *Shooting & Conservation* calling for a merger referendum. Both requests were declined by BASC council, whereupon Tice took the matter to court. With the question of merger now in the hands of the lawyers, it was starting to look less like a proposal of marriage and more like an attempt at a hostile takeover. BASC resisted, and resolved to let the dispute go to trial. Legal wrangling dragged on for nearly a year, with Tice pursuing his action all the way to the High Court, but in the end he failed to win either of his claims and the case was concluded at no cost to BASC.

This was not the end of the matter, however, for at the 1996 AGM Tice, who had run a pro-merger campaign in the sporting press, proposed yet again a referendum on the subject, whilst his colleague Colin Tett tabled a resolution to allow proxy voting at general meetings. In addition, Tice put himself forward for election to council. There was no doubt that the meeting was going to be a big one, and arrangements at Warwickshire College were attended to in every last detail, with a marquee erected to seat one thousand members and careful, courteous but firm stewarding on hand to prevent any irregular entry through the fire exits. After long debates, both Tice's and Tett's motions were overwhelmingly defeated, while of the 3,286 ballot forms received in the council election, Tice polled just 867 votes, not enough to get himself elected. Graham Suggett summed up the mood when he expressed the view that the merger proposals had generated bad feelings and unnecessary divisions where there should have been harmony for the common good of field sports. It had been damaging that the debate should have been carried on in public with its attendant acrimony, litigation and squabbling, said Suggett. But it was not the end of co-operation, for John Pullen of Devon Wildfowlers' Association introduced yet another resolution which supported the decision of council to work closely with the BFSS and other organisations whilst continuing as an independent shooting and conservation body. Pullen added the rider that all moneys and reserves which had been raised by WAGBI/BASC were to be used for the development and defence of sporting shooting. His resolution was passed overwhelmingly, and the merger debate was effectively closed.

Merger had taken up an enormous amount of time and energy, but shooting sports had other matters to attend to, for on the morning of 13 March 1996 Thomas Hamilton, a disturbed loner who nursed a range of grievances against society, had entered Dunblane Primary School and in the space of just under five minutes murdered sixteen children and their teacher with firearms for which he held a certificate granted to him by Central Scotland Police. Public revulsion and repugnance at the crime swept the nation and the shock waves echoed all over the world: how could such a thing be allowed to happen? How could a deranged man find himself in lawful possession of firearms? Why should anyone be allowed to own such things at all?

Colin Shedden, who had taken over as BASC's Scottish director in September 1994 on the departure of David Cant, was standing in front of one hundred Scottish gamekeepers at Scone Palace when the telephone call came through from Swift. A number of the keepers were from the Dunblane area and some even had children at local primary schools. It was hard for any of them to believe that such a thing could have happened, but the enormity of the event sunk in soon enough.

Bill Harriman, BASC's director of firearms and an eminent authority on antique weapons' demonstrates the procedure for discharging a matchlock musket to an enthralled audience at the Midland Game Fair

BASC had two jobs to do. On the one hand it had to deal with the press and on the other it had to prepare for the inevitable political reaction. Mass communications had moved a long way since the time of the Hungerford tragedy in 1986. Media reaction to the Dunblane shootings was immediate and relentless and for the first time, BASC was caught up in a '24/7' news story which demanded instant decisions from Robin Peel and his press officer Lesley Ferguson. The two worked closely with their London public affairs consultancy, Advocacy, to deal with the tidal wave of demands from the media for comment and interviews. Meanwhile Bill Harriman, head of firearms, addressed the political fallout.

Little more than a week after the shootings, Parliament resolved to appoint a public inquiry, and Lord Cullen's investigation occupied the following six months. Shedden attended every single day of the public hearings at Stirling and reported back at the close of each day's session to Marford Mill by fax – at that time the most immediate way of communicating the written word – copying his daily reports to Pat Johnson, Secretary of the British Shooting Sports Council. Once more, BSSC was faced with co-ordinating the response from the shooting organisations, and it appointed as its lawyer Mark Scoggins, who had great experience of dealing with public inquiries, having been involved with that which followed the Piper Alpha disaster in the North Sea. Whilst the immediate heat was upon the private possession of handguns, Swift was fully aware of the gravity of the threat which faced all forms of shooting. 'This is a defining moment for shooting sports,' he told the executive and finance committee on 18 April. 'BASC should be acting firmly and decisively by giving its unequivocal support to BSSC. The defence of shooting in the present political environment is essential.' The committee responded by pledging £40,000 to the campaign. Shooters pinned their hopes on the Cullen Inquiry. They supported it with high quality evidence and expected that its response would be proportionate, not punitive.

It was not Cullen's findings, however, which turned the political tide against gun ownership, but the report of the House of Commons Home Affairs Committee. Under the chairmanship of Sir Ivan Lawrence MP, the committee ran its own inquiry into the possession of handguns, concluding on 24 July, two months before Cullen was due to report, that a ban on handguns was not the answer and that instead, more stringent procedures should be implemented for the licensing of firearms. It was not what the press wanted to hear and the Conservative members of the Committee, who supported the report, were torn to shreds in the tabloid newspapers. It is one of life's great mysteries why the committee chose to undertake its investigation whilst Lord Cullen already had his own public inquiry underway. Perhaps the prospect of being seen to address a matter of such huge public interest appealed to a group of MPs who knew that they would shortly have to fight a very difficult election. If so, then the publicity backfired badly upon them. The Government quickly realised the scale of the mauling that it would receive at the hands of the press if it did not opt for a ban in some shape or form, and by the time that Cullen reported on 30 September, his conclusion – that consideration should be given to restricting the possession of self-loading pistols and revolvers, preferably by their disablement when not in use – was, in political terms, largely irrelevant. The tidal wave of anti-gun hysteria in the media re-started and John Major's lame and limping Government found itself in a bidding war with Tony Blair's Labour Opposition over who would ban most handguns.

Even the Sports Council froze its support for shooting, and during the autumn Harriman and his BSSC colleagues worked feverishly to extend exemptions from the proposed ban for pistols that were required in various specific situations. BASC's executive and finance committee had stressed that there was a legitimate place for pistols in country shooting and that it must protect the right to use such firearms on behalf of its members, so they particularly backed amendments such as those which permitted pistols for the humane dispatch of animals and for pest control. BSSC battled in vain to move amendments on 'disassembly' – Cullen's preferred option whereby the cylinders or slides of pistols for target shooting would be removed and stored separately in secure accommodation in shooting clubs when not in use. Until the last moment it seemed as though the disassembly proposal, which would have averted an outright ban, might be acceptable to the Lords, but eventually even this last straw slipped from the pistol shooters' clutches and the Bill received Royal Assent early in 1997. Labour's procedural move for a total ban which would include .22 rimfire pistols was a portent of what was to come after the next general election, but Lesley Ferguson was struck by another manifestation which emerged from the Dunblane campaign – that of shooters marching through the streets of London. The rally in Hyde Park and the subsequent march up Piccadilly to Trafalgar Square on 23 February 1997 was organised by the newly-formed Sportsmans' Association of Great Britain and was attended by large numbers of BASC members, plus two regional officers. Prospects of a pistol ban had galvanised shooters to demonstrate and march in public, and the comment was made that perhaps if wildfowlers or game shooters were placed in a similar situation then they would react in the same way too. Certainly the BFSS was watching closely, for it had plans for a similar event just five months later to support the beleaguered sport of hunting.

During the course of the 1990s BASC's regional structure grew apace. Membership was now in excess of 110,000 and there was a constant job to be done in servicing the members'

David Myles (left) with BASC council member Jack Carter, who went on to become the association's chairman

requirements, organising shows and membership events and, increasingly, lobbying local authorities and constituency MPs. Regionalisation was further stimulated by the growing mood for political devolution which was sweeping both Scotland and Wales. Tony Laws, now deputy director, had held the reins in Scotland between the departure of David Cant and the appointment of Colin Shedden, and by the time of the 1994 AGM, which was held in Perthshire, he was able to report on a range of new work programmes which were being undertaken by the staff at Trochry. Estuary strategies, and in particular the Scottish Natural Heritage 'Focus on Firths' initiative, had been dealt with at the Scottish wildfowling conference in Inverness, while Colin Shedden's three-year study on deer in Scotland had highlighted the fact that the amateur stalker was now making a major input into Scottish deer management. Goose shooting was still an issue and development of a BASC approved goose guide scheme was proceeding, with a training course and licensing arrangement which would be administered by the association. Copies of a code of practice had been printed in English, French and Italian for distribution to visiting shooters. BASC was determined to stamp out bad practice and to set and maintain standards in goose shooting, and already forty individuals had completed the training and were prepared for certification as BASC approved goose guides.

Scottish members, however, were becoming unhappy about the constitutional manner in which their affairs were represented within BASC's governing body. Following his retirement from Marford Mill, Brian Hughes had moved north of the border and had been elected to council, where he became a well-respected chairman of the Scottish Advisory Committee. But while it was all very well having their interests represented by a Scottish resident who happened to have a council seat, what the grass roots Scottish members really wanted was a dedicated Scottish council seat to be voted for solely by Scots. The debate at the AGM was not unlike that which was taking place in the country at large, and while it was pointed out that the Scots could always put up their own candidate for election and then, just as other interest groups such the wild-fowlers and gamekeepers had done, ensure he was elected, the hare of regional representation on council was afoot and running.

Development of regional centres continued in England. Late in 1992 the executive and finance committee approved the development of property leased by BASC at Gisburn, Lancashire, for the improvement of Philip Pugh's Northern regional headquarters, while Alan Thomas was appointed as the first South East regional officer two years later. A regional office for Wales and the West Midlands had been established in the old railway station at Caersws, Powys, in December 1989 following a lengthy period of negotiation with the British Rail Property Board, and Glynn Cook had taken up the post of regional officer. By 1994 it was, however, becoming clear that Wales too was moving swiftly towards devolution, and Cook pointed out that there would be much sense in creating a separate Welsh identity, with Wales and the

BASC's South West regional office at Smokey Botton Lodge, near Taunton in Somerset

The Midlands regional office at the Doveridge shooting ground near Ashbourne in Derbyshire was opened in 1999

border counties only being served from Caersws and the remainder of his territory being added to an enhanced Midlands region. Marford Mill was of course situated within Wales, and little thought had previously been given to an independent Welsh office, but the idea now took root and in March 1998 a separate BASC Wales was set up. A Welsh advisory committee was created the following year under the chairmanship of John Graham, chairman of both the Dee Wildfowlers and the North Wales Joint Council. The following year Carl Cox moved into a new Midlands regional office at the Doveridge shooting ground near Ashbourne in Derbyshire.

Deer stalking was by now reckoned to be the fastest growing branch of shooting and it was estimated that even within BASC's membership there were as many as 14,500 deer stalkers, with another 20,000 non-stalking members expressing interest in the sport. Curiously enough, deer stalking had been given an added boost by the banning of pistols in 1997, for many dispossessed pistol shooters did not want to give up their firearm certificates altogether and decided to explore rifle shooting instead. Competitive target shooting was a natural home for some of them, but others were lured by the challenge of hunting wild game with a rifle. Training all these newcomers to the sport to stalk responsibly, humanely and above all, safely, was an issue which exercised the minds of all in the deer world in the mid 1990s, especially in England where there was no long tradition of stalker education. Peter Watson, BASC's deer officer, outlined his thoughts to the executive and finance committee in October 1996 and a long discussion ensued, resulting in

BASC's participation in a working group alongside the BFSS, British Deer Society, Game Conservancy and Red Deer Commission, the aim of which was to develop a system of stalker training which would be acceptable to professional and sporting organisations alike, and which would be appropriate both to the professional deer manager and the recreational stalker, who was taking responsibility for an ever-increasing proportion of the national deer cull. The British Deer Society had launched its own Woodland Stalker's Competence Certificate in 1982 and this had two years later been upgraded to the National Stalker's Competence Certificate to serve both the woodland and hill stalking interests. The NSCC had grown in stature and respect, but now a more comprehensive body was needed which could independently administer a system of qualifications which would continue to be delivered by the individual membership organisations, and indeed by others. Two Deer Stalking Certificate (DSC) awards were envisaged, along the lines of other national vocational qualifications: Level 1, which would be an entry level qualification broadly similar to the old NSCC; and Level 2, designed for the more experienced stalker and especially the stalking professional. What was needed now was an awarding body, an administrative and financial base and an assessor structure. The upshot was to be a new company, Deer Management Qualifications, which was established at Marford Mill in 1998 under a structure which was agreed with BASC's partner organisations. The first twelve months for DMQ proved to be a steep learning curve, and the amount of management time involved in administering DSC2 in particular was far greater than had been expected, but by the end of the century the new process of administration for stalker training was beginning to function effectively, with two thousand registrations for Level 1 and one thousand for Level 2. The DSC system went on to achieve recognition from every organisation involved in deer management, from the Government and its agencies such as the Forestry Commission to the voluntary nature conservation bodies like the RSPB and the Wildlife Trusts.

Co-operation in the deer world took a further step forward with the creation in 2000 of the Deer Initiative. When the Government's proposal to create an administrative structure for deer management in England was first broached by Tony Laws to BASC council in January of that year, it was realised that the DI's aims – improvement of public understanding of deer management and the promotion of best practice amongst deer stalkers – overlapped closely with those of BASC, and council quickly agreed to pay the £1,000 joining fee, detailing Laws to join the working group which was drafting the Initiative's 'articles of faith', the Deer Accord. BASC became a founder member of the Deer Initiative, and deer and deer stalking remain one of the association's core areas of activity.

Chapter 14
LEAD, PIGEONS AND PESTS

Since the time that hunters first employed firearms to kill birds, they had used lead shot. Lead was the most efficient substance available: it was effective, it had a low melting point and so could easily be made into shotgun pellets, and it was cheap. What was not appreciated at the time that wildfowlers first started to creep around the fens and marshes with shotguns, however, was that lead could have damaging effects if it was ingested by waterfowl. WAGBI was aware of the potential problem from an early date, indeed it was first raised by Lord Mansfield in his president's introduction to the WAGBI Annual Report in 1960. By 1974, levels of lead ingestion were being found on the Ouse washes similar to those which were already having political repercussions in the United States, but it was not until the late 1980s that the issue really started to become a serious one for wildfowl shooting in Britain. As John Anderton handed over to his successor, John Swift was only too well aware of the fact that Danish hunters were having to replace lead with non-toxic alternatives and that it would not be many months before similar changes were to face the Dutch. BASC did not accept at the time that there was a conservation problem arising from lead, but the matter was already being raised in Parliament and accurate, up-to-date information was needed, both on the scale of the problem and on the performance and efficacy of the potential alternatives.

John Harradine's research department was tasked with trawling the scientific literature and establishing exactly what the facts were. BASC's objective at the beginning of the 1990s was to retain the initiative so as to stand at least some chance of controlling the pace and extent of any change, thereby ensuring that it took account of genuine need rather than merely responding to unsubstantiated alarmism. One important job was to search for suitable alternatives to lead, for although there was practical experience with steel shot gained in the US, it was recognised that the shotguns used by European shooters tended to be rather different to the heavy barrelled semi-autos which were popular amongst American waterfowlers. Other ramifications quickly became apparent: what would be the impact of using non-lead alternatives in 'best' game guns, large bore shotguns, damascus barrels, punt guns? The need for information seemed endless, so in 1991 Harradine set up a series of trials at the Leicestershire WA's clay shooting ground at Kibworth, giving a number of experienced shooters the chance to try a range of non-lead cartridges – mostly high performance steel loads imported from the US. Increasing pressure on the use of lead shot was coming from Europe and also from the conservation organisations in Britain, but at the same time, Harradine was becoming aware of American reports demonstrating increased levels of wounding with steel. Was one conservation problem simply being traded off for another? Clearly there was an important balance to be struck.

Events in Europe were, however, moving very rapidly, and a crucial turning point occurred at a conference in Brussels on lead shot and waterfowl that took place in 1991. Speaker after speaker reinforced the conservation threat posed by lead, and BASC's Colin Shedden found himself in a minority of one when, in his presentation, he expressed the view that a ban on lead

BASC's work on shotgun ballistics grew out of the political issues surrounding lead shot. Bettina Markussen and Dr John Harradine conduct research into lethality and wounding using ballistic gelatine

would simply be a disproportionate response to the problem. Back in Britain, the Department of the Environment convened a meeting to discuss lead shot in wetlands and its effect upon water-fowl, and set up a working group to consider the UK's response. Whilst participating in the ongoing political discussions, Harradine at the same time set up a programme of research into the ballistics of lead and its alternatives. Although there existed a huge amount of historical informa-tion about the patterning of lead shotgun cartridges, very little research had been carried out into how a shot cloud actually travels through the air, and the way that pellet mass, muzzle velocity, barrel wall friction and a host of other variables subtly interplay with one another in order to deliver the energy of the burning propellant to the target. Harradine obtained the support of Holland & Holland, set up a test rig at the company's shooting ground in north-west London and conducted trials with lead, steel and bismuth, which was by now emerging as a potential alternative material. With the political pace against lead hotting up, BASC council decided that its duty was to help the shooting industry find a range of non-toxic, commercially viable, effective and safe alternatives which would enable the association to support the Government's latest proposal – a voluntary two-year moratorium on the use of lead over wetlands starting in September 1995. Council was determined, however, to ensure that the continuing process of change remained a voluntary one so far as was possible.

That possibility came to a rude end in June 1996 with the signing in The Hague of the Agreement on the Conservation of African-Eurasian Migratory Waterbirds, which included within its text, agreed to by the British Government, a pledge to phase out the use of lead shot in wetlands by the year 2000. Already the rumblings of discontent and dissatisfaction could be heard from the wildfowling clubs, and these were voiced in council by Alan Jarrett of Kent Wildfowlers, chairman of the wildfowling liaison committee. Viable alternatives were not yet available, said Jarrett. Moreover, there was a wide perception amongst fowlers that BASC had sold them down the river. But it was not just wildfowlers who would be concerned, pointed out Jack Carter: game shooting in sensitive wetlands was just as liable to be affected and BASC needed to investigate more ways in which to inform game shooters about lead replacement. Publicity from Marford Mill about lead shot and its alternatives increased substantially and the matter became a regular subject of heated debate at wildfowling and gamekeeping conferences and in the sporting press. BASC realised that improved communication to the entire shooting community was essential, but was starting to learn that this in turn meant that it became the bearer of an exceedingly unpalatable message. And as with all bearers of bad tidings, it was the messenger that was liable to be the one who got shot.

When the agreed two-year voluntary restraint period finished in 1997, BASC and the other shooting organisations played for time and sought a further extension, arguing that sufficient viable alternatives were not yet in place to allow a general move away from lead in wetlands. But they were under no illusion about prospects for a change in the law, and in May 1998 the Department of Environment, Transport and the Regions (DETR) confirmed that legislation would be introduced as soon as parliamentary time permitted. Marford Mill immediately convened a 'think tank' of staff and wildfowling representatives to decide upon the most acceptable and effective way forward. Four options were considered: a ban on lead over wetlands; a ban on shooting waterfowl with lead; a hybrid ban on lead over designated wetlands only plus the shooting of waterfowl with lead; and a ban on lead altogether. Debate was intense, and strong words were exchanged as those present wrestled with the problem of how to address the shooting of wildfowl over flight ponds which were outside the boundaries of SSSIs. Shooting pressure over such ponds was known to be considerable, and mainstream wildfowlers were bitter at the prospect of their having to shoulder the burden of change alone whilst the inland flight pond shooters escaped the legislation. Ministers were known to have no stomach for a complete ban on lead, so option three was the one which found favour. Council concluded that it had to pursue an effective and fair replacement programme over both coastal and inland wetlands which addressed the issue of lead shot poisoning whilst introducing the minimum of restrictions, and it agreed to put a hybrid wording forward to DETR.

Government issued its proposals on 8 April 1999 and a month later, council considered them in detail. BASC staff had undertaken an exhaustive consultation: detailed briefs had been submitted to all the association's relevant advisory committees and to every affiliated club and shooting syndicate, legal interpretations had been sought, meetings had been held with DETR and the lead shot advisory group which consisted of the Countryside Alliance, Game Conservancy Trust, Gun Trade Association, Shooting Sports Trust, CLA and NFU, and no fewer than 17 regional meetings of BASC members had been held, attracting over 600 individual members, 78 clubs and 61 syndicates. The prospect of a ban on lead over foreshores and SSSIs had been generally expected, but the species ban had been neither anticipated nor was it liked, while there was universal dismay over DETR's proposals for enforcement, which raised the spectre of non-Government 'interested parties' being authorised to police the ban. BASC realised that since the instrument for change which the Government had selected – a Regulation under the Environmental Protection Act 1990 – was unlikely to be modified a great deal, it resolved to attempt to mitigate the worst aspects of the proposals whilst ensuring so far as it could that the forthcoming ban could not be allowed to 'creep' into other areas of shooting. It thus argued for a better list of sites based on agreed criteria, the deletion of snipe and golden plover from the list of species which could not be shot with lead, agreement that the police only would enforce the new law, exemptions for pest control and more open definitions for acceptable alternatives. The Regulation was signed on 29 July 1999 and came into force for the start of the wildfowl shooting season on 1 September.

While those wildfowlers who had voluntarily moved away from lead since 1995 accepted the new law with relatively good grace, BASC took a great deal of criticism from those whom a decade and more of increasing debate about lead shot had passed by. Could it have done more – should it have done more – to prevent the ban? As an ethical shooting organisation, BASC's philosophy was that it had to do what was right for the long term future of both the sport and the quarry species upon which it relied. From the early 1990s it had been apparent that change would come sooner or later, so BASC committed itself to ensuring that change was as informed as possible and that it did not come before viable alternatives to lead were available. There can be little doubt that in running its intensive programme of research it helped to stay the hand of Government until the gun and cartridge industry was more or less prepared, but equally, despite the huge amount of publicity, large sections of the shooting community were not expecting that change would affect them. If there was any area in which more might have been done, it was in that of informing the wider shooting public.

Over the next few years, BASC and its partner organisations on the Lead Shot Working Group succeeded in having the snipe and golden plover dropped from the species list, while Harradine ensured that the schedule of sites to which the Regulation applied comprised only those to which strict scientific criteria applied. In due course the legislation, which had initially covered only England, was extended to other parts of the UK.

While big issues like the replacement of lead shot and the struggle over the Firearms Bill dominated BASC's activities in the latter part of the 1990s, there was a host of other initiatives on the boil, several of them emanating from the conservation department. Much of the department's workload was devoted to maintaining shooting opportunity for BASC members over areas of high conservation importance, and in particular the coastal wetlands over which the association had a long legacy of interest. Since John Anderton's agreement with the Crown Estates Commissioners in the early 1960s, BASC members and affiliated wildfowling clubs had enjoyed access to Crown foreshore on a largely unregulated basis. Those carefree days were coming to an end, however, and in 1997 the Crown proposed a cessation of the general agreement with BASC and its replacement with a series of properly controlled leases. Now clubs would be obliged to strike local agreements with the Crown and pay an annual rental for their sporting rights based on the length of shoreline which they sought to shoot over. Clubs were given greater control over the foreshore, for the lone fowler would no longer have the right, simply as a BASC member, to shoot on intertidal land that was owned by the Crown. But with rights came responsibilities, and along with annual rents came management agreements and bag returns. Anxiously, wildfowling clubs joined the scramble with local and national conservation groups for control over the last remaining stretches of unregulated Crown foreshore, and as a member of the Crown's Joint Tidal Group, BASC found that there was a great deal of hand-holding to be done in order that affiliated clubs could maintain shooting over their traditional areas.

It would be a great mistake to think that the department's entire caseload related to wildfowling and wetlands. Even the major national conservation bodies were aware of the very considerable benefits which shooting could lend to the management of the wider countryside, and BASC recognised that in its large and active membership it had literally tens of thousands of individuals running thousands of individual small shoots, many of which were making a positive impact on rural biodiversity. The conservation department decided that this contribution was worth quantifying and so the 'Green Shoots' programme was born. Based initially in Cheshire, the Green Shoots project used detailed mapping systems to plot the land managed by BASC members in the county, to identify the landscape elements which shooting had enhanced and the species – both quarry and non-quarry alike – which benefited from their work. The project forged new links with local wildlife trusts and these were extended into other areas of common interest, such as the campaign to halt the decline of water voles on river systems in the south-west of England. BASC gamekeepers supplied the expertise in trapping the mink which were largely responsible for the water vole's decline while shooters and conservationists worked together to restore local habitats.

Upland land management, which was the focus of intense political debate because of its implications for issues such as countryside access and the illegal killing of raptors, was also a matter of great interest to BASC, and in 1997 it received an approach from North West Water to enter into a joint agreement to manage Arnfield moor in Cheshire as a demonstration site where grouse moor management and conservation work could be developed hand in hand. Tony Laws

*The Green Shoots project has helped many BASC members to make their own shoots more attractive to game and wildlife. Biodiversity officer Ian Danby (*centre*) advises members on controlling reed mace*

Green Shoots demonstrates shooting's conservation credentials to politicians. On 14 September 2004 the project was launched in North Wales. (left to right) BASC biodiversity officer Ian Danby; Glenda Thomas, FWAG Cymru; Carwyn Jones, Welsh Assembly Minister for Environment, Planning and Countryside; Joanna Robertson, Countryside Council for Wales; BASC director of conservation Tim Russell

and John Phillips of the Heather Trust produced a full management plan and agreed to sublet the sporting rights to a sympathetic tenant. Their proposals included a public information centre, opportunities for scientific research and the chance to establish closer links with the farming community. Council backed the plan and agreed unanimously that the Arnfield project should go ahead. It lasted for just three years. The annual cost of managing the moor had been considerable and the original sporting tenant had pulled out. While a second syndicate was keen to be involved, the complexities of the project and the responsibility which they placed on BASC eventually became more than the benefits to be gained.

Just as gundogs are a central feature of the shooting scene, they have always been an important aspect of the association's activities. Gundog events have been run at countless shows and country fairs from the WAGBI Safaris of the 1970s onward, while BASC's honorary gundog adviser Roy Jordan was always on hand to dispense support and advice to members. A rather special arena of gundog interest took a more central role, however, during the mid 1990s with the reorganisation of the gamekeepers' ring at Crufts. The first supporters of the world's greatest dog show were shooting sportsmen, and for decades after Crufts achieved much wider popularity the original gamekeepers' classes were maintained, though at a low key. When WAGBI took over the old Gamekeepers' Association in 1973 the classes continued to be organised by members of the association's old committee, but in 1989 they decided to call it a day and BASC agreed to take over. Unlike the remainder of the classes at Crufts, the gamekeepers' classes are structured not on the basis of adherence to breed standards, but instead they enable professional gamekeepers to exhibit in the show ring the dogs which they use for beating and picking up throughout the shooting season. Thus the gamekeepers' ring is the only place at Crufts where it is possible to see dogs that have been bred not purely for show, but for their working abilities. There is also the added attraction of watching the dogs and the professional keepers from some of the country's most prestigious estates, including the royal estates of Windsor and Sandringham. While Crufts continued to be held during the shooting season the gamekeepers' classes were thinly attended, but in the mid 1990s the show moved to a new date in March and switched venues to Birmingham's National Exhibition Centre. At the same time it achieved huge new public interest through television, and this opened up big new opportunities to promote working gundogs to a mainstream public audience. BASC's south-west regional office under John Dryden took a central role in developing the gamekeepers' classes into an important public platform for working gundogs, and in 1997 new classes were added for pickers-up, with teams competing against each other representing shooting estates from all over the country. The range of breeds exhibited in the game-keepers' classes also increased to encompass not only the traditional retrievers and spaniels but the new hunt point retrieve breeds, with dogs worked on both deer and small game being shown side by side, making Crufts a firm fixture in the BASC calendar.

Nick Lyle was elected chairman in January 1998. An accountant with an extensive business background, Lyle had a direct and forceful personality that did not suffer fools gladly, but he also had an unswerving determination to ensure that BASC got its financial and administrative house in order. Reserves had been drained the previous year during the long and exhausting battle with the Government over its new firearms legislation. Lyle regarded it as a priority to rebuild them as quickly as possible, and this he did. Despite the feeling that many areas of membership recruitment were now at saturation point, and with numbers of shotgun and firearm certificate holders on the decline, BASC buttressed its membership by working to ensure that existing members continued to rejoin. By April 1998 membership retention had reached 98%, up 3% on the previous year, and membership itself had climbed to one hundred and twenty-four thousand, a figure which was to be virtually unaffected even by the negative impact of the lead shot regulations in 1999. Improved service to members was high on the agenda. Public liability cover for members was increased to £5 million and a series of recommendations followed for the appointment of additional staff to the media and firearms departments – requirements that had been highlighted by the bruising Dunblane episode – together with further boosts for the gamekeeping and information technology departments. One of the priorities for the latter was to establish a BASC website. There were mixed views on this when the executive and finance committee had first considered the matter early in 1997: some had felt that the internet could soon render the publication of *Shooting & Conservation* redundant, thus saving the association a fortune in printing and distribution costs, but others regarded the usefulness of the internet as a means of communication as limited, with the main objective being to provide information to students and to market BASC to non-members.

Communications, or lack of them, were at least a partial reason for the furore which emerged in the first few weeks of the new millennium, though in fact the background to the row over the National Gamekeepers' Organisation's woodpigeon and corvid day can be traced back to 1996 when Ian Grindy, whose keepering job at Halsall was becoming increasingly precarious, decided to resign from the BASC gamekeepers' committee. Soon the committee lost its cohesion and quickly it started to fall apart. The gamekeepers had been extraordinarily successful at raising

BASC chairman Nick Lyle masterminded the association's structural review in 2000

money, both for the Gamekeepers' Welfare Trust and for other BASC activities such as the funding of the game and gamekeeping department, but it was when the committee requested that some of the money that it raised should be put towards the funding of three local projects, in particular a songbird conservation project at Raby, Co Durham, that tensions started to arise. The conservation and research committee did not favour the project and the modest grant was turned down by council. At this the gamekeepers objected, pointing out that it was they who had raised the money. For their part, the council were adamant that it was they who rightly managed the association's purse-strings. The resulting row about who controlled BASC's finances was followed by a series of resignations from the gamekeepers' committee and the setting up of a new gamekeeping body, the National Gamekeepers' Organisation.

When in February 2000 the NGO decided to organise a national woodpigeon and corvid shoot, BASC became alarmed. Marford Mill's concerns were founded upon the fact that the system of open general licences under which pigeons and pest species were killed, which itself had been fought for by BASC ten years previously, was still under threat from Europe. Were there to be a high profile national shoot with lots of attendant media publicity, then this could put the open general licences under renewed scrutiny and lead to an official review with the imposition of stricter conditions. The consequences for BASC members would be unpredictable. John Swift contacted David Clark of the NGO to express his concerns. Relations between the two organisations were still strained following the split four years previously, and BASC's attempts to damp down coverage of the day in the media were poorly handled. It appeared to all the world as though Britain's national shooting association was criticising the shooting of wood-pigeons and pest birds. Members were dismayed, *Shooting Times* was merciless in its criticism and again relations between the magazine and BASC sank to the lowest possible ebb.

Curiously, though, the debacle – which should perhaps have been foreseen and avoided – had two long-term positive repercussions for BASC. Firstly, the matter of the association's communications with its membership was completely readdressed. Initially it decided to suspend its quarterly magazine *Shooting & Conservation* and replace it with a new and more frequent tabloid news-oriented publication '*thevoiceofshooting.com*'. This, however, did not prove to be a long-term solution and instead BASC put its publications out to tender and opted for a brighter, more attractive and informative glossy magazine published every other month. Added to this was a redesign of the website.

Naturally there was robust criticism at the 2000 AGM over the stance which BASC's management had taken on the woodpigeon day and a realisation amongst council members that the issue of management at Marford Mill simply had to be addressed. When Lyle sat down to chair the July 2000 council meeting, he brought with him a wholesale review of BASC's management structure. The association, he said, was seen as an organisation staffed by underpaid employees and volunteers who were doing 'a jolly good job'. However, increased membership and, more particularly, the political environment of a long-term Labour administration, had rendered that rather amateurish culture redundant. Lyle argued that the chief executive was under-equipped to manage an organisation of BASC's size, and recommended a strengthening of the communications, public affairs, media and education function, the appointment of a director of operations who would deliver the required levels of service to members, delegation of responsibility and accountability to heads of departments and a focus upon succession within BASC's management. Council debated Lyle's proposals and accepted that part of the responsibility for poor management lay at its own door – in particular it was paying too much attention to day-to-day activities and not concentrating sufficiently on overall strategy.

Lyle's structural review, born out of a cauldron of discontent, was accepted in full. By the end of 2000, job descriptions had been drafted for the three senior management posts of director of communications, director of operations and director of business management, and the appointments of Christopher Graffius, Simon Hamlyn and Philippa Marshall-Purves were confirmed early in 2001. With a re-invigorated senior management team, BASC was ready to face a new century.

Chapter 15
POSTSCRIPT

W here does the past end and the present begin? When my generation studied modern British history, the textbooks finished in 1945. Nowadays, events that had yet to unfold when we sat our 'O' and 'A' levels are picked over and analysed by school-children, and it will not be long before the inexorable march of time consigns these opening years of the twenty-first century to the history books. So far as the story of BASC is concerned, how-ever, I have drawn a line around the turn of the millennium. Much of what has happened since is still history in the making and it will be for others to record and analyse it at some time in the future.

But this centenary history must nevertheless take account of the years up to 2008 – or 2007 if you believe what 'young' Stanley Duncan confided to John Anderton forty years ago – so it is important at least to sketch a picture of BASC in the noughties. BASC is, and has been for the

As the House of Commons debated the Animal Welfare Bill on 8 February 2006, BASC head of press Simon Clarke spoke to the media in Westminster about the threatened ban on tail docking

past thirty years, both a service organisation and a representative one. The two roles are complementary, for it is through communication and interaction with its membership, the largest in any voluntary shooting association within Europe, that the staff and management are informed of the needs, desires and demands of the ordinary shooter. In the final event, though, it is the political role which is the more important. A decade ago, BASC adopted the phrase 'The Voice of Shooting'. There are of course as many voices of shooting as there are shooting disciplines, but BASC can certainly argue convincingly that it speaks on behalf of the broad mass of live quarry shooters, be they game shooters – as most members are these days – rough shooters, pigeon shooters, deer stalkers or of course wildfowlers. Theirs is the authentic voice of shooting which it is so important that legislators and regulators must hear and understand if the sport is to survive and flourish. It is for this reason that, following the management restructuring of 2000 to 2001 BASC has put more effort into its media relations and political lobbying than ever before.

Ten years of Labour administration has required every rural lobbying group to reassess the way it

NICK RIDLEY

In protest at the proposed ban on tail docking, gundogs and terriers gathered in front of the Palace of Westminster. An exemption for working dogs was won by just eleven votes

addresses Government, and it is fair to say that BASC has done as well as any and better than some. Countryside politics was dominated during the opening years of the present century by the hunting debate. While BASC committed genuine support to hunting, with hundreds of clubs and syndicates and tens of thousands of its members turning out on the streets under its banners during the huge Countryside Alliance marches through London, and with political support lent through the Burns Inquiry and the tortuous process which followed it, the association did not sever communications with the governing party. Though this undoubtedly proved hard for many in the countryside to swallow, working with Government has undoubtedly been the right thing to do. For shooting has to be defended not on one front but on many, and the past half dozen years have seen a host of political skirmishes where close relations with Government have proved crucial.

*In 2003 BASC launched its initiative to encourage more women into the sport of shooting. Director of business management Philippa Marshall-Purves (*centre*) played a prominent role in the programme of activities*

The Anti-Social Behaviour Act 2003 and the Violent Crime Reduction Act 2006 have both tightened the ratchet on firearms ownership, and especially the possession and use of airguns. BASC has worked consistently to ameliorate the worst excesses of both pieces of legislation, and it has done so in the now-traditional manner, both through the consortium of shooting bodies which is the British Shooting Sports Council and by way of its own independent contacts with ministers and civil servants. Bill Harriman's firearms department is the largest of any shooting organisation in Britain, handling around five thousand membership enquiries a year. This enables BASC to keep its finger on the pulse of what is happening from day to day within firearms ownership and licensing, which in turn informs the policy-making process.

A further political achievement was the securing of tail docking for working dogs in England and Wales by just eleven votes during the passage of the Animal Welfare Act 2006. As ever, the victory was the result of a combined effort by many within the rural lobby, but the determination with which Christopher Graffius and his press and political team worked to win what many believed was impossible deserves great credit. The ink is not yet dry on either the Violent Crime Reduction Act or the Animal Welfare Act, while the final outcome of the docking debate in Scotland and Wales has yet to be decided. The effect which these pieces of legislation will have upon BASC members will be for others to judge.

What is certain, though, is that continued pressure upon firearms ownership has, over the past twenty years, slowly reduced the number of certificate holders. Thus the heady growth in membership which BASC experienced in the 1980s has long levelled out, and membership currently rests at around 124,000, in other words just over a quarter of all those who shoot live quarry in Britain today. Certain sections of the membership, though, continue to grow. Deer stalking remains a steadily growing area of recruitment within BASC, while I like to think that my own efforts to encourage council in 2003 to devote greater attention to women shooters gave some small measure of support to Midlands regional officer Liz Lamb and her women's shooting programme. More women are taking an active part in shooting than ever before, and not just in the beating line or picking up. The impact of that could have very beneficial political consequences for the sport, quite apart from making it a much more enjoyable activity to participate in, for both sexes.

Research continues to play a fundamental role in BASC's activity. There was a time when shooters used to ask why Marford Mill had its own research department when the Game Conservancy Trust had a much better one at Fordingbridge. The answer of course is that while the GCT helps us understand more about our quarry and its interaction with the natural and farmed environment, John Harradine's department is geared to helping BASC understand more about our sport, and to provide the vital answers that are needed when the next fight has to be fought, whether the question be how many shooters have docked spaniels, HPRs and terriers or what gun and cartridge combination used at what range is most likely to result in a dead pigeon rather than a wounded one. For although the research department is still deeply involved in the issues surrounding the replacement of lead, the ethical shooting debate has increasingly moved on into the avoidance of wounding, which in turn has implications for the education and training of shooters.

Encouragement of good standards and a responsible attitude within shooting has remained at the heart of BASC throughout its history, right from the days of Stanley Duncan. And while the founder of WAGBI could never have envisaged the lines of shotgun coaching stands at the Game Fair, the intensive training courses for deer stalkers or the Young Shots activity days which

BASC coaching at country shows has introduced thousands of newcomers to shotgun shooting

BASC Scotland's new building development at Trochry was opened on 12 May 2006 by BASC Scottish committee chairman Andrew Macfarlane assisted by former Scottish rugby captain Rob Wainwright

are part of hunter education today, such things mirror one of the very objects of the association as it was first envisaged – to foster good practice within the sport. Today the highest of standards are not an aspiration, they are an essential, for bad or unsafe practice in sporting shooting is quite capable of bringing down unwanted restriction or regulation. Good practice, on the other hand, enables the sport to show its face to the world and to encourage newcomers into its ranks.

Devolution has markedly changed the culture of BASC within the regions. What was once an unashamedly centralist organisation has had to change and adapt, and the country offices in Trochry, Caersws and Lisburn now hold a greater degree of independence even than was the case in 2000. Although the process of self government in Northern Ireland remains tentative, BASC Scotland and BASC Wales have become much more closely enmeshed with the Scottish Parliament and the Welsh Assembly and it seems inevitable that this process will continue. Development of individual national identity within BASC has had a rejuvenating effect, but more than a decade after the Dunblane tragedy the possession and use of firearms remains a sensitive subject in Scotland, and in the present climate the devolution of firearms legislation could have a very serious impact indeed upon shooting sports.

Just as regional government grows in importance, so does international legislation increasingly hold sway over our affairs, whether in the form of the Brussels Directive or the United Nations Convention. Thus BASC's involvement in international affairs, which started in response to the pan-European approach to the conservation of migratory birds which developed during the

Thousands of BASC members turned out to support Countryside Alliance marches. Essex wildfowlers were among the 250,000 marchers who descended upon London on 1 March 1998 in protest at Labour back-bencher Michael Foster's anti-hunting Bill

Director John Swift and chairman Alan Jarrett carried Marford Mill's banner during the Liberty and Livelihood March on 22 September 2002. This time the marchers numbered over 400,000 and BASC offered free banners to all 1,600 affiliated clubs and syndicates. But Tony Blair's Labour Government went ahead with a ban on hunting all the same

1950s, continues to grow. Now it is no longer merely wildlife legislation which has an international dimension, but almost every aspect of BASC's work, from animal welfare and firearms licensing to health and safety legislation. BASC remains a committed member of FACE UK, the channel through which British field sports interests are represented at European level.

It also remains a member of the other long-standing multi-organisational groupings, the Standing Conference on Countryside Sports and the British Shooting Sports Council. Through these, and through its own bilateral contacts, it works alongside other shooting and countryside bodies, though not always without differences of emphasis or even friction, for field sports remains a multi-party state. And while the talk in the mid 1990s was of merger, the past decade has if anything seen the opposite occurring as new organisations form in response to the march of devolved government.

Outbreaks of unrest continue within BASC Council, just as they have done down the decades. Council remains at the heart of the association's constitution and its democratic election process certainly lends BASC valuable political credibility. It doesn't always get things right, and it can occasionally make some quite perverse decisions. However, it remains a sounding board for the shooting community as a whole, with representation that reflects the diversity of live quarry shooting and firearms ownership in Britain today. Representation of the countries within the United Kingdom and the English regions has evolved quite rapidly in the twenty-first century, and nowadays members have the opportunity to elect council members from their own area to serve alongside those elected nationally.

TOM WYLIE

At the AGM on 11 June 2005, BASC chairman John Graham presented a .22 Hornet rifle to Patrick Lichfield in recognition of his services as BASC president

Meanwhile the conservation team has likewise had to adapt to the constantly shifting structure of agencies which regulate nature conservation. English Nature and the Countryside Agency have become Natural England, with new officers and staff who have their own ideas about the relationship between shooting and the natural environment. At the same time, the spotlight has turned upon increased access to the countryside and the refining of government schemes which link agriculture with the improvement of wildlife habitats. All of these things have an impact upon shooting, and the suggested extension of the 'right to roam' to coasts and woodlands in England has the potential to cause very serious problems indeed for the sport. Tim Russell's conservation staff therefore maintain their established focus on ensuring shooting opportunity for individual BASC members and affiliated clubs over areas of high nature conservation importance, while at the same time attempting to influence policy within central government, the devolved administrations and the national conservation agencies.

Throughout its history WAGBI and BASC has kept one boot firmly in the mud and doggedly remained a mass market organisation. In doing so it has given the lie to the common misapprehension that shooting is a sport of the moneyed elite. There have been certain disadvantages in doing so, for BASC has not always found it easy to attract glitzy funds from the rich and famous. Reliance on a solid subscription income topped up by the proceeds of raffles and draws has caused many a sleepless night to generations of finance officers. Politically, though, the tide of history has run in the association's favour as British society in general has become more egalitarian in nature. Even back in the 1950s, the successes which WAGBI achieved were won on the back of the admission by MPs of all persuasions that wildfowling was the sport of the working man. Nowadays the weight of numbers and a clear demonstration that shooting is a sport which draws the bulk of its support from ordinary people of ordinary means is essential to political success. Perhaps it is this which is at the heart of BASC's mission: to make shooting an activity which raises the hackles of neither the left nor the right, to make it a sport which is at one and the same time exciting and absorbing to its followers and unexceptional to its potential opponents.

Index